MARX, METHODOLOGY AND SCIENCE

To BDW *and* MMW
who have inspired with their unscientific method of living,
and in memory of the still much loved and missed LAM

Marx, Methodology and Science

Marx's science of politics

DAVID M. WALKER
Department of Politics, University of Newcastle upon Tyne

Routledge
Taylor & Francis Group

LONDON AND NEW YORK

First published 2001 by Ashgate Publishing

Reissued 2018 by Routledge
2 Park Square, Milton Park, Abingdon, Oxon OX14 4RN
711 Third Avenue, New York, NY 10017, USA

Routledge is an imprint of the Taylor & Francis Group, an informa business

Publisher's Note
The publisher has gone to great lengths to ensure the quality of this reprint but points out that some imperfections in the original copies may be apparent.

Disclaimer
The publisher has made every effort to trace copyright holders and welcomes correspondence from those they have been unable to contact.

A Library of Congress record exists under LC control number: 00111408

ISBN 13: 978-1-138-72579-9 (hbk)
ISBN 13: 978-1-138-72578-2 (pbk)
ISBN 13: 978-1-315-19171-3 (ebk)

Contents

Preface

The origins of this book lie in an undergraduate lecture on Marxism where the lecturer stated that Marxists believed Marxism to be scientific. The notion that a political ideology could be scientific seemed so self-evidently false to me that I could scarcely believe anyone seriously advanced this view. To my mind either this view was a misrepresentation of Marxists' views, or the claim was a crude attempt by Marxists to give their ideas an authority they did not warrant.

It has taken several years of study for me to realise that my lecturer was not outrageously misrepresenting Marxist views, and that the scientific Marxism claim was not simply a crude propaganda trick. It is plausible to argue that there is a Marxist method to investigating social reality, and that this method does have a serious claim to be considered scientific. I reached this conclusion by following two lines of research: first, identifying the component parts of Marx's method, and, second, looking at different characterisations of the scientific method. My understanding of both Marxism and science underwent considerable change in the process of studying them, leading to a little more respect for the former and a little less respect for the latter.

In the course of my research I encountered a range of arguments both for and against Marxism being a science. In general, those who have argued for Marxism being scientific have misunderstood Marx's method, and those who have argued against the claim have misunderstood both Marx's method and the nature of science. The intention in this book is to clarify both Marx's method and the method of science, and to present and assess the arguments for and against Marxism as a science.

It should be noted that concluding Marx's method is scientific is not the same as saying that Marxism is true. A theory may be both scientific and wrong. Therefore, any notion that to argue Marxism is scientific is to argue Marxism is true must be instantly dispensed with. The correctness of Marx's theories or of Marxist politics is not a concern of this book. What this book does show is that Marx made a number of invaluable methodological points, and highlighted numerous methodological errors of other thinkers and approaches to investigating history and society. Marx's method is worthy of the closest attention, and has a vital and relevant contribution to make to contemporary social science.

Acknowledgements

This book illustrates the social character of all production. It would never have emerged but for the varied and vital contributions of numerous people, only a few of whom are mentioned below.

The book is based on my Ph.D. research carried out at Manchester University, and I would like to thank my principal supervisor, Mr Michael Evans, for his patient and diligent supervision, my second supervisor, Mr Norman Geras, for his advice and help, and the Economic and Social Research Council for its financial assistance during my time at Manchester.

I would also like to thank the staff of the Department of Politics at the University of Newcastle upon Tyne for their friendliness and support during the period in which I attempted to combine work on my Ph.D. with undergraduate teaching. I would like to thank especially Professor Hugh Berrington for his generosity and example, and Professor Tim Gray for his encouragement and constructive comments.

In addition, I would like to acknowledge the help and support of my friends and family who refrained from telling me where to go when I was being a persistent pain in the arse. Above all, thanks to Deborah to whom I owe a greater debt than Brazil does to western financial institutions and governments.

Abbreviations

The following abbreviations are used in the text and footnotes:

CHPR	*Critique of Hegel's Philosophy of Right*
CHPR:I	*Introduction to Critique of Hegel's Philosophy of Right*
CPE	*Critique of Political Economy*
CPE:P	*Preface to a Critique of Political Economy*
CW	*Collected Works*
EPM	*Economic and Philosophical Manuscripts*
HF	*The Holy Family*
GI	*The German Ideology*
GR	*The Grundrisse*
Notes	*Notes on Adolph Wagner*
POP	*The Poverty of Philosophy*
TOF	*The Theses on Feuerbach*
TSV	*Theories of Surplus Value*

References take two forms: (i) author's surname, year of publication and page or chapter, e.g., Marx (1975) 5; or (ii) use of abbreviations listed above, e.g., CW. 5. 32 is *Collected Works*, volume 5, page 32. Where the *Collected Works* or *Early Writings* are referred to, the actual book, article or letter is noted in brackets after the reference. References to Hegel's *Logic* include section numbers, and the letter 'Z' indicates the extract is from the *Zusäte*.

Introduction

Political ideologies are usually distinguished from scientific theories by their lack of impartiality and their commitment to the implementation of a set of political ideals. Where science is factual and value-free, political ideologies deal in opinions and prescriptions. Science is about what is, and ideology about what ought to be.

Proponents of Marxism have distinguished it from other political ideologies precisely on the grounds that it is a science and not an ideology. This is a remarkable claim with far-reaching implications. It suggests a status and truth content for Marxism not possessed by other social theories, and implies Marxism is objective and factual where other theories are subjective and speculative.

Among those asserting the scientific status of Marxism are such leading Marxists as Kautsky, Bernstein, Plekhanov, Lenin, Bukharin, Stalin, and Trotsky, as well as whole schools of Marxism including Soviet Marxism, Austro-Marxism, and the Althusserians.[1] Engels labels Marxism as 'Scientific Socialism', and compares Marx and his work to Darwin and his. He makes it clear that Marxism's uniqueness and superiority lies in its scientificity, that where previous socialist doctrines were utopian, Marxism is scientific.[2] Marx himself refers to the scientific nature of his own work and criticises the scientific flaws of others on a number of occasions. In particular, Marx emphasises the scientific character of his work in the preface to the first edition of *Capital*, paralleling his approach to that of natural science.[3] He enthusiastically followed the scientific developments of his day and undoubtedly saw his work as apart of that general scientific advance. In short, the idea that Marxism is scientific is not just a view held by a few fringe followers; it is the view held by many if not most of its leading theorists and proponents from Marx onwards.

The accounts of Marx's scientific socialism utilise, usually unconsciously, different conceptions of science. Whichever is the dominant model of the time colours the portrayal of Marx's science being given. At different times Marxism has been interpreted to fit the models of science put forward by scientific positivism, critical rationalism, scientific conventionalism and scientific realism. In each case the philosophy of

1

science embraced has been taken to be the true account of science and Marxism has been taken to exemplify the particular conception of science. Thus Marxism has been 'proved' to be scientific.

The claim to scientific status has not been welcomed by all Marxists though. It has been rejected by many in the Western Marxist tradition, including Lukács, Marcuse, and Sartre, representing schools of Hegelian, critical and humanist Marxism respectively. Their rejection of the scientific claim is based on a perception of science as incompatible with dialectics, or as controlling and manipulative in character, or as inappropriate for the study of society.

Outside of Marxist circles the claim has been treated with considerable scepticism, indeed, it has largely been dismissed as empty rhetoric. With the recent collapse of Communist regimes (for whom Marxism's scientific status was a tenet of faith) in the Soviet Union and Eastern Europe the claim has seemed even more far-fetched.

There are problems with the positions of both the proponents and the opponents of the scientific claim. Given the significance and implications of the claim, it is surprising to note how little serious attention it has received. In the main it seems that both proponents and opponents of scientific Marxism have taken it to be self-evident that Marxism either is or is not a science. Examination of the claim has been infrequent, largely cursory and usually lacking depth. The notion of science has been left unexamined or receives only scant attention, and there has been a similar lack of thoroughness in establishing what constitutes Marx's method.

A survey of attempts to examine the scientific claims of Marxism illustrates this point. Eastman (1941) poses the question "Marxism: Is it science?" and replies in the negative. However, his reading of Marx combines the distortions of the Second International with a bizarre view of the German mind and philosophy ('primitively credulous and animistic').[4] Popper's rejection of the claim that Marxism is a science considers the scientific claim seriously, but a misreading of Marx and a narrow and distinctive conception of science mar his assessment.[5] Little (1986) endeavours to demonstrate Marxism's scientific status, but he does so only by ascribing methodological individualism to Marx, rejecting dialectics, restricting the science of Marx to *Capital*, and denying a unity of social and natural science. McCarthy (1988) interprets Marx as engaged in a critique of science, objectivity and foundationalism, and, therefore, as putting forward an alternative method to the scientific one. McCarthy, though, places undue stress on the influence of Hegel, Schelling and Aristotle on Marx, ascribing a dialectical and teleological approach to Marx, that fails to give due weight to his materialism and ignores the weight of evidence that

Marx was engaged in a scientific project. Murray (1988) portrays Marx's method as scientific but non-positivist, and Marx as a unique philosopher-scientist. However, he exaggerates the Hegelian character of Marx's method, confuses the method of enquiry with the method of presentation, and does not relate Marx's method to any other conceptions of science. A number of shorter pieces have looked at aspects of the question,[6] but overall the treatments of the scientific status of Marxism have been few and flawed.

There have also been some works where Marx's method receives significant attention, notably Carver (1975), Sayer (1979) and Wilson (1991), but in these the question of scientific status is not addressed at any length.

In this book attention will be given *both* to the nature of Marx's method *and* to the nature of science. The component parts of Marx's method will be identified and accounts given of the main philosophies of science. Particular attention will be given to the importance of dialectics and materialism as a basis for Marx's method and as giving it a distinctive character.

In the course of the book a number of subsidiary issues will be considered, including the relationship of Marx to Hegel and Feuerbach, the extent of continuity between the early and the later works of Marx, and the relationship of Marx's philosophy to his science. The considerable degree of continuity between the early and the later works will be highlighted (along with points of departure), as will the debt to both Hegel and Feuerbach (along with his criticisms of and differences from them). The continuing importance of philosophy throughout Marx's thought, and its role in underpinning Marx's science will also be underscored.

The question of the concordance between Marx's thought and that of Engels does not feature prominently in the book, because evidence used is almost entirely drawn from the writings of Marx. In some expositions of Marxism, the writings of Engels are used to represent the views of Marx, particularly on dialectics and materialism, and Marxism's 'scientism' is often attributed to Engels rather than Marx. To avoid this sort of dispute Engels is only referred to when he illuminates a certain point, or occasionally to point out some divergence between him and Marx. This focus on Marx's writings also means that it is a question of the nature and scientificity of Marx's method rather than of Marxism more generally. Later Marxists will be referred to inasmuch as their interpretations of Marx are relevant.

More centrally, there is the problem of the polarisation of views regarding dialectics and materialism. Orthodox Marxism sees dialectics and materialism as fused and as the basis of its scientificity. The interpretation of dialectical materialism given takes the form of laws or formulae, which marry well with both positivism and determinism. Opponents of the Marxism as science view who yet espouse Marxism (principally Western Marxists - with notable exceptions such as Althusser and Colletti) tend to view dialectics and materialism as separate and emphasise the former at the expense of the latter, even to the extent of being accused of slipping into a form of idealism (Lukács for example).

Interpretations of materialism and dialectics will be put forward that entail neither separation and emphasis of dialectics at the expense of materialism, nor rigid formulations that point to a deterministic scientism. In developing a coherent exposition of Marx's materialism, six theses will be identified and explored, and their relation to each other sketched out. In defending a credible understanding of dialectics the central notion of contradiction will be analysed, along with the dialectical conception of identity and teleology, and the relationship of dialectics to formal logic and analytical philosophy will be elucidated.

The survey of philosophies of science provided in this book identifies four principal conceptions of science: scientific positivism, critical rationalism, conventionalism and scientific realism. Of these scientific positivism has had the most influence, both on general perceptions of science and on interpretations of the scientificity of Marxism. Scientific positivism will be the starting point for discussing conceptions of science and interpretations of the scientific status of Marx's method. For the purpose of comparison a set of categories of key tenets will be outlined and applied to the four conceptions. The three later conceptions will be discussed as, in part, critiques of positivism, and scientific realism will be promoted as the most viable of the four views of science. The works of Popper, Kuhn, Feyerabend, Lakatos and Bhaskar will be the main sources drawn on in this section of the work.

Overall, the aims of the book are: (i) to provide an account of Marx's method, showing its development from early writings through what may be termed the transitional works, to the mature works, and clarifying its central features; (ii) to outline Marx's materialism and dialectics, identifying and elaborating the principal themes of each, and their role and significance in his thought as a whole; (iii) to give an overview of the main conceptions of science, describing and clarifying their characterising tenets; and (iv) to assess the scientific status of Marx's method via a comparison of his approach with the conceptions of science described, and an examination of the arguments put forward by proponents of Marxism as a science.

Briefly, the conclusions of the book are that Marx has a distinctive and coherent approach to investigating social reality. His method is built on materialist and dialectical foundations, and these give it its essential character. Various components go to make up Marx's method, and most notable among these are the elements of critique, abstraction and the essence-appearance distinction.

Marx's method does not conform to three of the four conceptions of science identified in the book, namely, scientific positivism, critical rationalism and conventionalism. However, attempts to portray Marx's method as matching these models of science are themselves mistaken and misinterpret Marx. The fourth conception, scientific realism, does accommodate Marx's approach and gives credibility to the scientific status claim. Furthermore, Marx's method, with its critical, dialectical and materialist dimensions, is one from which valuable lessons can be drawn by contemporary social science.

The book will begin with an account of the elements and evolution of Marx's method in his early and his later works in chapters one and two. In chapters three and four Marx's dialectics and materialism will be clarified and their coherence and importance discussed. The different conceptions of science will be described and commented upon in chapter six, and in chapter seven the scientific standing of Marx's method will be assessed with reference to the four conceptions of science outlined. The conclusion will summarise the main points of the book, and offer some further reflections on method and science.

Notes

[1] More recent commentators who claim Marxism to be scientific include Callinicos (1983); Little (1986); Bhaskar (1986); and Farr (1991).

[2] See CW. 24. 281-325 (*Socialism: Utopian and Scientific*); ibid., 467 (*Speech at the Graveside*).

[3] For Marx on the scientific nature of his work see *Capital* I, 89, 90, 93, 94, 98, 100, 102, 104, and 105; for Marx on the scientific failings of others see *Capital* I, .96, 97,and 98; and TSV II, 36, 120, and 121.
Note: *Wissenschaft*, the German word for science and the word used by Marx, has a broader meaning than its English counterpart, and can be used to mean 'learning', 'scholarship' and 'erudition'. However, the context of Marx's comments suggests he saw no difference in status between his work and that of natural science. It is also worth noting that Bernstein and Kautsky, who were both presumably fully conversant in their native German tongue took Marx to mean science in the stronger English sense.

[4] Eastman (1941) 174

[5] Popper (1960) and (1963).

[6] See, for example, Ball (1984); Collier (1979); Edgley (1979); Farr (1984) and (1991).

1   Method in the Early Marx

The most common way of dividing up Marx's work is between the early and the later works with the dividing line usually put at 1845 and the writing of the pivotal piece, *The Theses on Feuerbach*. This chapter and the next will follow this practice, although in a modified form as will be seen in chapter two.[1]

These early works preceded elaboration of the 'materialist conception of history', and are considered by many to be representative of Marx before Marxism, i.e., Marx's thinking before he arrived at his own distinctive theory of history and society. This has led some commentators, most notably Althusser, to reject them or relegate them to a secondary status in the corpus of Marx's work.

In addition, supporters of the scientific claim have ignored the early works in favour of the 'more scientific' later works, with some, again most notably Althusser, dismissing the early works as 'pre-scientific'. Equally, those who have asserted the importance of the early works have favoured the view of Marxism as philosophy rather than as science. Fromm with his humanist interpretation of Marxism is typical of these writers.

Contrary to both these viewpoints Marx was developing his scientific method even in the early works. Following Hegel and the other Hegelians Marx was concerned to articulate a complete scientific system. Hegel and his disciples believed they possessed a method by which they could obtain objective knowledge and they contrasted their approach with the unscientific, speculative and intuitive approach of Romantic philosophers such as Schelling. Marx too aimed to produce an objective and true understanding of the world.

The main term used by Hegel and his followers to refer to the scientific enterprise they saw themselves as engaged in was *Wissenschaft*. This term, although it translates into English as science has a slightly different meaning to the English word. It is not so closely identified with the natural sciences as the English term, but, rather, has a broader sense encompassing a notion of organised knowledge obtained by some form of rigorous or disciplined method. *Wissenschaft* points to an activity that seeks to yield truth in an objective fashion. Hence, Hegel, his followers and Marx all have described their approaches as scientific without necessarily seeking to imply an identical method to that of the natural sciences.

During this period Marx gradually distances himself first from Hegel and then from the Left Hegelians as his own critical thinking made him aware of the contradictions within Hegelianism and its methodological failings. Hegel claimed his philosophy was the framework for all scientific work, but as the basis for scientific investigation it had serious shortcomings. Many of these were exposed by the Left Young Hegelians like Strauss, Bruno Bauer and Feuerbach who moved Hegelianism in a more scientific direction. It was left to Marx to develop a more fully scientific approach through a critique of these Left Hegelians.[2]

Correctly understood the early works constitute steps in the development of Marx's thought, important in their own right and necessary to an understanding of Marx's later work, but not the 'finished article'. In them Marx comes to terms with Hegelianism and speculative philosophy, and outlines his basic position with regard to political economic theory. Marx is in the process of formulating his approach and method, and of doing the philosophical groundwork which underlies his later writings.

It is clear from the *Grundrisse* and other evidence that Marx referred back to his early work and utilised ideas he outlined there in the writing of his later works. There is no 'epistemological break' or 'pre-science'-'science' divide. The early philosophising is not at odds with the later 'scientific' works; it is their necessary philosophical counterpart, the philosophy of Marx's science. The early works provide an insight into Marx's understanding of science.

In his early writings Marx devotes considerable attention to method and in particular to methodological criticisms of other thinkers. The thinking behind these comments remains pertinent throughout Marx's work and is part of his attempt to construct a truer and more scientific method of investigation of social reality.

Marx's Methodological Criticisms in the Early Works

Typically Marx develops his own thought through a critique of others, principally Hegel, the Left Hegelians, and the political economists (especially Adam Smith, David Ricardo, James Mill and J-B Say). Hegel features throughout Marx's early writings, most directly in the CHPR, but always in the background even when not the immediate subject of comment. By looking at Marx's critical comments about other writers something of his own approach may be discerned.

Marx and Hegel

According to Marx Hegel's most basic mistake is his inversion of subject and predicate which makes the Idea the subject and empirical reality the predicate. Marx writes in the CHPR, "The crux of the matter is that Hegel everywhere makes the Idea into the subject, while the genuine, real subject... is turned into the predicate."[3] This fundamental error of Hegel's has, according to Marx, various implications that Marx elaborates into a major critique of Hegel's methodology.

Hegel's starting point is the Idea and the abstract concepts he derives from 'pure being'. Hegel's abstractions assume the status of reality, they are hypostatised, the realisation of moments of the abstract concept becomes concrete fact. For example, on Hegel's analysis of the transition from the family and civil society to the political state Marx writes:

> ...the transition does not result from the *particular* nature of the family etc, and the particular nature of the state, but from the *universal* relationship of *freedom* and *necessity*. We find exactly the same process at work in the 'Logic' in the transition from the sphere of Essence to that of the Concept. In the 'Philosophy of Nature', the same transition can be observed from Inorganic nature to Life. It is always the same categories which are made to supply now one sphere and now another with a soul. The problem is merely to discover the appropriate abstract determinants to fit the individual concrete ones.[4]

Hegel's abstract treatment of society, i.e., starting from abstractions and treating the concrete as the embodiment of them, leads to the undifferentiated application of general concepts and terms. For example, Hegel applies the term 'organism' to the state without indicating any distinction between the state as organism and, say, an animal organism. As far as Hegel's account goes the respective structure and relation of parts of each may be the same. He defines his terms abstractly in relation to the state/political constitution not because of the specific characteristics of the state/political constitution, but because of the features of the Idea. Marx writes:

> The starting-point is the abstract Idea which then develops into the *political constitution* of the state. We are not concerned with a political Idea but with the abstract Idea in a political form, the mere fact that I say 'this organism (i,e. the state, the political constitution) is the differentiation of the Idea into various elements, etc' does not mean that I know anything at all about the *specific Idea*

of the political constitution; the same statement can be made with the same truth about the organism of an *animal* as about the organism of the *state*.[5]

Hegel's abstract and idealist starting point leads him to be more concerned to establish concrete reality as a predicate of the Idea, than to establish the specific nature of actual things.

This critique in the CHPR of the abstract idealism of Hegelian philosophy is continued in the HF. In one passage in particular Marx lampoons 'speculative philosophy' by way of an analysis of fruit using the speculative method. Hegelian analysis, according to Marx, inverts the abstract and the concrete making the abstract idea of 'Fruit' the true essence, substance, origin and active subject of actual fruit. He writes:

> If from real apples, pears, strawberries and almonds I form the general idea *'Fruit'*, if I go further and *imagine* that my abstract idea *'Fruit'*, derived from real fruit, is an entity existing outside me, is indeed the *true* essence of the pear, the apple, etc., then - in the *language of speculative* philosophy - I am declaring that 'Fruit' is the *'substance'* of the pear, the apple, the almond, etc. I am saying, therefore, that to be a pear is not essential to the pear, that to be an apple is not essential to the apple; that what is essential to these things is not their real existence, perceptible to the senses, but the essence I have abstracted from them, and then foisted on them, the essence of my idea - *'Fruit'*. I therefore declare apples, pears, almonds, etc., to mere forms of existence, *modi*, of *'Fruit'*.[6]

The concrete is reduced to 'mere forms of existence' or 'semblances' of the abstract. The abstract idea 'Fruit' is derived from real fruit, but Hegelian speculative philosophy takes the abstract idea as the starting point and 'imagines' itself to be deriving real fruit from the idea 'Fruit'. As in the CHPR Marx makes the point that this approach denies significance to concrete distinctions, to the particular:

> My finite understanding supported by my senses does of course *distinguish* an apple from a pear and a pear from an almond, but my speculative reason declares these sensuous differences inessential and irrelevant. It sees in the apple the same as in the pear, and in the pear *the same* as in the almond, namely 'Fruit'. Particular real fruits are no more than semblances whose true essence is *'the* substance' - 'Fruit'.[7]

Closely related to this criticism of Hegel's abstract idealism is Marx's criticism of Hegel for imposing the formal categories of his 'Logic' on to concrete reality. Mediation is formal in Hegel, because it is the mediation of the 'Logic', and not derived from the particular, specific, actual reality.

For example, Hegel writes about the family and state and the transition from the one to the other as the mediation of freedom and necessity. The transition, according to Hegel, is the result of the universal relationship of freedom and necessity, not the particular nature of the family and state, i.e., it is merely formal. Marx writes of Hegel's account of the state:

> The concrete content and the real defining characteristics appear to be formal; the entire abstract, formal definition appears as the concrete content. The essence of the determining characteristics of the state is not that they define the state but that they are capable of being viewed in their most abstract form as logico-metaphysical determinations. Hegel's true interest is not the philosophy of right but logic.[8]

Marx sees Hegel as not being concerned with the concrete and the particular except to show that it is an expression or manifestation of the abstract categories of the 'Logic': "the entire 'Philosophy of Right' is no more than a parenthesis of the 'Logic'."[9] In other words, the *Philosophy of Right* is the application of the categories of the 'Logic' to the sphere of the state and constitution.

Marx also notes that Hegel obscures reality by depriving it of any nature or will except for the Idea. He denies any internal logic to reality by making its logic the logic of the Idea. For example, in the *Philosophy of Right* Hegel treats the monarch as a predicate of the Idea, and portrays his decisions as the self-determination of absolute free will, of the Idea. But if the monarch is treated as subject then his decisions may be seen for what they are, namely, the result of individual will, of caprice. Because Hegel's starting point is the Idea, and because concrete reality concerns him only as an expression of the Idea, real relations are mystified. Hegel's treatment of the political constitution is a further example. Marx writes:

> He has converted into a product, a predicate of the Idea, what was properly its subject. He does not develop his thought from the object, but instead the object is constructed according to a system of thought perfected in the abstract sphere of logic. His task is not to elaborate the definite idea of the political constitution, but to provide the political constitution with a relationship to the abstract Idea and to establish it as a link in the life-history of the Idea - an obvious mystification.[10]

This charge of mystification levelled by Marx against Hegel in the CHPR also finds an echo in the HF:

...Hegel very often gives a real presentation, embracing the thing itself, within the speculative presentation. This real development within the speculative development misleads the reader into considering the speculative development as real and the real as speculative.[11]

Concrete reality and its real development and nature are made obscure by entanglement in speculative philosophy and the abstract Idea.

Marx also accuses Hegel of dualism. Hegel's approach separates the material and the ideal by splitting subject and predicate, but makes the true subject, concrete reality, the predicate, and making the true predicate, the Idea, the subject. However, he cannot deny completely the independence of concrete reality, although his starting point and approach implies it. Concrete reality thus becomes both predicate and subject. For example, the monarch is sometimes treated as predicate (predicate of the idea), and sometimes as subject (self-creating sovereign). Empirical facts are sometimes treated as facts as such, and sometimes as predicates of the Idea. There is a dualism in Hegel's approach, caused by his inversion of subject and object, which he cannot overcome.[12]

One of the most serious charges that Marx makes against Hegel (as far as Marx himself is concerned) is that he is guilty of uncritical philosophising. In treating concrete reality as the expression of the Idea, the critical element is removed. By making the real the manifestation of the rational it is put beyond criticism. Hegel turns empirical fact into metaphysical axiom and thus disarms critical philosophy. For example, the empirical fact that the will of the monarch is the final decision is turned by Hegel into the metaphysical axiom: the final decision of the will is the monarch.[13] Hegel seeks only to apprehend the present and actual to fit the actual into his logical categories.[14] Furthermore, contradictions identified in reality are seen to be transcended in the ideal realm.

Following on from his comments in the CHPR Marx, in the EPM, accuses Hegel of 'uncritical idealism' emptying the empirical world of meaning and significance by treating it as the manifestation of the Idea, and of 'uncritical positivism'.[15] Because of the need for empirical content for the categories of the Idea, the empirical world is returned to by Hegel, but in uncritical fashion. In other words, Hegel is guilty of a double inversion: first, being is held to be nothing but thought; second, thought, of necessity, becomes whatever being is. Hence, uncritical idealism and uncritical positivism.

In the EPM Marx also criticises Hegel for failing to distinguish alienation from objectification, and by conflating them absolutising alienation. Because his starting point is the Idea alienation is treated as objectification of the Idea and a critical view of alienation and its causes is prevented.[16]

A final methodological criticism made by Marx concerns Hegel's orientation to practice. According to Marx, Hegel's approach leads to no practical implications, and the failure to resolve contradictions and imperfections in reality. This is because Hegel posits thought as primary, and distinctive human activity is understood as activity in thought. The inversion of subject and predicate makes thought the active subject.[17]

Hegel seeks to transcend the world in thought, Marx in practice. Hegel's inversion of reality ultimately leads to his leaving the world unchanged; his philosophy is not only non-critical but also non-practical, thus reinforcing existing social reality and failing to reject and transform it. Hence, Hegel, recognising alienation only as objectification of the Idea/self-consciousness sees its transcendence as occurring in thought-activity alone, and the actual world remains unchanged.

Marx and the Young Hegelians

The Young Hegelians were followers of Hegel in the generation immediately after his death. The label is usually used to refer to his more radical interpreters who sought to take Hegelianism beyond its existing parameters and to transform it into a critical, humanist philosophy. However, as Toews has pointed out, the generation of Hegelians after Hegel's death diverged on various issues and only the Left Hegelians adopted this radical interpretation.

As a student in Berlin Marx embraced Left Hegelianism and was particularly influenced by Bruno Bauer and radical atheism. Marx was attracted to the emphasis on criticism.[18] However, by 1843 Marx was developing his own position distinct from that of the Left Hegelians. In the CHPR his criticism of Hegel goes beyond that given by the Left Hegelians. Where they criticise Hegel for not pushing his philosophy to its logical radical conclusions, Marx criticises Hegel's philosophy for being inherently 'conservative'. Where the Left Hegelians argued that Hegel had compromised his philosophy in the face of the pressures of a conservative establishment, Marx argues that Hegel's thought is intrinsically uncritical and non-radical. So long as Hegel's philosophy remains idealist and speculative, and inverts reality it can do no other than reinforce the status quo.

As a consequence of Marx's different view of Hegel he is led to criticise the Left Hegelians themselves, and in particular the limited nature of their critical approach. In one sense the Left Hegelians fail to step outside of the parameters of Hegelianism in their criticisms of Hegel. They remain within an idealist, speculative paradigm. Marx, largely by an immanent critique, shows they, like Hegel, cannot offer a radical, 'true' critique of society. Marx, in the EPM, describes Bruno Bauer and his associates as 'critical theologians'. He writes:

> *Their failure to go to the root of the matter* is inevitable, since even the *critical* theologian is still a theologian...On close investigation *theological criticism*, although it was a truly progressive factor at the beginning of the movement, is in the final analysis nothing more than the culmination and consequence of the old *philosophical*, and especially *Hegelian, transcendence* distorted into a *theological caricature*.[19]

Bauer, as a Hegelian, is an idealist and his critique of religion remains in the realm of thought. He fails to produce a material critique, a critique that goes beyond the theological issues to an understanding of why they arise, what their roots are in the material world, i.e., he fails to go to the root of the matter. The resolution of the theological issue is a transcendence in thought just like Hegel's.

In the HF Marx shows the limitations of the idealist perspective retained by the Left Hegelians, even those who radically criticise Hegel. He writes:

> ...*Absolute Criticism* has learnt from Hegel's *Phänomenologie* at least the art of converting *real objective* chains that exist *outside me* into *merely ideal*, merely *subjective* chains, existing merely *in me* and thus of converting all *external* sensuously perceptible struggles into pure struggles of thought.[20]

The approach of the Left Hegelians, as with Hegel, denies the importance of practice, of practical activity, by transforming the real and concrete into the ideal and abstract. Hence, according to Marx, their treatment of the estrangement and debasement of workers:

> According to Critical Criticism, the whole evil lies only in the workers' 'thinking'...Critical Criticism...teaches them that they cease in reality to be wage-workers if in thinking they abolish the thought of wage-labour; if in thinking they cease to regard themselves as wage-workers...Critical Criticism teaches them that they abolish real capital by overcoming in *thinking* the category Capital, that they *really* change and transform themselves into real human beings by changing their '*abstract ego*' in consciousness and scorning

as an un-Critical operation all real change of their real existence, of the real conditions of their existence, that is to say, of their *real ego*. The 'spirit', which sees in reality only categories, naturally reduces all human activity and practice to the dialectical process of thought of Critical Criticism.[21]

Marx's movement away from Left Hegelianism is influenced by the work of Feuerbach. His influence is evident in the CHPR, and Marx is explicit in the EPM regarding his admiration for Feuerbach: "It is only with *Feuerbach* that *positive* humanistic and naturalistic criticism begins." And again: "Feuerbach is the only person who has a serious and a critical attitude to the Hegelian dialectic and who has made real discoveries in this field. He is the true conqueror of the old philosophy."[22]

The Left Hegelians remain within the 'old philosophy,' i.e., Hegelianism. Feuerbach steps outside of it, and Marx follows him. A truly critical attitude to the world requires a critique of Hegelianism the Left Hegelians cannot provide.

The Left Hegelians also believed that they could apply rational criticism at a philosophical level to any and every issue and area, without requiring knowledge of the subject to any great degree. Rational criticism rather than empirical criticism was their approach. At the beginning of the EPM Marx feels it necessary, "to assure the reader who is familiar with political economy that I arrived at my conclusions through an entirely empirical analysis based on an exhaustive critical study of political economy."[23] Marx is at pains to indicate his departure from the speculative method of the Left Hegelians, and to emphasise the empirical nature of his study. This is an important development of his methodology.

Marx and Political Economy

Marx devotes his attention to political economy and to the various writings of political economists in the EPM. To a large extent his approach parallels the approach he adopted in the CHPR and his criticisms also bear comparison. In each case Marx's comments have a strong methodological emphasis. In each case he uses an immanent critique - a critique from within - as his principal weapon. In each Marx uses the texts of his subjects (Hegel and the political economists) as his starting point, and via a critique of the writers makes a critique of society. Both Hegel and the political economists are accused by Marx of being intrinsically uncritical. Their accounts do not provide 'real', adequate explanations, i.e.; they do not describe the origins and necessity of the phenomena under scrutiny. Marx writes:

> Political economy proceeds from the fact of private property. It does not explain it. It grasps the *material* process of private property, the process through which it actually passes, in general and abstract formulae which it then takes as *laws*. It does not *comprehend* these laws, ie it does not show how they arise from the nature of private property. Political economy fails to explain the reason for the division between labour and capital, between capital and land. For example, when it defines the relation of wages to profit it takes the interests of the capitalists as the basis of its analysis; ie it assumes what it is supposed to explain. Similarly, competition is frequently brought into the argument and explained in terms of external circumstances. Political economy teaches us nothing about the extent to which these external and apparently accidental circumstances are only the expression of a necessary development.[24]

Marx criticises the political economists for only explaining how the economic system operates, and not how its component parts have arisen. Because interconnections are not grasped the inevitability of monopoly, overproduction and the immiseration of the worker is not appreciated, and the true nature of social reality is hidden and mystified by the political economists. They take the viewpoint of private property/alienated labour, which leads to a mystification of the situation.

Marx accepts the basic account provided by the political economists, and uses it as his starting point. However, he seeks to demonstrate (i) internal contradictions in their accounts, for example, the ascription of primacy to labour in wealth creation, but the poverty of the labourers; (ii) the failure to see the economy as an interconnected totality, where apparently accidental circumstances are in reality necessary developments, for example, the struggle between labour and capital; (iii) the ahistorical approach of the political economists, which absolutises private property and the system based on it.

The standpoint of the political economists conceals the true nature of the economic reality, and in particular the alienation at its heart. Hence, the political economists, like Hegel and the Hegelians, adopt an uncritical position.

Marx's Method in the Early Works

The components and character of Marx's own method may now be outlined, partly drawing on the criticisms of other writers described above and partly looking at his more positive methodological comments.

Critique

As has been emphasised 'critique' is a key notion in Marx's early writings. Indeed, throughout them Marx is seeking to arrive at an adequate notion of critique, and a definite development of a critical approach may be traced from the 'rational critique' of his Left Hegelian days through to a material-practical critique in the 'Theses on Feuerbach'. Marx developed his own critical method primarily through critiques of other thinkers, most notably Hegel, the Left Hegelians (particularly Strauss and Bauer), Feuerbach and the political economists.

In the CHPR Marx is already breaking with Hegelian critical method. He writes:

> A criticism that still *struggles* with its object remains dogmatic. For example, it was dogmatic to attack the dogma of the Holy Trinity by pointing out the contradiction of the three that were one. True criticism shows the inner genesis of the Holy Trinity in the brain of man. It describes its birth. Similarly, a truly philosophical criticism of the present constitution does not content itself with showing that it contains contradictions: it *explains* them, comprehends their genesis, their necessity. It grasps their *particular* significance.[25]

At this stage Marx still refers to 'philosophical criticism', but he seeks to go beyond the mere identification of contradictions to an explanation of their origins. There is something necessary about the contradictions identified; they are not just accidental, mere errors of reasoning. So Marx is here moving away from the Left Hegelian approach, but has yet to make a definite break.

In a letter to Ruge in 1843 Marx explicitly discusses the role and nature of critique. He notes how the religious criticism with which the Left Hegelians began has turned to political issues. But Marx also argues that the religious and political struggles are manifestations of the theoretical and practical struggles of humanity. He writes:

> Just as religion is the table of contents of the theoretical struggles of mankind, so the *political state* enumerates its practical struggles. Thus the particular form and nature of the political state contains all social struggles, needs and truths within itself.[26]

Once again criticism must go beyond the immediate issues, beyond the identification of 'rational' errors or contradictions. As Marx writes about a proposed new journal, "to sum up the credo of our journal in a *single word*: the self-clarification (critical philosophy) of the struggles and wishes of the age."[27] Critical philosophy means the self-clarification of the religious and political struggles in terms of what they represent from a humanist perspective.

In the CHPR:I Marx is clearer in his views. He begins, "For Germany, the *criticism of religion* has been essentially completed, and the criticism of religion is the prerequisite of all criticism."[28] In other words, the criticism put forward by the Left Hegelians, such as Bauer, was necessary, but has been completed, and is only the beginning of all criticism. Marx continues:

> [Religion] is the *fantastic realization* of the human essence since the human essence has not acquired any true reality. The struggle against religion is therefore indirectly the struggle against *that world* whose spiritual *aroma* is religion.[29]

Marx is saying that criticism must go beyond religion to the oppression and suffering it stems from in the real world. This is the self-clarification of which Marx talked in his letter to Ruge as being the aim of critical philosophy. True criticism can but lead from religion to the secular and political. Marx writes:

> It is the immediate *task of philosophy*...to unmask self-estrangement in its *unholy forms* once the *holy form* of human self-estrangement has been unmasked. Thus the criticism of heaven turns into the criticism of earth, the *criticism of religion* into the *criticism of law* and the *criticism of theology* into the *criticism of politics*.[30]

The criticism of religion ends with humanism, religion being a form of human self-estrangement. But as Marx puts it, it is the task of philosophy to move beyond the revealing of religious self-estrangement to the unmasking of self-estrangement in its 'unholy forms', i.e., in the political and social world. More than this criticism must be material and practical:

> Clearly the weapon of criticism cannot replace the criticism of weapons, and material force must be overthrown by material force. But theory also becomes a material force once it has gripped the masses. Theory is capable of gripping the masses when it demonstrates *ad hominem*, and it demonstrates *ad hominem* as soon as it becomes radical. To be radical is to grasp things by the root. But for man the root is man himself.[31]

And again:

The critique of religion ends with the doctrine that for man the supreme being is man, and thus with the categorical imperative to overthrow all conditions in which man is a debased, enslaved, neglected and contemptible being...[32]

Radical critique leads from religion to politics to dehumanisation, and to practice. So critique demystifies (clarifies) the issues, contradictions and struggles manifest in religion, transcends them by grasping the roots of the problem in the political/secular world, and issues in practical activity as a categorical imperative to change the world. Note this is in stark contrast to Hegel who transcends contradictions in the empirical world by resolving them in the ideal world.

To sum up Marx's notion of critique, it displays the three characteristics of being:

(i) immanent - it is a critique from within. For example, he criticises Hegel on the basis of internal contradictions irresolvable in the context of Hegel's philosophy. Marx does not use an archimedean point outside of his subject as a viewpoint from which to judge. The internal criticism propels itself to transcendence.

(ii) transcendent - the critique must transcend its object of criticism in order to comprehend it; it must grasp it by its roots - roots that according to Marx lead to 'man' and the 'human condition'. Thus a criticism of religion leads to the cause of religious consciousness, i.e., the dehumanised condition of humanity.

(iii) practical - the third element is the inevitable final step from immanence to transcendence to resolution. The religious/philosophical consciousness is immanently criticised, its contradictions identified and its mysticism torn away. It is transcended to its secular/political roots, and the condition of alienation and the culpability of the system of private property comprehended. Finally, if the original problem or contradiction is to be resolved it must be resolved by practical activity.

Practice

This last point concerning practical activity highlights another key element of Marx's method: practice. A practical orientation is a key and integral component of Marx's approach in the early writings. Prefiguring his comments in the TOF it is already clear in the early writings that Marx sees the origins of philosophical problems in material reality, and their resolution as requiring practical activity to transform these material conditions. His analyses of the thought of Hegel, the Hegelians and the political economists leads to the concrete reality - the state, society, economy - they describe, and from here to practical activity. The weight given to practice by Marx is illustrated in the following passage from the EPM:

> It can be seen how subjectivism and objectivism, spiritualism and materialism, activity and passivity, lose their antithetical character, and hence their existence as such antitheses, only in the social condition; it can be seen how the resolution of the *theoretical* antitheses themselves is possible *only* in a *practical* way, only through the practical energy of man, and how their resolution is for that reason by no means only a problem of knowledge, but a real problem of life, a problem which *philosophy* was unable to solve precisely because it treated it as a *purely* theoretical problem.[33]

This practical orientation also colours Marx's view of the role of the philosopher and of philosophy, and stands in marked contrast to that of Hegel and speculative philosophy. The Hegelian approach is passive rather than practical in its implications; it is a philosophy of inaction rather than of action. History is for observing and interpreting rather than for participating in. Marx writes:

> Already in Hegel the *Absolute Spirit* of history has its material in the *Mass* and finds its appropriate expression only in *philosophy*. The philosopher, however, is only the organ through which the maker of history, the Absolute Spirit, arrives at self-consciousness *retrospectively* after the movement has ended. The participation of the philosopher in history is reduced to this retrospective consciousness, for the real movement is accomplished by the Absolute Spirit *unconsciously*. Hence the philosopher appears on the scene *post festum*.[34]

For Hegel the owl of Minerva does indeed only spread its wings at dusk; the role of the philosopher is to express the self-realisation of the Absolute Spirit, a role that can only be fulfilled after the events of the day have taken place, after the 'real movement is accomplished'. Marx wants to participate in the real movement as it is happening, to create this movement.

Materialism and 'Empiricism'

A further aspect of Marx's method is its materialist and empirical character. These aspects are counter-posed to the idealism and abstraction of speculative philosophy and are implicit in Marx's critical comments on Hegelianism. In more positive form the empirical theme is suggested in the

EPM: "I arrived at my conclusions through an entirely empirical analysis," and, "Sense perception must be the basis of all science."[35]

His adoption of materialism is suggested in his description of Feuerbach's 'great achievement' as, "To have founded true materialism and real science by making the social relation of 'man to man' the basic principle of his theory."[36]

Marx's empiricism and materialism are bound up together, but their natures and relationship are vague.[37] Marx up until 1845 is very much influenced by Feuerbach, who is also ambiguous in his attitude to and understanding of materialism.[38] Indeed, Marx seems to view materialism as one side of a contradiction to be superseded, the antithesis of idealism, which whilst it may need emphasis against the dominance of idealist philosophy, ultimately must be overcome. In the EPM Marx writes:

> Here we see how consistent naturalism or humanism differs both from idealism and materialism and is at the same time their unifying truth. We also see that only naturalism is capable of comprehending the process of world history.[39]

If we are to define Marx's materialism at this stage it consists in the following:

(i) an opposition to abstract idealism and the ascribing of primacy to the ideal-spiritual realm.

(ii) an emphasis on the senses, 'man', and nature over (but not to the exclusion of) thought and spirit.

(iii) an emphasis on material social conditions in causal explanations and the resolution of theoretical problems.

Marx's criticisms of abstract idealism have been described above. They are the substance of point (i). Point (ii) represents the Feuerbachian influence, which runs throughout the early writings. The theme is aired in the EPM, for example:

> *Sense perception* (see Feuerbach) must be the basis of all science. Only when science starts out from sense perception in the dual form of *sensuous* consciousness and *sensuous* need - i.e. only when science starts out from nature - is it *real* science. The whole of history is a preparation, a development, for *'man'* to become the object of *sensuous* consciousness and for the needs of 'man as man' to become [sensuous] needs. History itself is a *real* part of *natural history* and of nature's becoming man. Natural science will in time

subsume the science of man just as the science of man will subsume natural science: there will be *one* science.[40]

The emphasis on material social conditions, noted in point (iii), is clear from Marx's notions of critique and practical activity. It can also be seen in Marx's approach to the issue of the political emancipation of the Jews. In *On The Jewish Question* Marx criticised the approach of Bauer to this issue for casting it in religious terms. Marx looked at the issue in terms of the social grounds of religion, the material conditions, which must be changed for not only political emancipation, but religious and human emancipation also.[41]

Marx's atheism combines (ii) and (iii). An earlier militant atheism has given way by the time he was writing the CHPR and CHPR:I to an effort to explain religion in social, humanist terms.[42] Implicit in it is a denial of the supernatural but his main concern is with religion as a symptom; what it betokens and what lies at its root is of more concern to Marx:

> Religious suffering is at one and the same time the expression of real suffering and protest against real suffering. Religion is the sigh of the oppressed creature, the heart of a heartless world and the soul of soulless conditions. It is the opium of the people.[43]

There is also evidence that Marx held a realist-materialist viewpoint in this early period, i.e., that he maintained the world exists independently of thought or perception. In the EPM Marx writes:

> *Man* is directly a *natural being*. As a natural being and as a living natural being he is on the one hand equipped with *natural powers*, with *vital powers*, he is an *active* natural being; these powers exist in him as dispositions and capacities, as *drives*. On the other hand, as a natural, corporeal, sensuous, objective being he is a *suffering*, conditioned and limited being, like animals and plants. That is to say, the *objects* of his drives exist outside him as *objects* independent of him...*Hunger* is a natural *need*; it therefore requires a *nature* and *object* outside itself in order to satisfy and still itself. Hunger is the acknowledged need of my body for an *object* which exists outside itself...[44]

Marx in this passage says that objects of human need exist independent of human beings, outside of 'man'. Elsewhere in the EPM he draws materialist (realist) conclusions from scientific evidence against creationism:

> The creation of the *earth* received a heavy blow from the science of *geogeny*, i.e. the science which depicts the formation of the earth, its coming to be, as a

process of self-generation. *Generatio aequivoca* is the only practical refutation of the theory of creation.[45]

A comment on Bauer in the HF also implies a realist position:

> Since the *'religious world as such'* exists only as the world of *self-consciousness*, the Critical Critic [Bauer] - the theologian *ex professo* - cannot by any means entertain the thought that there is a world in which *consciousness* and *being* are distinct; a world which continues to exist when I merely abolish its existence in thought, its existence as a category or as a standpoint; i.e., when I modify my own subjective consciousness without altering the objective reality in a really objective way, that is to say, without altering my own *objective* reality and that of other men.[46]

Marx strikes a more ambiguous note in other parts of the early works,[47] but, at the very least, he is leaning towards a realist position, which he unambiguously assumed in later writings.

Dialectics

Another positive element in Marx's method is its dialectical character. The early works are replete with the language and concepts of dialectics: dialectical unity, contradiction, antitheses, negation of the negation, interconnection, internal relations, and supersession for example. A few examples will suffice to give the flavour of this dialectical character:

> Hegel's chief error is to conceive the *contradiction of appearances* as *unity in essence, in the idea*, while in fact it has something more profound for its essence, namely, an *essential contradiction*, just as here this contradiction of the legislative authority within itself, for example, is merely the contradiction of the political state, and therefore also of civil society within itself.[48] (CHPR)

> The antithesis between *lack of property* and *property*, so long as it is not comprehended as the antithesis of *labour* and *capital*, still remains an indifferent antithesis, not grasped in its *active connection*, in its *internal* relation, not yet grasped as a *contradiction*.[49] (EPM)

> Private property as private property, as wealth is compelled to maintain *itself*, and thereby its opposite, the proletariat, in *existence*. That is the positive side of the antithesis, self-satisfied private property...Within this antithesis the private property-owner is therefore the *conservative* side, the proletarian the

destructive side. From the former arises the action of preserving the antithesis, from the latter the action of annihilating it.[50] (HF)

The first quotation is part of Marx's criticism of the Hegelian dialectic but shows he is not thereby rejecting dialectics as such when he criticises it in the hands of Hegel. In the second, from the EPM, the significance of the notion of contradiction in Marx's method of analysis is again suggested, along with some hint of the broader dialectical character of his method, namely, an emphasis on change and connectedness ('active connection') and the doctrine of internal relations. The HF extract shows the application of the concept of contradiction to political economy and its link with practical activity. Marx's dialectics will be discussed and elaborated further in a later chapter.

The elements of Marx's developed scientific method are beginning to emerge in the early works. His general approach has a dialectical character, is materialist (albeit loosely), critical and emphasises the concrete, specific and empirical. Marx, in the course of the early works, also utilises three specific techniques in particular: the transformative method, textual analysis, and the historico-genetic method.[51]   All are evident in the CHPR.

The first, largely inspired by Feuerbach, involves inverting the subject and predicate (or object) as they are presented to reveal the true, unmystified nature of things. The application of this method assumes that some inversion has already taken place, and it is the primary criticism levelled by Marx against Hegel and speculative philosophy that he and it systematically invert real relations. A simple illustration of the inversion or transformative method is the transforming of the assertion "God made man" into "Man made God". Subject and predicate are inverted in the original statement thus obscuring the true relation between 'God' and 'man'. As Feuerbach writes, "We have only to always make the predicate into the subject, and thus as subject to object and principle - ie, only to invert the speculative philosophy, and thus we have the undisguised, the pure blank truth."[52] An example of Marx using the technique occurs in the CHPR: "Just as religion does not make man, but rather man makes religion, so the constitution does not make the people, but the people make the constitution."[53]

Marx's textual analysis identifies contradictions in Hegel's arguments, contradictions partly arising from Hegel's approach, but also reflecting actual contradictions in society. Marx basically accepts Hegel's account of society as accurate, albeit in a mystified manner of presentation. Therefore, contradictions in Hegel's account point to contradictions in reality. So

Marx moves from the pages of Hegel's *Philosophy of Right* to existing society, from an internal critique of Hegel's philosophy to an external critique of society. At this point Marx draws on his historical research, particularly regarding the origins of the state, to criticise state and society. Marx focuses on the dichotomy of state and civil society, which he criticises from a radical democratic position.

These techniques and the general method described characterise Marx's approach in the early writings and form the basis of his later method.

Notes

[1] The principal pre-1845 works of methodological interest are the *Critique of Hegel's Philosophy of Right* (CHPR), *A Contribution to the Critique of Hegel's Philosophy of Right:Introduction* (CHPR:I), the *Economic and Philosophical Manuscripts* (EPM), and *The Holy Family* (HF).

[2] For an account of the development of Hegelianism and use of the term *Wissenschaft* within it see Toews (1980).

[3] Marx (1975) 65 (CHPR)

[4] ibid., 64-65 (CHPR)

[5] ibid., 66-67 (CHPR)

[6] CW. 4. 57 (HF)

[7] ibid., 57 (HF)

[8] Marx (1975) 73 (CHPR)

[9] ibid., 74 (CHPR)

[10] ibid., 69-70 (CHPR)

[11] CW. 4. 60 (HF)

[12] See Howard (1972) 53 on this point.

[13] ibid., 82

[14] See O'Malley (1970) xxxv

[15] See Colletti (1975) 20

[16] See Bhaskar (1989) 126-27

[17] See Maguire (1972) 4

[18] See, for example, Marx's doctoral thesis, CW. 1. 85 and 86. Also, Maguire (1972) 4

[19] Marx (1975) 281-282 (EPM)

[20] CW. 4. 82-83 (HF)

[21] ibid., 52-53 (HF)

[22] Marx (1975) 281; ibid., 381 (EPM)

[23] ibid., 281 (EPM)

[24] ibid., 322-23 (EPM)

[25] ibid., 158-59 (CHPR)

[26] ibid., 208 (Letter to Ruge, September 1843)

[27] ibid., 209 (Letter to Ruge, September 1843)

[28] ibid., 243 (CHPR:I)

[29] ibid., 244 (CHPR:I)

[30] ibid., 244-45 (CHPR:I)

[31] ibid., 251 (CHPR:I)

[32] ibid., 251 (CHPR:I)
[33] ibid., 354 (EPM)
[34] CW. 4. 85-86 (HF)
[35] Marx (1975) 281; ibid., 355 (EPM)
[36] ibid., 381 (EPM)
[37] Colletti (1975) 11, is incorrect when he describes Marx as 'clearly materialist' in 1842.
[38] See McLellan (1969) 101-13
[39] Marx (1975) 389 (EPM)
[40] ibid., 355 (EPM)
[41] See Suchting (1983) 28
[42] See McLellan (1973) 42 on Marx's early atheism.
[43] Marx (1975) 244 (CHPR:I)
[44] ibid., 389-90 (EPM)
[45] ibid., 356 (EPM)
[46] CW. 4. 192-93 (HF)
[47] A point acknowledged by Ruben, who is the most forceful advocate of a realist Marx in the early works. See Ruben (1979) 91
[48] CW. 3. 91 (CHPR)
[49] ibid., 293-94 (EPM)
[50] CW. 4. 35-36 (HF)
[51] See O'Malley (1970)
[52] Feuerbach in Howard (1972) 19
[53] Marx (1975) 87 (CHPR)

2   Method in the Later Marx

In the previous chapter an outline was given of Marx's method in his early work. Various key themes were identified, most notably materialism, dialectics, an emphasis on the empirical and concrete, and use of the inversion technique. The aim of this chapter is to show how Marx developed and departed from these methodological features in his later work, and to provide a clear and thorough account of Marx's method in his later writings.

Before beginning the clarificatory account of Marx's method in his later writings a brief comment on the issue of periodisation and continuity is appropriate. There is a continuing debate among commentators as to the relationship between Marx's early and later writings. Did the same ideas persist from the earlier writings into the later ones or was there a break of some kind between the two?

Periodisation and Continuity

Marx's work is commonly periodised into the pre-1845 'early works' and the 1845 onwards 'later works'. The date of 1845 has been held to be pivotal in Marx's work because the *Theses on Feuerbach* (TOF) is, in the words of Engels, "the first document in which is deposited the brilliant germ of the new world outlook,"[1] i.e., it heralds the birth of historical materialism and, hence, of Marxism proper.

However, even while accepting the major innovation signified by the TOF, it is not necessary to view this writing as constituting an absolute break with Marx's previous thought. Any periodisation of Marx's work necessarily has blurred edges, because even the most radical changes in his ideas are accompanied by continuities with his earlier thinking. In particular, the view that an absolute (or epistemological) break divides the early from the later works should by now have been discredited by the wide dissemination of the *Grundrisse* (GR). In this work themes and concerns from the early works, particularly relating to dialectical philosophy, feature prominently.   This, along with comments scattered throughout the later works, points firmly towards a continuity in Marx's work.

The case for continuity has been persuasively made by various commentators,[2] so it will suffice here to present just some of the supporting evidence relating to the one theme of dialectics. Those who have argued that there is a break between the early and later Marx have often focussed on the theme of dialectics, arguing that it is present only in the early writings. However, in a letter to Engels written in 1858 Marx suggests the continuing influence of Hegel on him:

> I am by the way discovering some nice arguments. E.g., I have completely demolished the theory of profit as hitherto propounded. What was of great use to me as regards *method* of treatment was Hegel's *Logic* at which I had taken another look BY MERE ACCIDENT...I should very much like to write in two or three sheets making accessible to the common reader the *rational* aspect of the method which Hegel not only discovered but also mystified.[3]

In other letters Marx describes *Capital* as having a "dialectical structure", as involving a "dialectical method of exposition", and as "this first attempt at applying the dialectical method to Political Economy"; while in the *Theories of Surplus Value* (TSV) Marx accuses Thomas De Quincey of lacking "dialectical depth".[4]

Hegel's influence on Marx's later works is further acknowledged in the famous 1873 postface to the second edition of *Capital* where Marx writes that he is a pupil of Hegel whom he describes as "that mighty thinker." He also notes that there is a 'rational kernel' within the 'mystical shell' of Hegel's dialectic, and refers to his own 'dialectical method.'

The question is clearly not continuity *or* break, but rather of *the extent* of the continuity between the early and the later works. The evidence suggests that not only was there no categorical break in Marx's thought, but also that themes of the early works, most notably dialectics, continued right through the later works. In describing the method found in the later works the extent of continuity will become more apparent.

Given the continuity of themes from the early to the later Marx, there is an argument to be made for amending the usual 'early'/'later' periodisation of Marx's work. Adopting the dividing line of 1845, the later works begin with the TOF, *The German Ideology* (GI) and the *Poverty of Philosophy* (POP). These works written in 1845, 1846 and 1847 respectively, along with Marx's other works up to 1857 may be considered transitional between the early and the mature writings of Marx - a 'middle Marx'. While marking the birth of the materialist conception of history and a departure from that work strongly Hegelian or Feuerbachian in character, they still involve Marx looking over his shoulder at his philosophical roots, and 'settling accounts' with the speculative philosophy embraced in his youth; they still have a substantial philosophical content, and they do not have the economic focus of the mature works from the GR onwards.[5] The later works, then, may themselves be divided into transitional works (1845-57) and mature works (1857 on). It is this scheme that will be used in the rest of this chapter.

The Transitional Works

Materialism and Practice

One of the principal themes to be found in the transitional works (and also one of the most significant areas of development in the later Marx) is materialism. Up until 1845 Marx's views on materialism were ambiguous and under-developed. With the TOF and the GI Marx elaborates his view of materialism in a much clearer and more emphatic manner.

The TOF demonstrates Marx's philosophical materialism. Following on from the early works they continue his implied philosophical realism, his opposition to idealism and his view that the ultimate resolution of philosophical/theoretical problems is achieved in the material world. But the main theme of the TOF is practice or human activity, and his main criticism of the materialism of Feuerbach and thinkers like him is its inattention to practice. Old materialism views reality in passive terms, as consisting of objects separate from us, which we observe and contemplate. Activity is seen in terms of thought, and the distinctively human as theory or consciousness. In other words, activity is essentially restricted to thought - the territory of idealism. The material and the ideal are separated as passive object and active subject; Marx denies this independence and asserts the importance of practical human activity (or practice) in reality. Practice is (mis)conceived in Feuerbach's materialism as the realm of egoism, commerce and utility; and so it is not considered significant.

The source of Marx's ambiguity in the early works regarding materialism becomes a little clearer now. In the Economic and Philosophical Manuscripts (EPM) Marx at times seemed to regard materialism as one side of a contradiction (the other side being idealism) to be overcome: "consistent naturalism or humanism differs both from idealism and materialism and is at the same time their unifying truth."[6] And elsewhere in the same work:

> It can be seen how subjectivism and objectivism, spiritualism and materialism, activity and passivity, lose their antithetical character, and hence their existence as such antitheses, only in the social condition; it can be seen how the resolution of the *theoretical* antitheses themselves is possible *only* in a *practical* way...[7]

In the transitional works Marx develops the idea, only fleetingly touched on in the early works, that the ideal-material dichotomy may be overcome through practice. His position is still clearly materialist, but differs from previous materialism because of the element of activity that it takes from idealism. In the TOF Marx enunciates his notion of the unity of theory and practice:

> The question whether objective truth can be attributed to human thinking is not a question of theory but is a *practical* question. Man must prove the truth, i.e., the reality and power, the this-worldliness of his thinking in practice. The dispute over the reality or non-reality of thinking which is isolated from practice is a purely *scholastic* question.[8]

So, thoughts traceable in the EPM are here laid down emphatically: idealism is rejected, but so is passive, abstract materialism. Old dichotomies between ideal and material and subject and object are overcome, and practice (unified with theory) is made central.

Marx's comments on philosophical materialism lay the foundations for his 'materialist conception of history', which he outlines in the GI. In this materialist conception practice, the central theme of the philosophical materialism outlined in the TOF, is discussed in more concrete terms as production. Production is how human beings distinguish themselves from animals (they are not to be distinguished according to such abstract idealist criteria as consciousness), and production is the primary determining factor of the form of intercourse and of society more generally. The very nature of human beings is in a sense determined by production.

The materialist conception of history makes material production the starting point for historical study. Production is the key to understanding societies; it is the basis on which the form of economic intercourse, civil society, religion, philosophy - in short all society - arises. To understand or explain society or history the process of production must be examined.

Production has primacy over consciousness; it is determining of consciousness. Marx contrasts his materialist conception of history with that of idealism:

> It has not, like the idealist view of history, to look for a category in every period, but remains constantly on the real *ground* of history; it does not explain practice from the idea but explains the formation of ideas from material practice, and accordingly it comes to the conclusion that all forms and products of consciousness cannot be dissolved by mental criticism, by resolution into "self-consciousness" or transformation into "apparitions", "spectres", "whimsies", etc., but only by the practical overthrow of the actual social relations which gave rise to this idealistic humbug; that not criticism but revolution is the driving force of history...[9]

The idealist approach marginalises or ignores the most important aspect of history; it confuses cause and effect, explaining material phenomena in terms of consciousness instead of the other way around. It imposes abstract categories on reality, and it can only criticise, not change society, because it operates at the level of theory and neglects practice. For Marx, practical intervention is a consequence of the materialist approach, and in political terms that translates into revolution.

Critique

It is clear then that Marx in the transitional works espouses a strong practical materialism. This materialism is also characterised by its emphasis on critique. This feature figured prominently in the early works and is now integrated into his materialism. Indeed, Marx grounds it in materialism and shows the road from Feuerbachian critique to materialism and *actual* critique:

> Owing to the fact that Feuerbach showed the religious world as an illusion of the earthly world - a world which in his writing appears merely as a *phrase* - German theory too was confronted with the question which he left unanswered: how did it come about that people "got" these illusions "into their heads"? Even for the German theoreticians this question paved the way to the materialistic view of the world, a view which is *not without premises*, but which empirically observes the actual material premises as such and for that reason is, for the first time, *actually* a critical view of the world.[10]

According to Marx, Feuerbach was sufficiently critical to expose the religious consciousness as an illusion, but his criticism remained at the level of theory. He failed to push the criticism to its materialist conclusion, that is, he did not seek the cause of the illusion in material circumstances. Feuerbach's was only a 'semi-materialism' because he did not incorporate the aspect of human practice into it. According to Marx, Feuerbach is inclined to "relapse into idealism" just when the point of practice, i.e., of actual criticism is reached. This point concerning Feuerbach's lack of genuine criticism bears comparison with Marx's comments in the EPM regarding Hegel's uncritical positivism and uncritical idealism.[11] In the GI Marx writes of Feuerbach:

> In the first case, the *contemplation* of the sensuous world, he necessarily lights on things which contradict his consciousness and feeling, which disturb the harmony he presupposes, the harmony of all parts of the sensuous world and especially of man and nature. To remove this disturbance, he must take refuge in a double perception, a profane one that perceives "only the flatly obvious" and a higher, philosophical, one that perceives the "true essence" of things.[12]

Feuerbach, by only perceiving "the flatly obvious", by ignoring activity, does not penetrate to the material contradictions that cause the illusion he identifies - the result: a form of uncritical positivism. The second perception in which he takes refuge from contradictions is a philosophical one that perceives the "true essence" of things. The realm of true essence is unsullied by concrete human practice and its contradictions; it is a realm of uncritical idealism.

For Marx, critique is a matter of getting to the truth beyond the illusion. Idealism is flawed in this respect because it is uncritical. The idealist conception is only able to:

> ...see in history the spectacular political events and religious and other theoretical struggles, and in particular with regard to each historical epoch they were compelled to *share the illusion of that epoch*. For instance, if an epoch imagines itself to be actuated by purely "political" or "religious" motives, although "religion" and "politics" are only forms of its true motives, the historian accepts this opinion.[13]

Only the materialist approach allows the illusions of any epoch to be penetrated, because it examines the cause of those illusions in the material base. Idealism, or any approach that does not appreciate the significance of human practice, must be limited in its capacity for critique and tend towards 'uncritical positivism'.

Marx's critical method in the early works was immanent, transcendent and practical (see chapter one). That is, it was a critique from within on the basis of internal contradictions in the writer's thought; its aim was to transcend the object of criticism by grasping the root of the contradiction; and it resolved the contradiction through practice. These same features apply to his critical method in the transitional works. This is illustrated by the fourth thesis on Feuerbach:

> Feuerbach starts out from the fact of religious self-estrangement, of the duplication of the world into a religious world and a secular one. His work consists in resolving the religious world into its secular basis. But that the secular basis lifts off from itself and establishes itself as an independent realm in the clouds can only be explained by the inner strife and intrinsic contradictoriness of this secular basis. The latter must, therefore, itself be both understood in its contradiction and revolutionised in practice. Thus, for instance, once the earthly family is discovered to be the secret of the holy family, the former must then itself be destroyed in theory and in practice.[14]

An immanent critique of the religious world leads to the root of its contradictions in the contradictions of the material world, and then to practice in order to destroy the causes of the religious consciousness in the material world. The difference from the critical method of the early works lies in the replacement of a Feuerbachian inspired humanism by the materialist conception of history.

'Empiricism'

In his account of the materialist method Marx is at pains to emphasise its empirical character.[15] In stressing the empirical nature of his method Marx's main concern is to contrast his materialist approach with that of German idealist (and 'semi-materialist') philosophy. In order to do this, he uses the term 'empirical' in at least three slightly different, although closely related ways. First, he describes the premises of his approach as being "verified in a purely empirical way" in contrast to German idealist philosophy, the premises of which are derived from philosophical reasoning, and are not a matter of empirical fact. The facts of production, the main materialist premise, can be verified empirically.

Secondly, Marx uses the term to highlight the starting point and primary focus of his approach. For Marx, his approach is empirical in that instead "of setting out from what men say, imagine, conceive," he sets out "from real, active men, and on the basis of their real life-process."[16]   Here 'empirical' denotes the material, the concrete, real individuals engaged in production. Marx's empirical approach starts with the living, producing individual in contrast to 'German philosophy' that starts from consciousness, people's ideas about themselves. Empirical in this context means starting from what people do, not from what they say (or think), from the facts of production rather than the speculations of consciousness.

The third nuance of 'empirical' as used by Marx implies the importance of specific empirical data over general concepts, the importance of historical detail over philosophical generalisation. According to Marx, German philosophy employs abstract concepts devoid of empirical content. Here empirical is counter-posed to ahistorical and non-specific.   For example, the notion of the family, according to Marx is not a static one, but rather one that changes over time. So, great attention must be given to the empirical nature of the family in any given historical context, or as Marx puts it, it must "be treated and analysed according to the existing empirical data, not according to 'the concept of the family.'"[17]

In short, German philosophy, according to Marx, has "never left the realm of philosophy". Its premises are derived philosophically rather than empirically, its starting point is consciousness rather than the more 'factual' material world, and its method is based on speculation and *apriori* reasoning with insufficient attention to empirical data.

Abstraction

Marx's stress on the empirical connects with his views on abstraction. A major criticism of Feuerbach is that his materialism is abstract.   In particular his conception of 'man' is abstract:

> ...because he still remains in the realm of theory and conceives of men not in their given social connection, not under their existing conditions of life, which have made them *what* they are, he never arrives at the actually existing, active men, but stops at the abstraction "man"...[18]

> Feuerbach's "conception" of the sensuous world is confined on the one hand to mere contemplation of it, and on the other to mere feeling; he posits "Man" instead of "real historical man". "Man" is really "the German".[19]

Here Marx criticises Feuerbach for his passive, contemplative attitude and for his abstractness in making 'Man' his subject rather than 'real historical man', i.e., human beings in specific social relations. Feuerbach does not conceive human beings in terms of their activity, their production. The abstraction 'Man' hides 'the German' that Feuerbach takes to be universal.

Marx similarly criticises other thinkers for their employment of abstract concepts. As with his criticism of Hegel in the early works, he criticises the undifferentiated application of general concepts without regard to the specific subject. For example Stirner is criticised for transforming private property "into the abstract notion of property,"[20] Stirner also transforms a specific historical form of liberation, namely liberation from serfdom, into a general, abstract category of 'freedom'. According to Marx, Stirner "transforms a definite historical act of self-liberation into the abstract category of 'freedom,' and this category is them defined more closely by means of totally different historical phenomenon which can likewise be included under the general conception of 'freedom.'"[21] In other words, Stirner empties the empirical content from a specific historical event, and in the space created inserts the meaning from another specific idea of freedom, thus making the abstraction even more of a distortion. Marx complains that in the process of abstraction applied by Stirner and others, concepts are detached from the historical situations that give them their content, have their meanings changed and are misapplied elsewhere.

Marx also criticises Proudhon for his method of abstraction:

Is it surprising that everything, in the final abstraction - for we have here an abstraction, and not an analysis - presents itself as a logical category? Is it surprising that, it you let drop little by little all that constituted the individuality of a house, leaving out first of all the materials of which it is composed, then the form that distinguishes it, you end up with nothing but a body; that, if you leave out of account the limits of this body, you soon have nothing but a space - that if, finally, you leave out of account the dimensions of this space, there is absolutely nothing left but pure quantity, the logical category?...Thus the metaphysicians who, in making these abstractions, think they are making analyses, and who, the more they detach themselves from things, imagine themselves to be getting all the nearer to the point of penetrating to their core - these metaphysicians in turn are right in saying that things here below are embroideries of which the logical categories constitute the canvas.[22]

Here Marx explicates the link between abstraction and idealism, how the process of abstraction allows the idealist inversion to take place. Idealist philosophers, including here the anarchist Proudhon, strip away from real things everything that gives them their specific identity, leaving nothing more than an abstract category or concept. This abstract category or concept they take to be the core or essence of the real object, the true reality, while the real object becomes little more than a shadowy impression of the category or concept. Marx's practical, empirical materialism is directly opposed to this idealist abstraction, which makes logical categories the core of things and the prime mover. The method of idealist abstraction gives an abstract dialectics also. In the POP Marx criticises the abstract idealism that produces a purely formal dialectical movement. If dialectics is treated in an abstract idealist way it becomes the empty formula thesis, antithesis, synthesis, which is applied to reality in a purely abstract or formal way. Dialectical movement and contradiction which is abstract in this way, is not rooted in concrete reality, and as such becomes a set of categories imposed on reality instead of drawn from the material world.

However, Marx's attacks on misuses of abstraction do not mean he eschewed all abstraction himself. Indeed, given that any process of conceptualisation and analysis involves abstraction, Marx could hardly have rejected it entirely. He discusses his own method of abstraction in the mature works, which will be considered later in this chapter.

Dialectics

Marx's method in these transitional works retains its dialectical nature (see chapter four for a fuller account of dialectical philosophy) from the early works, and in particular its use of the concept of contradiction. This is suggested in the TOF:

> Feuerbach starts out from the fact of religious self-estrangement, of the duplication of the world into a religious world and a secular one. His work consists in resolving the religious world into its secular basis. But that the secular basis lifts off from itself and establishes itself as an independent realm in the clouds can only be explained by the inner strife and intrinsic contradictoriness of this secular basis. The latter must, therefore, itself be both understood in its contradiction and revolutionised in practice.[23]

Feuerbach, according to Marx, fails to identify the material contradictions that give rise to religion and consequently can neither explain nor dissolve religion.

The central role of contradiction continues in the GI, where Marx takes it to be fundamental in the development of history and the eruption of revolution. Marx writes:

> The contradiction between the productive forces and the form of intercourse, which...has occurred several times in past history...necessarily on each occasion burst out in a revolution, taking on at the same time various subsidiary forms, such as all-embracing collisions, collisions of various classes, contradictions of consciousness, battle of ideas, political struggle, etc...Thus all collisions in history have their origin, according to our view, in the contradiction between the productive forces and the form of intercourse.[24]

The principal contradiction Marx identifies is that between productive forces and form of intercourse. From it spring other contradictions - of consciousness, ideas, political struggles, etc. - which are the form (but not the basis) of revolutionary struggles. The main and most prevalent contradiction stemming from that between productive forces and the form of intercourse is class contradiction, a primacy emphasised by Marx:

> ...society has hitherto always developed within the framework of a contradiction - in antiquity the contradiction between free men and slaves, in the Middle Ages that between nobility and serfs, in modern times that between the bourgeoisie and the proletariat.   (GI)

> The history of all hitherto existing society is the history of class struggles.[25]
> (*Manifesto*)

Class contradiction, along with various other contradictions, is implied by the division of labour, which in turn is determined by the development of the productive forces. These various contradictions are material contradictions rooted in a material framework - the mode of production. They do not exist just in consciousness and they cannot be overcome just by exhortation, by changing ideas. Hence Marx's criticism of Stirner for trying to ignore the basic contradiction between the bourgeoisie and the proletariat. According to Marx, Stirner believes that if individuals can banish the notion of class contradiction from their heads, then the contradiction will cease to exist:

> [Stirner] does not want...two individuals to be in "contradiction" to one another as bourgeois and proletarian...he would like to have them enter into a purely personal relation, to associate with one another merely as individuals. He does not take into consideration that in the framework of division of labour personal relations necessarily and inevitably develop into class relations and become fixed as such and that, therefore, all his talk amounts simply to a pious wish, which he expects to realise by exhorting the individuals of these classes to get out of their heads the idea of their "contradiction"...[26]

The contradictions Marx identifies are in this sense necessary: they are intrinsic to the state of society, to the division of labour and the development of the productive forces. His criticism of Stirner, Feuerbach and others is that they do not show (because they do not understand) the necessity of these contradictions and, hence, believe they can be resolved simply by wishing it, by changing opinions.

Just as Marx's materialism underpins his dialectics, so his dialectics informs his materialism. One example is the dialectical element of change. In his criticism of Feuerbach the absence of change in his materialism is expressed as a lack of history:

> He does not see that the sensuous world around him is not a thing given direct from all eternity, remaining ever the same, but the product of industry and of the state of society; and, indeed a product in the sense that it is an historical product, the result of the activity of a whole succession of generations, each standing on the shoulders of the preceding one, developing its industry and its intercourse, and modifying its social system according to the changed needs.[27]

This criticism echoes the ones Marx makes against Feuerbach and the political economists for using static abstractions. Change or movement must be incorporated into our understanding of the world, into the concepts and categories we employ. Just as a dialectics that is idealist rather than materialist is flawed, so a materialism that lacks the key dialectical feature of movement is inadequate.

Inversion

A final element of Marx's method in the transitional works deserving of mention is the technique of inversion. This technique featured in the early works and was taken from Feuerbach. In the transitional works Marx repeatedly identifies the inversions made by idealist and bourgeois thought.

Hegel and the Hegelians invert the material and the ideal attributing activity and primacy to the latter, and viewing the former as the expression or manifestation of the ideal. Cause and explanation are misattributed as a result. Marx writes in the GI, "for Bruno [Bauer], along with all philosophers and ideologists, erroneously regards thoughts and ideas - the independent intellectual expression of the existing world - as the basis of this existing world."[28]

Proudhon is similarly criticised in the POP for inverting conceptual categories and material relations of production:

> Economic categories are only the theoretical expressions, the abstractions of the social relations of production. M. Proudhon, holding things upside down like a true philosopher, sees in actual relations nothing but the incarnation of these principles, of these categories...[29]

Marx is not content simply to note the inversion. He locates its cause in the material base. The inversions Marx notes are ultimately products of the 'historical life-process':

> If in all ideology men and their relations appear upside-down as in a *camera obscura*, this phenomenon arises just as much from their historical life-process as the inversion of objects on the retina does from their physical life-process.[30]

If ideology inverts reality then the inversion technique must be applied to put it right side up. However, some care should be taken with the inversion method since Marx does not merely invert subject and predicate in a straightforward manner. The TOF shows that Marx did not wish to simply reverse the relationship of the material and the ideal in order to prioritise the former. Previous materialists had already done this, and Marx criticises them for not retaining the active side of idealism. Activity must be integrated into materialism, and consciousness seen as part of the individual; the separation of ideal and material must be replaced by the unity of theory and practice. So the inversion technique is only the first step, and once turned right side up the separated elements of reality must be reintegrated.

*

The transitional works display considerable continuities with the early works, but also significant developments. Marx continues his criticisms of idealism - its abstraction, inversion of reality, and uncritical perspective - and he develops his criticisms of existing materialism - its contemplative attitude, its lack of an active side and its neglect of human activity (the separation rather than unity of theory and practice). He introduces his materialist conception of history, which is characterised by its materialism, centrality of practice (production), empirical component, concreteness, sense of history and change, critical approach, use of the key dialectical concept of contradiction, and employment of the inversion technique. In the mature works these themes recur and undergo further development.

The Mature Works

In the mature works Marx shifts his attention to political economy. From a methodological point of view the key works are the *Grundrisse* (GR), *A Contribution to the Critique of Political Economy* (CPE), *Preface to a Critique of Political Economy* (CPE:P), *Theories of Surplus Value* (TSV), *Capital*, and the *Notes on Adolph Wagner* (*Notes*). These span the period 1857-1880 and show Marx's method at its most developed.

Materialism

Much of the transitional works were taken up with discussing materialism, and in particular the materialist conception of history. Having covered this ground already, there is little direct discussion of materialism in the mature works. However, the mature works remain strongly materialist in both focus and approach; in this sense they develop out of the transitional works using the foundation established by Marx in those writings. The introduction to the GR sets the tone: "The object before us, to begin with, *material production*...Individuals producing in society - hence socially determined individual production - is, of course, the point of departure."[31] The investigation of material production is the dominant theme of the later works, and in the famous *Preface to a Critique of Political Economy* (CPE:P) Marx reiterates the materialist conception of history, the method he developed in the GI.

The primacy of social production is at the heart of the materialist approach and in the mature works Marx sets out to investigate social production. Marx employs this approach throughout his analysis of capitalism in *Capital*. In a rare direct mention of the materialist method in *Capital* (and this in a footnote) it is clear the importance he attaches to it:

Technology reveals the active relation of man to nature, the direct process of the production of his life, and thereby it also lays bare the direct process of the production of the social relations of his life, and of the mental conceptions that flow from those relations. Even a history of religion that is written in abstraction from this material basis is uncritical. It is, in reality, much easier to discover by analysis the earthly kernel of the misty creations of religion than to do the opposite, i.e. to develop from the actual, given relations of life the forms in which these have been apotheosized. The latter method is the only materialist, and therefore the only scientific one. The weaknesses of the abstract materialism of natural science, a materialism which excludes the historical process, are immediately evident from the abstract and ideological conceptions expressed by its spokesmen whenever they venture beyond the bounds of their own speciality.[32]

An approach that ignores the material base is uncritical, and an approach that ignores history is abstract and ultimately inadequate. Furthermore, only a materialist method is scientific.

Critique

Marx's linking of materialism and critique follows on from the transitional works, and it is evident that Marx continues to place great emphasis on the critical character of his method. His main work, *Capital*, is subtitled *A Critique of Political Economy*, and the immanent-transcendent-practical critique of the early works continues to apply. A non-critical approach glosses over contradictions and accepts the mystified appearance of things. It fails to pierce the world of illusion, and assumes an inverted view of reality. In the mature works the element of critique is truly integral in the sense of having been integrated into the method and no longer requiring explicit highlighting. It runs throughout the other elements of Marx's method, an ever-present thread.

Practice

The closely linked theme of practice also receives little direct attention, although again it remains crucial to Marx's approach. Its continuing significance for Marx throughout the later works is demonstrated by the *Notes on Adolf Wagner* of 1879-80. Here Wagner is reproached for his inattention to practice and production in much the same way that Marx criticised previous materialism in the TOF and 'German philosophy' in the GI:

But with a schoolmaster-professor the relations of man to nature are not *practical* from the outset, that is relations established by action; rather [for Wagner] they are *theoretical* relations...on no account do men begin by 'standing in that theoretical relation to the *things of the external world*'. They begin, like every animal, by *eating, drinking* etc., hence not by 'standing' in a relation, but *by relating themselves actively*, taking hold of certain things in the external world through action, and thus satisfying their need[s]. (Therefore they begin with production.)[33]

Wagner is guilty of separating theory and practice, of failing to appreciate that consciousness exists in and develops through practice. Human beings relate to the world through activity, and, in particular, through production to satisfy their life needs.

'Empiricism'

Another theme that does not receive the emphasis it did in the earlier works is his empirical approach. In the GI in particular Marx was keen to assert the empirical character of his work. By the time of the mature works there is less need for Marx to stress this point. His 'opponent' is no longer speculative, idealist philosophy, but political economy and the unduly empirical and insufficiently theoretical approach of most recent and contemporary political economists (e.g., Ricardo, Smith, Say, Bastiat, Carey). Hence, his criticism of Ricardians for 'crass empiricism,' while Carey comes under fire for "massive and uncritical use of statistics, a catalogue-like erudition." More generally bourgeois economists are rebuked for "lack of theoretical understanding" and for "coarse grabbing at and interest in the empirically available material."[34]

In short, Marx criticises what he considers to be unsophisticated and uncritical use of empirical data. This is a thread that runs right through Marx's works from his criticism of Hegel for 'uncritical positivism' to the charge of 'crass empiricism' against political economists. Marx remains committed to an empirical approach (he uses a wealth of empirical data in his research), but not to an empiricist one.[35]

Essence and Appearance

Closely related to this point is Marx's use of the essence-appearance distinction, which incorporates his criticism of crude empiricism. In *Capital*, volume III, Marx writes:

If, as the reader will have realised to his great dismay, the analysis of the actual intrinsic relations of capitalist production is a very complicated matter and very extensive; if it is a work of science to resolve the visible, merely external movement into the true intrinsic movement, it is self-evident that conceptions which arise about the laws of production in the minds of agents of capitalist production and circulation will diverge drastically from these real laws and will merely be the conscious expression of the visible movements.

And again, "But all science would be superfluous if the outward appearance and the essence of things directly coincided."[36] What these quotations suggest is the centrality of a particular version of the essence-appearance distinction to Marx's conception of science. The inadequacy of the bourgeois political economists' scientific method lies largely in its failure to go beyond appearance to the 'intrinsic movement'. Their empirical approach focuses on the 'visible movements', and leads them to develop an 'inverted' conception of the world. Capitalism is characterised by a mismatch between appearance and essence, the outward appearance and the inner essence of things tend not to coincide. This means that if things are taken at 'face-value' (i.e., purely on the basis of their appearance), and if concepts and laws are derived directly from their appearance, then these concepts and laws will 'diverge drastically' from the 'real laws' and essential concepts. This is not to say that outward appearance is in some way a chimera or not real, but it can be deceptive. For example, profit as the surface appearance of surplus-value obscures the latter and misleads as to the origin of the extra value in profit:

In effect, profit is the form in which surplus-value presents itself to the view, and must initially be stripped by analysis to disclose the latter. In surplus-value, the relation between capital and labour is laid bare; in the relation of capital to profit, i.e., of capital to surplus-value that appears on the one hand as an excess over the cost-price of commodities realised in the process of circulation and, on the other, as a surplus more closely determined by its relation to the total capital, *the capital* appears *as a relation to itself*, a relation in which it, as the original sum of value, is distinguished from a new value which it generated. One is conscious that capital generates this new value by its movement in the processes of production and circulation. But the way in which this occurs is cloaked in mystery and appears to originate from hidden qualities inherent in capital itself.[37]

It is the connection between essence and appearance that is hidden, the mechanism generating the outward phenomena from the inner essence which is unseen. Marx makes the connection through analysis.

This use of the essence-appearance distinction marks something of a methodological innovation for Marx. The terms appear in the early works, particularly with reference to human essence, but barely feature at all in the transitional works. In the CHPR Hegel comes under fire for viewing Spirit as essence and material reality as mere appearance. In the TOF Feuerbach is criticised for positing abstract, static human essence. The term is only retrieved in the mature works to refer to the inner relations, intrinsic movement, inner connection - the structure, processes and mechanism that generate the appearance or external phenomena. This is a clear departure from earlier use of the terms.[38]

Inversion

The essence-appearance theme draws in another element from Marx's earlier works, namely, inversion. Inversion was originally seen as a method for turning misconceptions right side up; now it is seen as a characteristic of capitalism, a systemic phenomenon that makes appearance diverge from essence. The process of production inverts subject and object, for example, reversing and obscuring the relationship between surplus-value and profit:

> The way in which surplus-value is transformed into the form of profit by way of the rate of profit is, however, a further development of the inversion of subject and object that takes place already in the process of production...

> If the rate of surplus-value is known and its magnitude given, the rate of profit expresses nothing but what it actually is, namely a different way of measuring surplus-value...But in reality (i.e., in the world of phenomena) the matter is reversed. Surplus-value is given, but given as an excess of the selling price of the commodity over its cost-price; and it remains a mystery where this surplus originated...[39]

The process of capitalist production inverts economic relationships. The outer appearance of inner relations is inverted along with conceptions derived from that appearance. Hence, Marx writes, "everything appears reversed in competition, and thus in consciousness of the agents of competition."[40]

That the thread of inversion runs from the early works through the later works is evident from the reference Marx makes in *Capital* I comparing inversion in production with that in religion:

> Hence the rule of the capitalist over the worker is the rule of things over man, of dead labour over the living, of the product over the producer. For the commodities that become the instruments of rule over the workers...are mere consequences of the process of production, they are its products. Thus at the level of material production...we find the *same* situation that we find in *religion* at the ideological level, namely the inversion of subject into object and *vice versa*.[41]

Here Marx harks back to his original use of the inversion technique in his Feuerbachian days, and his early theological concerns.

Abstraction

From a methodological point of view, one of the most prominent themes of the late works as a whole and of the mature works in particular is abstraction. In the transitional works it was noted how Feuerbach, Stirner and Proudhon were criticised by Marx for their use of abstract concepts. This negative view of abstraction would appear to persist in the mature works where Marx criticises the political economists for 'simple formal abstraction', 'forced abstractions' and 'false abstraction'.[42] Further, in the *Notes* Marx criticises Wagner for his abstract starting point. Marx's comments on Wagner's use of the abstract concept 'man' strongly resemble those he makes in the GI on Feuerbach's use of the abstraction 'man'. In each case 'real historical man' or determinate social man is overlooked, and the empty abstraction 'man' is filled with 'the German' in Feuerbach's case and 'professorial man' by Wagner. The abstractions to which Marx is objecting are ones that are too general and assumed to apply too widely. Wagner's 'man' is assumed to embody universal features and to be universally applicable.

Marx also notes that Wagner's 'man' is not as abstract as Wagner himself assumes. At the very least, by virtue of ascribing language to this 'man', Wagner has placed him in society. Marx makes the criticism on a number of occasions that historically specific features are implicit in abstractions made by various writers. For example, Marx accuses political economists, such as J.S. Mill, of furtively inserting bourgeois relations into the general concept 'society'. Marx accuses Mill of presenting production "as encased in eternal natural laws independent of history," and then treating capitalist relations "as the inviolable natural laws on which society in the abstract is founded."[43]

Marx makes a very similar point against the presentation of that which is historically specific as something eternal. He claims that an important failing of classical political economy is that it sees capitalist production not "as a *historical* form but as a *natural form* of social production."[44]

In other words, Marx identifies a number of abstractions which are imagined to be general, eternal and/or natural, but which in fact contain historically specific assumptions. A related criticism concerns the failure to distinguish different forms of a thing, and, in particular, the failure to distinguish the general (abstract) form from its specific forms. For example, Marx notes Adam Smith fails to distinguish between surplus value and its specific forms of rent and profit.[45]

As well as objecting to the use of inadequate abstractions and to the inappropriate use of (what may be) adequate abstractions, Marx finds fault in abstract reasoning. As with Hegel, so with some of the political economists, who circumvent reality by abstract reasoning in order to deny the existence of contradictions in the material world. For example, Marx criticises James Mill's abstract logic that he uses to eliminate contradictions existing in reality. Like his earlier criticisms of Hegel and the idealists, Marx is here criticising efforts to present reality as conflict free, by reconciling in thought the very real contradictions existing in reality.[46] Abstract reasoning allows the resolution of real contradictions in thought, but this is merely a form of mystification since the contradictions continue to exist in reality. Of course the ideological motive behind this abstract reasoning is to demonstrate the harmony, and, hence, the 'good' and eternal character, of the contemporary economic system.

The above criticisms by Marx relate to the manner and use of abstractions and not to abstraction as such. Indeed, it is a measure of the importance that Marx attaches to abstraction that he devotes the attention he does to criticising bad abstraction. Elsewhere it is apparent that Marx embraces abstraction as a method: "...in the analysis of economic forms neither microscopes nor chemical reagents are of assistance. The power of abstraction must replace both."[47] This comment from the preface to the first edition of *Capital* suggests the centrality of abstraction to Marx's method, which he is also implicitly comparing to the method of natural science (biology to be precise).

That it is only poorly executed abstraction rather than abstraction as such to which Marx objects is further illustrated by his criticism of

Ricardo's use of abstraction. Far from criticising Ricardo for being too abstract, Marx reproaches him for not being abstract enough. Like those political economists Marx criticises for importing historically determinate features into their abstractions, Ricardo retains too much of the concrete in his abstraction of value. He is then also criticised by Marx for formal abstraction, i.e., for deriving general laws from the phenomenal without adequate theoretical interpretation. In this instance it is again the *manner* of abstracting that is criticised.[48]

Marx discusses his views on abstraction in the introduction to the GR. He begins by discussing the use of very general abstractions such as the concept 'production'. While having some value Marx sets strict limits on the usefulness or applicability of such general, transhistorical abstractions. Such abstractions can obliterate crucial differences leading to a rewritten history that presents a seamless development up to the present day, and projects elements of modern capitalism, such as capital itself, into former societies. Modern economists, according to Marx, use abstraction to portray the capitalist economy as harmonious and eternal. These criticisms are familiar from the account already given of Marx's catalogue of misuses of abstraction.

Marx goes on to discuss the role of abstraction in the method of political economy, making an implicit distinction between the method of inquiry and the method of presentation. In the method of inquiry, that is to say in the process of investigation into any aspect of political economy, the starting point is the concrete world around us. Or to put this another way, the method of inquiry starts from our observations and conceptions of the world, our experiences and theories of the world, "what is given, in the head as well as in reality".[49] From this starting point we develop abstractions as we analyse and theorise 'what is given'. In short, the method of inquiry proceeds from the concrete to the abstract.

The method of presentation, on the other hand, is a reversal of this; it proceeds from the abstract to the concrete. That is to say, in presenting the results of our investigations, according to Marx, we must start from the abstract and gradually work our way to concrete reality. The concrete appears as the result rather than as the starting point.

Marx distinguishes between the concrete as starting point and the concrete as end point. The concrete reality with which the method of inquiry begins is what he terms the 'immediate concrete', that is reality as we immediately perceive it, whereas the concrete with which the method of presentation ends is what Marx terms the 'concrete totality' or 'the product of thinking and comprehending.'

This distinction between method of enquiry and of presentation is made more explicitly by Marx in the postface to the second edition to *Capital* I:

> Of course the method of presentation must differ in form from that of inquiry. The latter has to appropriate the material in detail, to analyse its different forms of development and to track down their inner connection. Only after this work has been done can the real movement be appropriately presented. If this is done successfully, if the life of the subject-matter is now reflected back in the ideas, then it may appear as if we have before us an *a priori* construction.[50]

The *a priori* appearance stems from the abstract starting point in the method of presentation, which demonstrates the necessary links between aspects of the subject matter (political economy). However, it is worth noting that Marx changes his view of what the abstract starting point for presenting his political economy should be. Initially (that is in the GR) Marx's abstract starting point for the method of presentation seems to be general abstraction: "The order obviously has to be (1) the general, abstract determinants which obtain in more or less all forms of society..."[51] By the time of *Capital* I the starting point is the much less general 'commodity'. The change is from a notion of the abstract as the general, common characteristics of production to the abstract as the particular essential features of capitalist production, located in the commodity. It is a matter of abstracting the essential from the inessential.[52]

The GR and postface to *Capital* extracts on method may be usefully read along side a comment Marx makes in the TSV:

> Classical economy is not interested in elaborating how the various forms come into being, but seeks to reduce them to their unity by means of analysis, because it starts from them as given premises. But analysis is the necessary prerequisite of genetical presentation, and of the understanding of the real, formative process in its different phases.[53]

Classical economy accepts forms of appearance uncritically as its premises or starting point. It then analyses (abstracts from) these, reducing them to general abstractions consisting of their common features. So, wealth, for example, in its various forms, such as rent and interest, is reduced to profit. What classical economy does not do is to show how the forms of appearance arose, their formative process, i.e., their inner relations and underlying mechanisms. This genetical method of presentation is what Marx seeks to achieve, and in it the (concrete) forms are the result rather than the point of departure. Marx is interested in showing the genesis of capital, its formation and development, its essential features and the necessary connections between them. He wishes to capture the dynamic of capitalism, the contradictions that drive it, and the direction in which it is moving. These aims produce and are part of a method of abstraction very different from the thinkers he criticises.

Abstraction is not only a method, it is also a process in reality. For example, the reduction of diverse labours to simple labour is a process of abstraction in reality:

> To measure the exchange values of commodities by the labour time they contain, the different kinds of labour have to be reduced to uniform, homogenous, simple labour, in short to labour of uniform quality, whose only difference, therefore is quantity.
>
> This reduction appears to be an abstraction, but it is an abstraction which is made every day in the social process of production. The conversion of all commodities into labour time is no greater an abstraction, and is no less real, than the resolution of all organic bodies into air.[54]

Furthermore, abstractions in thought are themselves the product of historical relations. Abstractions in thought reflect abstractions in reality:

> As a rule, the most general abstractions arise only in the midst of the richest possible concrete development, where one thing appears as common to many, to all. Then it ceases to be thinkable in a particular form alone...[A]bstraction of labour as such is not merely the mental product of a concrete totality of labours. Indifference towards specific labours corresponds to a form of society in which individuals can with ease transfer from one labour to another, and where the specific kind is a matter of chance for them, hence of indifference.
>
> This example of labour shows strikingly how even the most abstract categories, despite their validity - precisely because of their abstractness - for all epochs, are nevertheless, in the specific character of this abstraction, themselves likewise a product of historic relations, and possess their full validity only for and within these relations.[55]

Certain conditions are necessary in order for abstractions in thought to be made, and certain abstractions are the product of the specific historical conditions reached. Marx is here referring to those, such as the political economists, who abstract in an unthinking way. They abstract with insufficient awareness of their own historical specificity and they reflect abstractions in reality unquestioningly and uncritically.

Marx's own abstractions show an acute awareness of how they are created. It is this conscious approach to abstraction and the dialectical character of Marx's abstractions which makes them distinctive. Dialectics is the final aspect of Marx's method in the mature works to be considered.

Dialectics

Some mention of Marx's continuing use of dialectics in the later works has already been made at the beginning of this chapter. In the transitional works Marx made significant use of the dialectical notion of contradiction, but as a whole dialectics did not feature prominently. What direct discussion there was tended to be critical, for example, in the POP. This lack of prominence is, perhaps, largely due to Marx's desire to distance himself from speculative, idealist dialectics, and from Hegelianism more generally. By the time of the mature works, though, Marx's principal opponent was no longer German idealist philosophy, but contemporary political economy, and here it is the dialectical approach which needs asserting. Hence, dialectical language is more pervasive, particularly in the GR.[56]

The central dialectical theme, as in the earlier writings, is contradiction. The *Preface to a Critique of Political Economy* takes up where the GI left off by identifying the key contradiction as that between the forces and relations of production.[57] Historical development is driven by the dialectical contradiction between the forces and relations of production which are both united and opposed. In *Capital* III Marx identifies this contradiction in capitalism as the cause of its passing as a mode of production:

> The capitalist mode of production is...a historical means of developing the material forces of production and creating an appropriate world-market and is, at the same time, a continual conflict between this its historical task and its own corresponding relations of social production.[58]

More often, though, Marx focuses on less general contradictions. The contradictions identified by Marx in the mature works are extensive and mainly economic. Some of the principal ones are (examples of references in brackets): exchange value and use-value (*Capital* I, chapter 1; TSV II, p.509); production and consumption (TSV I, p.283); buying and selling

(TSV III, p.101); capital and labour (TSV III, pp.97-98); and labour and property (TSV III, pp.422-23). For Marx capitalism is riven with contradictions, each ultimately containing the possibility of crisis. The link between contradictions and crises is dealt with at length by Marx (especially in TSV II), and the consequences for capitalism are spelled out:

> The fact that bourgeois production is compelled by its own immanent laws, on the one hand, to develop the productive forces as if production did not take place on a narrow restricted social foundation, while, on the other hand, it can develop these forces only within these narrow limits, is the deepest and most hidden cause of crises, of the crying contradictions within which bourgeois production is carried on and which, even at a cursory glance, reveal it as only a transitional, historical form.[59]

Contradictions cause crises and crises reveal contradictions. Those who seek to justify capitalism ('the apologists') deny contradictions exist or deny their deep-rootedness and immanence. For example:

> In the crises of the world market, the contradictions and antagonisms of bourgeois production are strikingly revealed. Instead of investigating the nature of the conflicting elements which erupt in the catastrophe itself and insisting, in the face of their regular and periodic recurrence, that if production were carried on according to the textbooks, crises would never occur. Thus the apologetics consist in the falsification of the simplest economic relations, and particularly in clinging to the concept of unity in the face of contradiction.[60]

Contradictions imply change. They themselves exist in processes as tendencies, which, in the form of crises, are liable to precipitate dramatic change. The idea of everything being in motion is central to dialectics, and Marx's method incorporates this. 'Process', 'movement', 'metamorphosis', 'development', 'moment' and 'becoming' are the kind of terms Marx uses throughout his mature works to indicate that the subject-matter being dealt with is in a state of flux.[61]

The 'long view' makes the process and moments more apparent. From within capitalism, for example, the changing nature of the system as a whole is not so evident even if movement within the system is acknowledged. Change tends to be hidden beneath the surface until the eruption of crisis. Marx's method aims to 'see' the change in things, especially the hidden change, and to incorporate it into its abstractions and analyses. Hence, the description of Marx's abstractions as dialectical -

they incorporate change: 'capital' includes its history and its tendencies, it is not just the actual means of production. The specifically dialectical term '*aufheben*' (here translated as suspension) implies the dialectical view of change used in Marx's method:

> ...our method indicates the points where historical investigation must enter in, or where bourgeois economy as a merely historical form of the production process points beyond itself to earlier historical modes of production...This correct view likewise leads at the same time to the points at which the suspension of the present form of production relations gives signs of its becoming - foreshadowings of the future. Just as, on one side the pre-bourgeois phases appear as *merely historical*, i.e. suspended pre-suppositions, so do the contemporary conditions of production likewise appear as engaged in *suspending themselves* and hence in positing the historic presuppositions for a new state of society.[62]

Marx has a sense of history in his method. The present contains suspended elements of the past, pointing to the origins of contemporary society. The present is also in the process of itself becoming history, with contemporary conditions of production 'engaged in *suspending themselves*'. The translation of '*aufheben*' as suspension is helpful in conveying the presupposition of motion; the halting and retention of things in process is suggested, motion itself is suspended with regard to these things.[63] Also worthy of note in this extract is the term 'becoming', another dialectical term implying immanent change. The suspension of present production relations is part of the process of becoming of future production relations. Things, in this instance production relations, are always becoming something else, they are not static.

*

The method in the mature works is a continuation of that in the transitional works (which is itself a development of the method found in the early writings). The familiar themes of materialism (particularly historical materialism), critique, practice, an empirical approach, inversion, abstraction and dialectics, all apparent in the transitional works, recur in the mature writings. Materialism, critique, practice, and 'empiricism' recede into the background, having been asserted and argued for at length already. Their presence is no less powerful but they have become more assimilated, fully absorbed into the method. Abstraction, essence and appearance, and dialectics come to the fore in Marx's methodological discussions. With greater distance from the Hegelianism of his youth with which accounts have now been settled, and with a target of attack other than German speculative philosophy, Marx is able to express a more positive view of dialectics. The GR shows how much his published works owe to the dialectical approach, although the question of how successfully Marx stripped the dialectic of its mystical Hegelian shell is open to debate. His reflections on abstraction show the importance he attached to a correct method and use of abstraction, and his use of an essence-appearance distinction is a significant and distinctive feature of his method in the mature works.

Conclusion

It is clear that Marx paid a great deal of attention to method, and that his own approach was a fusion of several key elements. He sought to overcome the limitations of the Hegelian, idealist approach - principally its lack of a practical, empirical, materialist foundation - while retaining its principal strength, namely, its critical dialectical dimension.

Indeed, it is the dialectical component that binds the very different elements of Marx's method together. Every aspect of his method has a dialectical character to it: dialectics lends a dynamic, practical-critical character to his materialism; it prevents his empirical approach lapsing into empiricism by incorporating it into the essence-appearance distinction that he develops; and it ensures his abstraction technique does not fall into the trap of simply producing empty generalisations rather than identifying the essential in any given structure or process. Marx's method is, then, above all a dialectical method, and it is precisely in its dialectical character than its strength lies.

A fuller discussion of Marx's dialectical approach will be given in chapter four after looking more closely at his understanding of materialism in the next chapter.

Notes

[1] Engels quoted in W. Suchting, "Marx's 'Theses on Feuerbach' in Issues in Marxist Philosophy, vol.II, Materialism, ed. J. Mepham and D.-H. Ruben (Brighton: Harvester Press, 1979), p.5

[2] See C. Arthur, *Dialectics of Labour* (Oxford: Blackwell, 1986), and D. McLellan, *Introduction to 'Marx's Grundrisse'* (London: Macmillan, 1980) for example. Authors arguing for the continuing influence of Hegel/dialectics on Marx in the later works include Carver (1975); S. Meikle, *Essentialism in the Thought of Karl Marx* (London: Duckworth, 1985); M. Nicolaus in "Foreword" to Karl Marx, *Grundrisse* (London: Penguin, 1973); R. Rosdolsky, *The Making of Marx's 'Capital'*, tr. P. Burgess (London: Pluto, 1977); and H. Uchida, *Marx's Grundrisse and Hegel's Logic*, ed. T. Carver (London: Routledge, 1988).

[3] *CW*, volume 40, p.249 (correspondence)

[4] *CW*, volume 42, p.173; ibid., p.390; ibid., p.464 (correspondence); and Karl Marx, *Theories of Surplus Value* (hereafter *TSV*), volume II (London: Lawrence and Wishart, 1969b), p.123

[5] See Arthur (1986), pp.102-26 for a very similar periodisation. He also includes *The Holy Family* (1844) in the transitional works, a point that serves to illustrate the early work - late work continuity.

[6] Karl Marx, *Early Writings* (Harmondsworth: Penguin, 1975), p.389 (EPM)

[7] ibid., p.354

[8] *CW*, volume 5, p.3 (TOF)

[9] ibid., pp.53-54 (GI)

[10] ibid., p.236 (GI)

[11] See Marx (1975), p.385 (EPM)

[12] *CW*, volume 5, p.39 (GI)

[13] ibid., p.55 (GI)

[14] *CW*, volume 5, p.4 (TOF)

[15] There are at least nine assertions of the empirical character of his method by Marx in the *German Ideology* alone.

[16] ibid., pp.36-37 (GI)

[17] ibid., p.43 (GI)

[18] ibid., p.41 (GI)

[19] ibid., pp. 38-39 (GI)

[20] ibid., p.229 (GI)

[21] ibid., p.302 (GI)

[22] *CW*, volume 6, p.163 (POP)

[23] *CW*, volume 5, p.4 (TOF)

[24] ibid., p.74 (GI)

[25] ibid., p.432 (GI); CW, volume 6, p.485 (*Manifesto*)

[26] *CW*, volume 5, pp.436-37 (GI)

[27] ibid., p.39; ibid., p.41 (GI)

[28] ibid., p.99 (GI)

[29] *CW*, volume 6, p.165 (POP)

[30] *CW*, volume 5, p.36 (GI)

[31] Marx (1973), p.83 (GR)

[32] Marx (1976), pp. 493-94 (*Capital* I)

[33] Carver (1975), p.190 (*Notes on Wagner*)

[34] K. Marx, Theories of Surplus Value, volume I (London: Lawrence and Wishart, 1969a), p.89; Marx (1973), p.888 (GR); Ibid., p.92.

[35] One indication of Marx's continuing commitment to an empirical approach is noted by McLellan: "As in the 1850s and 1860s, Marx [after 1870] amassed a huge amount of

material...After his death Engels was amazed to find among Marx's papers more than two cubic metres of documents containing nothing but Russian statistics." D. McLellan, *Karl Marx: His Life and Thought* (London: Macmillan, 1973), p.422

[36] K. Marx, *Capital*, volume III (London: Lawrence and Wishart, 1974), pp.312-13; ibid., p.817

[37] ibid., p.48

[38] Meikle (1988) discusses essentialism extensively, but overstates the case when he claims essentialism to be the 'essence' of Marx's method.

[39] Marx (1974), p.45; ibid. p.47 (*Capital* III)

[40] ibid., pp.224-25

[41] Marx (1976), p.990 (*Capital* I)

[42] Marx (1969a), p.89 (TSV I); K. Marx, *Theories of Surplus Value*, volume II (London: Lawrence and Wishart, 1969b), p.437

[43] Marx (1973), p.87 (GR)

[44] K. Marx, *Theories of Surplus Value*, volume III (London: Lawrence and Wishart, 1971), p.501

[45] Marx (1969a), p.92 (TSV I)

[46] Marx (1971), p.101 (TSV III)

[47] Marx (1976), p.90 (*Capital* I)

[48] See Marx (1969b), p.106 (TSV II)

[49] D. Sayer, *Marx's Method* (Hassocks, Sussex: Harvester, 1979), p.102

[50] Marx (1976), p.102 (*Capital* I)

[51] Marx (1973), p.108 (GR)

[52] For a full discussion of this point see Sayer (1979), pp.96-103

[53] Marx (1971), pp.500-01 (TSV III)

[54] *CW*, volume 29, p.272 (*Critique of Political Economy*)

[55] Marx (1973), p.104 (GR); ibid., p.105

[56] Marx's published works still tend to avoid too explicit a use of dialectical terminology in order to be more accessible to readers.

[57] *CW*, volume 29, p.263 (CPE:P)

[58] Marx (1974), p.250 (*Capital* III)

[59] Marx (1971), p.84 (TSV III)

[60] Marx (1969b), p.500 (TSV II); for further examples of 'apologist' denials of contradictions see also Marx (1969a), p.89 (TSV I); Marx (1969b), p.150 and p.495 (TSV II); Marx (1971), p.29, p.55 and pp.84-85 (TSV III)

[61] See, for example, Marx (1973), p.712 (GR); ibid., p.258; ibid., p.263

[62] ibid., pp.460-61

[63] Suspension is how Marx himself translated *aufheben* (see Marx (1973), p.750), although it is not clear from the context that any dialectical connotation is intended.

3   Marx and Materialism

The great basic question of all, especially of latter-day, philosophy, is that concerning the relation of thinking and being...[W]hich is primary, mind or nature [?]...Answers to this question split the philosophers into two great camps. Those who asserted the primacy of the mind over nature and, therefore, in the last instance, assumed world creation in some form or other...comprised the camp of idealism. The others, who regarded nature as primary, belong to the various schools of materialism.[1]

According to Engels the history of philosophy may be understood in terms of materialism and idealism. In looking at any given philosopher or philosophy we should ask to which do they give primacy: the ideal or the material? All philosophy, according to Engels, may be divided into the two camps of idealism and materialism. He and Marx fall into the materialist camp, a prerequisite for any truly scientific theory, according to Engels. Furthermore, Engels claims, the flaws inherent in previous materialist philosophies have finally been overcome in Marxism.

However, the precise nature of Marx's materialism and its role and significance in his thought is not as straightforward as Engels' categorisation of philosophy. To understand it some appreciation of philosophical materialism as a whole is required to help put Marx's materialism in context.

Materialism in Philosophy

The term 'materialism' encompasses diverse propositions and, as with all philosophical positions, it has a history in which its nature has changed. However, from a survey of those who have described themselves as materialists or who have been commonly held to espouse such a philosophy, a set of propositions associated with it may be identified.[2] Some of these propositions are compatible with non-materialist thought, but they have all historically been strongly linked with materialism. These propositions are not precise and allow some leeway for interpretation.

They incorporate terms such as 'primacy', 'dependency', and 'matter' and 'mind', all of which may be construed in different ways. Nevertheless, they do give a sense of what materialism is, and of what it is not.

Before describing these characteristic tenets of materialism, it should be noted that materialism is most commonly opposed to idealism (especially in the Marxist tradition), but it is also the case that historically materialism has been counter-posed to dualism, i.e., the doctrine that the world is composed of two constituents: spiritual/mind and corporeal/body (e.g., Augustine, Descartes). Marx's materialism opposes itself to both idealism and dualism.

Seven Tenets of Materialism

(i) Everything that exists is matter The first tenet asserts that the sole reality is material reality. The mental is a form of matter; there is no dualism between mind and matter. This tenet is sometimes expressed as naturalism, where nature is held to be the sole reality.

(ii) Matter is prior to mind The second tenet assigns primacy to matter by asserting that before there was mind there was matter. This rules out the possibility of theism which asserts the existence of a spiritual being as creator, and, therefore, it implies atheism. This tenet also entails the third tenet, that matter is independent of mind, in that matter could not be dependent on mind if it existed before mind.

(iii) Matter is independent of mind Tenet three expresses the notion of realism, that (material) reality exists independently of thought or perception. This is often identified as the defining proposition of materialism, but is logically distinct from a materialist position. For example, Kant held a position both realist (the 'thing-in-itself') and idealist. Also realism may posit the reality of the mental/spiritual as well as the material.[3]

(iv) Everything that exists is dependent on matter The proposition that everything that exists is dependent on matter begs the question of what is meant by dependent. However, it is clear that once again some kind of primacy is being ascribed to matter to the extent that nothing exists or happens without matter. The dependency in question is sometimes held to be a causal one, i.e., that movement of matter is the primary and ultimate

cause operating in the universe, and often understood in a reductive way to mean everything can be reduced to matter, thus linking it with tenet one.

(v) Only sensible entities, processes or content exist The stressing of the sensible in tenet five provides the basis for empiricism, but because the exact nature of the sensible entities is not specified, it may be either the basis for a materialist empiricism or for an idealist empiricism (e.g. Berkeley's empiricism).

(vi) Everything is composed of atoms The atomism expressed in the sixth tenet is a key feature of the materialism of Democritus, Epicurus, Gassendi and Hobbes, but nevertheless it is not intrinsic to materialism as such. Whether matter is composed of atoms or not does not affect the materialist position in essence.

(vii) The universe is not governed by intelligence, purpose, or final causes Finally, tenet seven's rejection of teleology is a pre-requisite for *a posteriori* investigation of the world. The notion of teleology is associated with the existence of a deity, a supernatural being that gives purpose to the world and its inhabitants. Hence, the association of the rejection of teleology with materialism, although, again, adherence to this tenet is not essential for a materialist.

Marx's Materialism

If we take these seven tenets as sketching out the broad character of materialist philosophy, what then is Marx's materialism and how does it compare?

Materialism appears to lie at the heart of Marxist theory. The principal terms and labels for the elements of Marx's theory seem to suggest this: 'the materialist conception of history', 'historical materialism' , 'dialectical materialism' (the latter two were not used by Marx himself though). Yet materialism remains ill defined in much of Marxist literature, and its definition hotly disputed in the rest. Indeed, it is even contended by some commentators that Marx was not a materialist.[4] Nevertheless, six basic theses of Marx's materialism can be identified in his work.

(i) The Realism Thesis

This is the thesis that there does exist a world independent of our perception of it; that material objects exist separately and independently of thought/mind/spirit. The evidence for Marx's realism from the early works has already been rehearsed (see chapter one, "Method in the Early Marx"). Further evidence may be drawn from the later works:

> The totality as it appears in the head, as a totality of thoughts, is a product of a thinking head, which appropriates the world in the only way it can...The real subject retains its autonomous existence outside the head just as before...[5] (GR)

> Use-values like coats, linen, etc., in short, the physical bodies of commodities, are combinations of two elements, the material provided by nature, and labour. If we subtract the total amount of useful labour of different kinds which is contained in the coat, the linen, etc.. a material substratum is always left. This substratum is furnished by nature without human intervention.[6] (*Capital*)

The realism thesis is also implied by the primacy of matter thesis, since if matter existed before mind then it must have existed without mind, and, therefore, must be mind independent.

It is noteworthy that the centrality of the realism thesis to Marxism is disputed. Ruben and Bhaskar put it at the very heart of Marx's thinking, but as Wood points out, and Ruben acknowledges, many commentators, implicitly or explicitly, deny Marx held the realism thesis.[7] According to Wood, these commentators hold one form or another of the view that "for Marx either there is no natural world apart from human beings and their subjectivity as practical beings, or else apart from man natural things have no determinate properties."[8]

However, this non-realist interpretation of Marx seems to be based on two points of confusion. First, Marx quite clearly believed that human beings transform nature/reality by praxis, and that in this sense they have a creative role with regard to nature. But a creative role is not the same as actually creating nature as such. Secondly, Marx's epistemological views argue against a passive, contemplative materialism or empiricism, and in favour of the view that human beings are active in the knowing process, and do not just receive knowledge as a pure 'given'. But to acknowledge an active element in the process of obtaining knowledge, or even to accept that knowledge is in some sense and to some extent 'produced' is not to deny a 'given' element based on the independent external reality.

To put this argument another way, nature may be viewed as always mediated when human beings confront it, but this does not entail the denial of an unmediated existence. Nature may no longer be 'natural' when human beings confront it now, because it has been changed and shaped by human practice to such a large extent, but its existence is still independent of human beings.

The non-realism case is put more strongly in terms of cognition and mediation, rather than praxis and mediation. If cognition is an active process then the knowledge process may be seen as inevitably involving mediation of the external world through: (i) the human activity required in the knowing process, and (ii) the conceptual framework inherent in the individual. Bhaskar suggests a useful distinction between intransitive and transitive objects of knowledge. The former are, "the real things and structures, mechanisms and processes, events and possibilities of the world...[which are not] in any way dependent upon our knowledge, let alone perception of them."[9] The latter (transitive objects of knowledge) are:

> ...the raw materials of science - the artificial objects fashioned into items of knowledge by the science of the day. They include the antecedently established facts and theories, paradigms and models, methods and techniques of inquiry available to a particular scientific school or worker.[10]

Bhaskar's distinction suggests an intransitive dimension corresponding to objective, independent reality and a transitive dimension consisting of socially produced knowledges which act as part of the mediating element in the process of knowledge acquisition. Thus, nature/reality may exist independently of human beings/mind in an unmediated form, and yet always be mediated in the experience of human beings because of the framework of transitive knowledge through which cognition of intransitive objects of knowledge must operate. So the realism thesis is maintained intact, whilst also accepting the inevitability of the mediation of the external world when we experience it, and that knowledge incorporates a produced component.

(ii) The Primacy of Matter Thesis

Marx's extended critique of idealism through the early and transitional works embodies an attack on the idealist assertion of the primacy of the mind over matter. The idealists invert the material and the ideal, and in transforming these back Marx turns the primacy of the ideal into the primacy of matter. This critique of Hegelian idealism has already been noted (see chapter one, "Method in the Early Marx"). The clearest positive statements of the thesis are to be found in Engels' *Feuerbach and the End of Classical German Philosophy* (LF):

> ...the material sensuously perceptible world to which we ourselves belong is the only reality and...our consciousness and thinking, however suprasensuous they may seem, are the product of a material, bodily organ, the brain. Matter is not a product of the mind, but mind itself is merely the highest product of matter.[11]

The primacy of matter thesis has been central in orthodox and Soviet interpretations of Marxist materialism. For example, the authoritative Stalinist text *Problems of Leninism* summarises Marxist materialism as follows:

> ...the Marxist materialist philosophy holds that matter, nature, being, is an objective reality existing outside and independent of our mind; that matter is primary, since it is the source of sensations, ideas, mind, and that mind is secondary, derivative, since it is a reflection of matter which in its development has reached a high degree of perfection, namely, of the brain, and the brain is the organ of thought; and that therefore one cannot separate thought from matter without committing a grave error.[12]

In similar vein (and representative of Second International orthodoxy) Bernstein writes:

> To be a materialist means first of all to trace back all phenomena to the necessary movement of matter. These movements of matter are accomplished according to the materialist doctrine from beginning to end as a mechanical process, each individual process being the necessary result of preceding mechanical facts.[13]

This interpretation of the primacy thesis (and of Marx's materialism more generally) goes further than either Marx or Engels would wish in its reductiveness. Neither Marx nor Engels reduced the mental to the material. For Marx and Engels, matter and mind may constitute a unity, but not an identity; matter is primary in that it can exist without mind

(mind, though, cannot exist without matter), and, as Engels noted, mind emerges from matter.

However, there is something in Engels' writings on materialism that does lend itself to the kind of rigid and reductive materialism quoted. Engels seeks to create a materialist philosophical system, encompassing a complete cosmology.[14] He seeks to fill in the philosophical background to Marx's social and historical analyses, doing the work Marx had not the time or inclination to do. Indeed, Engels was better informed in such topics as natural science, so it seems a natural division of labour between the two of them. Inevitably, then, Engels goes beyond what Marx actually wrote, and, in his desire to formulate a philosophical underpinning for historical materialism, he comes close to creating a *prima philosophia*. Engels work is susceptible to a reading that takes such philosophical abstractions as 'matter' as the starting point from which the more practical, concrete historical materialism is derived. As Schmidt writes:

> Wherever matter is brought in to provide an all-embracing, metaphysical explanation of the world, one is compelled willy-nilly to proceed from it as a universal principle and not from one of its concrete modes of existence.[15]

However, it should be noted that Engels is not unaware of this danger:

> Matter as such is a pure creation of thought and an abstraction. We leave out of account the qualitative differences of things in lumping them together as corporeally existing things under the concept matter. Hence matter as such, as distinct from definite existing pieces of matter, is not anything sensuously existing.[16]

Nevertheless, Engels seems happy to leap from the primacy of matter thesis to the historical materialism thesis without a pause to establish the connection between the two. It seems the verbal parallel between 'matter' in philosophical materialism and 'the material' in historical materialism (with 'mind' corresponding to the 'ideological superstructure') is enough for Engels to claim that the historical materialism thesis is but an extension or application to the concrete social world of the more general primacy of matter thesis.

(iii) The Naturalism Thesis

In this context naturalism denotes the thesis that the natural world constitutes the entirety of reality, with the natural world being opposed to the supernatural, so nature (reality) is not derived from or dependent upon any supernatural entity.   This thesis embraces Marx's atheism (and what may be termed his 'post-atheism'),[17] and with the first two theses constitutes Marx's materialist ontological beliefs.   Again the early works incorporate this thesis, for example this expression of it in the EPM:

> But since for socialist man the *whole of what is called world history* is nothing more than the creation of man through human labour, and the development of nature for man, he therefore has palpable and incontrovertible proof of his self-mediated birth, of his *process of emergence*.   Since the *essentiality* of man and of nature, man as the existence of nature for man and nature as the existence of man for man, has become practically and sensuously perceptible, the question of an alien being, a being above nature and man - a question which implies an admission of the unreality of nature and of man - has become impossible in practice.   Atheism, which is a denial of this unreality, no longer has any meaning, for atheism is a negation of God, through which negation it asserts the existence of man.   But socialism as such no longer needs such mediation.[18]

The naturalism thesis is the third of Marx's 'philosophical' materialism theses.   This thesis is made central to Marx's philosophical materialism by such commentators as Wood and Callinicos.[19]   For Wood the core of this thesis is the assertion that the sole reality is the natural world, and the natural world is made up solely of matter.   For Callinicos the thesis is understood as meaning that 'man' is a dependent part of nature, and the basic unity of the natural and social world makes for a basic unity of natural and social science.

Callinicos' interpretation presents a weaker version of the thesis. According to him, Marx wishes to deny the existence of the supernatural, and that the world is the product of God or *Geist*.   Wood's interpretation is stronger and needs to be construed with care.   It could be read as implying Marx was a reductive materialist, but rather than seeking to reduce everything to the material, Marx's aim is to oppose idealist and dualist assertions regarding the independence of the mental.   As Marx writes in the HF, "It is impossible to separate thought from matter that thinks."[20]

Both Wood and Callinicos see Marx as endeavouring to emphasise the natural world, and the fact that human beings are a part of nature, they share a common 'essentiality'.   Marx often uses the term 'nature' as a synonym for reality, because for him the natural world constitutes the entirety of reality, and the natural world encompasses human beings.

However, Marx does not reduce human beings to nature; he just appreciates that they are a part of nature as well as apart from nature. He sees them as both like and unlike animals. Timpanero catches this thought when he writes, "to reduce man to what is specific about him with respect to other animals is just as one-sided as to reduce him (as vulgar materialists do) to what he has in common with them."[21] Or as Schmidt puts it, "Natural and human history together constitute for Marx a differentiated unity. Thus human history is not merged in pure natural history, natural history is not merged in human history."[22]

In other words, Marx uses the term 'nature' to refer both to the totality of reality and to nature as opposed to society/human beings. For Marx, nature and society constitute a unity and are interwoven in concrete reality. As Labriola writes:

> Men, living socially, do not cease to live also naturally, They are certainly not bound to nature as are animals... But nature is always the immediate subsoil of the artificial terrain of society, and is the ambience which envelops us all. Technique has interposed modifications, diversions and attenuations of natural influences between ourselves as social animals and nature, but it has not thereby destroyed their efficacy, which on the contrary we experience continuously.[23]

Callinicos notes that naturalism as a term is also used to refer to the unity of science thesis, i.e., the view that the same scientific approach or concepts or laws or language is appropriate to both the natural and social worlds given their basic unity. Human beings are part of nature and nature is the sole reality; there is ultimately a unity of the social and natural, hence, unity of the sciences. There is strong evidence to suggest Marx's naturalism incorporated some form of the unity of science thesis:

> Natural science will in time subsume the science of man just as the science of man will subsume natural science: there will be *one* science. (EPM)

> ...the development of the economic formation of society is viewed as a process of natural history... (*Capital*)

> ...a scientific analysis of competition is possible only if we can grasp the inner nature of capital, just as the apparent motions of the heavenly bodies are intelligible only to someone who is acquainted with their real motions, which are not perceptible to the senses. (*Capital*)[24]

Marx's views will be discussed further in chapter seven, 'Marx and Science', suffice it to say here that his naturalism includes some form of unity of science.

The naturalism thesis is also linked to the anti-teleology tenet associated with materialism. Marx's anti-teleology is bound up with his (post) atheism, and in particular his opposition to any notion of a God created earth. The religious theory of creation implies teleology (a God-given purpose), and the rebuttal of this theory undermines such a teleology:

> The creation of the *earth* received a heavy blow from the science of *geogeny*, i.e. the science which depicts the formation of the earth, its coming to be, as a process of self-generation. *Generatio aequivoca* is the only practical refutation of the theory of creation.[25]

However, a teleology has been imputed to Marxism in the more deterministic interpretations of historical materialism, which imply an inevitable movement towards the goal of socialism, as if history's purpose was the attainment of communism. This view cannot be attributed to Marx. The determinist interpretation is at best one-sided and conflicts with the praxis thesis. The idea of a Marxist teleology is based on a positivist misinterpretation of Marx's 'laws of history,' and a superficial inversion of Hegel's idealist dialectics, replacing the realisation of Spirit with the realisation of communism. A slightly different sense of teleology attributed to Marx will be discussed in chapter five on dialectics.

(iv) The Historical Materialism Thesis

The fundamental thesis of historical materialism is that social production determines (or conditions) the existence of human beings and of society in general. It ascribes causal primacy to the mode of production, the material base of society, over ideas/the ideological sphere in social life. The classic statement of this thesis is to be found in the CPE:P:

> In the social production of existence, men inevitably enter into definite relations which are independent of their will, namely relations of production appropriate to a given stage in the development of their material forces of production. The totality of these relations of production constitutes the economic structure of society, the real foundation, on which rises a legal and political superstructure and to which correspond definite forms of social consciousness. The mode of

production of material life conditions the general process of social, political and intellectual life. It is not the consciousness of men that determines their existence, but their social existence that determines their consciousness. At a certain stage of development, the material productive forces of society come into conflict with the existing relations of production, or - this merely expresses the same thing in legal terms - with the property relations within the framework of which they have operated hitherto. From forms of development of the productive forces these relations turn into their fetters. Then begins an epoch of social revolution. The changes in the economic foundation lead sooner or later to the transformation of the whole immense superstructure.[26]

The historical materialism thesis is the heart of Marxism, and has largely been elaborated in chapter three, "Method in the Later Marx". Whilst compatible with the philosophical materialism of the first three theses it is not entailed by them. When Marx talks about 'the material' he is usually discussing the concrete social form of means and mode of production, i.e., materialism for Marx is historical materialism rather than philosophical materialism.

Historical materialism is an explanatory thesis put forward by Marx to demystify history and politics, to guide analysis of and research into society. In historical materialism Marx counter-poses 'material' not to spiritual or mental (as in philosophical materialism), but to ideological, or even more strictly to the non-economic. The material basis of society consists of those elements involved in the immediate production and reproduction of life, i.e., nature and the means of production of (in the first instance) the basics of life, e.g. food, clothing and shelter. Thus, tools, technology, techniques and productive organisation take centre-stage, and institutions, laws, etc. are held to be basically secondary to the means of production. Ideas (the ideological superstructure) are held to be ultimately derivative from the material base.

(v) The Praxis Thesis

This asserts the constitutive role of human practice in changing nature, society, social being, and social consciousness, and the unity of theory and practice. Praxis is central in the production and reproduction of social life and as such is an integral part of Marx's critique of idealism and contemplative philosophy. The 'Theses on Feuerbach' embody Marx's praxis thesis, notably the 2nd and 8th theses:

The question whether truth can be attributed to human thinking is not a question of theory but is a *practical* question. In practice man must prove the truth, that is, the reality and power, the this-sidedness of his thinking. The dispute over the reality or non-reality of thinking which is isolated from practice is a purely *scholastic* question.

All social life is essentially *practical*. All mysteries which lead theory to mysticism find their rational solution in human practice and in the comprehension of this practice.[27]

The praxis thesis in some ways spans both philosophical and historical materialism. Its origins lie in the dispute with idealism and contemplative philosophy. Praxis acknowledges the active side of idealism, but rejects its idealist setting. Praxis accepts the material basis of contemplative materialism, but rejects its passivity. In arguing against these two tendencies Marx developed his thesis of praxis, i.e., that human practice has a constitutive role in changing the world including nature, society, social being and social consciousness. Praxis is active social being, rather than active thought. Inasmuch as praxis involves beings in the act of self-creation it rejects the passive, mechanistic/contemplative materialist view of human beings as mere products of their environment. Praxis is practical materialism that focuses on human beings engaged in productive activity - the starting point of historical materialism. It is the unity of theory and practice, thinking not considered in isolation from matter that thinks - a component of Marx's naturalism. Praxis emphasises the practical, human labour and production, and rejects the idealist notion of the primacy of thought - Marx's primacy thesis - and emphasises the concrete - part of Marx's materialist methodology.

Human beings act upon their environment and in changing it change themselves. Human beings distinguish themselves as human beings through praxis. No other animal has this capacity for conscious action. Marx writes in *Capital* I:

A spider conducts operations that resemble those of a weaver, and a bee would put many a human architect to shame by the construction of its honeycomb cells. But what distinguishes the worst architect from the best of bees is that the architect builds the cell in his mind before he constructs it in wax. At the end of every labour process, a result emerges which had already existed ideally. Man not only effects a change of form in the materials of nature; he also realizes his own purpose in those materials.[28]

Marx grounds his notion of praxis in the production and reproduction of the means of life. He does not say human beings are different because they have consciousness. He says human beings distinguish themselves from animals in the process of production, an activity involving consciousness, but not in abstract form. Praxis is at the heart of historical materialism.

Some commentators, such as Gramsci, seem to view praxis as being at odds with materialism, and that the former is to be favoured:

> It has been forgotten that in the case of [historical materialism] one should put the accent on the first term - 'historical' - and not on the second - which is of metaphysical origin. The doctrine of praxis is absolute humanism of history.[29]

However, as Timpanero writes:

> ...in the expression 'historical materialism', the noun was a polemic against Hegel and a whole philosophical tradition which affirmed the primacy of the spirit over any economic structure, whereas the adjective was a polemic against Feuerbach and English classical economy, in short against any statically naturalist conception of human society.[30]

A failure to ground praxis in materialism risks lapsing into idealism by forgetting the extent to which human beings are conditioned by nature and their surroundings and that whilst praxis incorporates the notion of human creation and transformation of society and nature, nevertheless the world exists independently of human beings. Timpanero writes:

> A philosophy which is, even in the broadest and most comprehensive sense a methodology of human action always runs the risk of evading or underestimating that which is passivity and external conditioning in the human condition.[31]

The use of the term 'praxis' rather than the English 'practice' is intended to denote something more than practice or activity. In the first place it denotes the activity by which human beings distinguish themselves from other creatures, a practice informed by consciousness and purpose. This is in contrast to much philosophy that identifies the distinctiveness of human beings in terms of abstract human reason or consciousness. Secondly, it denotes practical materialism as opposed to passive or abstract materialism. The latter conceives material reality as an object of observation or contemplation, as something essentially passive and separate from thought (which is active). Marx's praxis makes the point that human activity is part of the material world. Thirdly, praxis denies the existence of thought separate from thinking matter, i.e., the premise of idealism. The unity of theory and practice is a rejection of the abstractions of idealism as well as of contemplative materialism. Fourthly, it denotes practical philosophy, both in terms of the practical application of philosophy to reality, and in terms of the resolution of theoretical problems through and in practice. Finally, it denotes the role of human practice in constituting both society and human beings themselves.

The praxis thesis also has epistemological implications. Marx is keen to emphasise the role of human practice in the knowledge process, ruling out a passive theory of knowledge where external reality leaves its imprint on the blank sheet of the human mind. The praxis thesis also implies that a principal object of study must be human practice itself. In addition, it requires that knowledge be related to practice, or to put it another way, knowledge must matter, be of practical purpose.

However, two dangers lurk: first, that knowledge may be considered to be created by human activity, i.e., knowledge is entirely 'produced', there is no 'given'. Second, that the proof of the pudding is considered *only* to be in the eating, i.e., the truth criterion is entirely pragmatic (a possible reading of some of Engels' comments, or even of the TOF, especially thesis eight). Praxis does not entail omission of the given, i.e., the external, independent reality, or neglect of the socially produced character of knowledge. Bhaskar's intransitive and transitive objects of knowledge allow for both a given component and a produced component of knowledge, and usefully ground praxis in realism. As for pragmatism, this also is not required by praxis. Praxis may imply knowledge be related to practice, and it may suggest that human practice is vital in the production of knowledge, but this does not entail that the ultimate criterion of truth is practice. Marx's notion of praxis is not about establishing a criterion of truth; it is not about justifying or grounding knowledge. If anything it is precisely a denial of the validity of that kind of philosophising, which seeks by philosophical reasoning to establish ultimate criteria for knowledge.

Marx assumes, but does not argue for, a correspondence theory of truth. The realism thesis requires such a theory.[32] Reflection theory implies some kind of independent reality that is being reflected, i.e. the reflection theory of truth entails realism. Any non-classical (non-reflection) theory that suggests knowledge/truth is produced without a 'given' component is liable to fall into idealism. Adjukiewicz writes:

...nonclassical definitions of truth...became one of the points of departure for idealism according to which the world accessible to cognition is not taken to be the true reality; that world is reduced to the role of a construction of thought and thus to a kind of fiction different from poetic fiction only in being constructed according to some regular criteria on which we finally rely in making judgements.[33]

(vi) The Materialist Methodology Thesis

This consists in a method of enquiry that takes as its starting point, concrete determinate forms of life, the empirical, rather than abstractions or *a priori* categories. The insistence on concrete premises is emphasised in the GI (noted in chapter one, 'Method in the Early Marx'), and the methodological discussions in the GR (noted in chapter two, 'Method in the Later Marx') reinforce the importance Marx attaches to a materialist method. The primacy of the practical and of material production are incorporated into this thesis.

The materialist methodology thesis has in a sense been outlined already in the two previous chapters, where Marx's methodology and its development have been described. It gives a focus for study: the material world and specifically the material base of society. In human beings' practice, their productive activity, lies the key to understanding the social world. Marx considers material production to be fundamental, the foundation of society, and all else, notably ideology, is derived from this foundation. The starting point for explanation and understanding is this material base, not people's ideas about themselves, and not God, *Geist* or pure being. Marx also repeatedly stresses the importance of an empirical and concrete approach that does not substitute theory for history or abstract generalisation for concrete fact. This, of course, is not to say that Marx eschewed theory and abstraction as such (see chapter two, 'Method in the Later Marx'), but he was aware from his knowledge of speculative philosophy that history and the concrete could be treated as secondary and derivative if an idealist approach is adopted.

Marx's materialist methodology follows on from the other materialist theses. Its basic orientation is informed by Marx's philosophical theses, which preclude an idealist approach; they provide a natural background for a materialist methodology. The praxis and historical materialism theses more directly give the materialist methodology. They point to the relationship of human beings with nature (material production) as central, and highlight history and human activity as crucial elements overlooked in other approaches.

*

This set of Marxian theses may be compared with the materialist propositions outlined earlier. The realism thesis embodies the materialist tenet that matter is independent of mind, while the priority of matter to mind and the dependency of everything on matter tenets reappear in the primacy thesis. The naturalism thesis contains the first listed tenet of materialism, that everything that exists is matter, and the atheism implied by the naturalism thesis accommodates the anti-teleology tenet. Something of the empiricism suggested in the assertion that only sensible entities and processes exist, is contained in the materialist methodology thesis, but no room is found for atomism in Marx's materialism. The two distinctive theses Marx puts forward are the historical materialism and praxis theses, suggesting where the originality of his materialism lies.

The absence of atomism in Marx's materialism is worth noting. Some commentators have argued that Marx's approach was not just non-atomistic but anti-atomistic.[34] Atomism here is taken to mean the assigning of primacy to the smallest constituents of phenomena or of experience, the privileging of parts over wholes. Marx, they contend, favoured an approach that privileged essences or totalities, assuming things to have inner natures and to be interconnected with other things in organic totalities. Marx himself was well acquainted with the philosophies of atomism and essentialism from his doctoral thesis, and in a passage in the HF Marx argues against viewing civil society in an atomistic way, an approach which he sees as itself a product of alienation:

Speaking exactly and in the prosaic sense, the members of civil society are not *atoms*. The *specific property* of the atom is that it has *no* properties and is therefore not connected with beings outside it by any relationship determined by its own *natural necessity*. The atom *has no needs*, it is *self-sufficient*; the world outside it is an absolute *vacuum*, i.e., is contentless, senseless, meaningless, just because the atom has *all fullness* in itself. The egoistic individual in civil society may in his non-sensuous imagination and lifeless abstraction inflate himself into an *atom*, i.e., into an unrelated, self-sufficient, wantless, *absolutely full*, blessed being. Unblessed *sensuous reality* does not bother about his imagination, each of his senses compels him to believe in the existence of the world and of individuals outside him, and even his *profane* stomach reminds him every day that the world *outside* him is not *empty*, but is what really *fills*...it is *natural necessity*, the *essential human properties* however estranged they may seem to be, and *interest* that hold the members of civil society together...[35]

Marx seems to be saying here that the atom has no essential properties that connect it with other things; its relations with other things are accidental rather than necessary, they do not stem from inner essential properties. Human beings, on the other hand do possess essential properties, and their relations in civil society result from these properties; their relations are the product of natural necessity rather than accident. Natural necessity here means stemming from a thing's nature (its essential properties), rather than being merely contingent. Viewing things atomistically means seeing them as unconnected except by chance or circumstance, and as lacking essential properties.

The Marx as essentialist and anti-atomism interpretation links up with his dialectical approach and use of the essence-appearance distinction. It is not necessary to accept the Manichean world-view (atomists versus essentialists) put forward by proponents of this interpretation to appreciate that a strict atomistic approach is at odds with Marx's views.

Linked to this point is the only partial acceptance of the materialist tenet that only sensible entities or processes exist. If this tenet is construed in a purely physicalist or behaviourist way, if it is understood to deny the existence of things not directly discernible to the human senses, then it diverges from Marx's materialism. Marx posits the existence of entities and processes, (the hidden essential properties), which are not directly discernible, but the existence of which explains the sensible.

Of the six materialist tenets attributed to Marx here three may be described as philosophical: the realism thesis, the primacy of matter thesis, and the naturalism thesis. These theses do not feature prominently in Marx's works, and particularly not in the later works. Marx's philosophical materialism generally lies very much in the background, and it is largely a question of inferring it from his critique of idealism. The primacy of matter thesis, as a part of his philosophical materialism, is a background assumption that is largely subsumed in the realism thesis. The concrete, practical materialism of the materialist conception of history (and society) is of far greater importance for Marx than the philosophical materialism, and he does not seek to join the two. Marx's historical materialism thesis, praxis thesis and materialist methodology are consistent with his philosophical materialism, but they are not entailed by it.

It was noted earlier that the historical materialism thesis was one of the points of departure from the general materialist tenets described at the outset of this chapter. By its emphasis on history and on production it distinguishes Marx's materialism from other forms. The elements of history and production bring materialism down from general abstractions to concrete specifics; they introduce change and activity into materialism, a point elaborated further in the praxis thesis.

The centrality of materialism to Marx's thought is evident, although it does not form a systematically developed philosophy. Rather it takes the form of several interconnected theses, which, while they do not logically entail one another, do accord and cohere with each other. Marx, though, was not just a materialist; he also embraced a dialectical philosophy that gave his materialism much of its distinctive character, and this will be discussed in the next chapter.

Notes

[1] CW. 26. 365-66 (LF)

[2] A list of thinkers who may be labelled materialist or as contributing to materialist thought would include Democritus, Epicurus, Bacon, Hobbes, Locke, Gassendi, Helvétius, and Holbach. On materialism generally see Passmore (1957), especially chapters 11 and 12; Russell (1961), especially chapters on atomists, Epicurans and Hobbes; Copleston (1966), Quinton (1973), and Ayer (1976), especially chapter 6.

[3] See Ajdukiewicz (1973) 111

[4] See, for example, Dupre (1966) 223.

[5] GR. 101-02

[6] *Capital*, I. 133

[7] Wood lists the following as interpreting Marx as a non-realist: Lukàcs (1971); Avineri (1968); Hook (1936); Rotenstreich (1965);Gregor (1965); and Calvez (1957). See Wood (1981) 183-86

[8] Wood (1981) 183. See also Ruben (1979) 63

[9] Bhaskar (1978) 22

[10] ibid., 21

[11] CW. 26. 369 (LF). The primacy of matter thesis can also be found in *Anti-Dühring*, which Engels states he read in its entirety to Marx, providing further evidence of Marx's subscription to this thesis. See Engels (1976) 43 for example.

[12] Stalin (1947) 576

[13] Bernstein (1961) 6

[14] See *Anti-Dühring* and *Ludwig Feuerbach and the End of Classical German Philosophy*.

[15] Schmidt (1971) 35

[16] Engels (1969) 322-23

[17] See Schmidt (1971) 38

[18] Marx (1975) 357 (EPM)

[19] See Wood (1980) chapter 11, and Callinicos (1983) chapter 4.

[20] CW. 4. 129 (HF)

[21] Timpanero (1971) 16

[22] Schmidt (1971) 45

[23] Labriola (1966) 217

[24] Marx (1975) 355 (EPM); *Capital*, I. 92; ibid., 433

[25] Marx (1975) 356 (EPM)

[26] CW. 29. 263 (CPE:P)

[27] CW. 5. 5 (TOF)

[28] *Capital* I. 284

[29] Gramsci (1971) 465

[30] Timpanero (1971) 40

[31] ibid., 36

[32] See Ruben (1979) for an extended account of this argument.

[33] Ajdukiewicz (1973) 21

[34] See Meikle (1985) and Wilson (1991)

[35] CW. 4. 120 (HF)

4 Marx and Dialectics

The position of dialectics in Marx's thought is a fiercely contested issue. Some commentators view dialectics as a defining characteristic of Marxism, and vital for an understanding of the world.[1] Others see dialectics as Hegelian mysticism either left behind by Marx when he developed historical materialism, or retained as a flawed component of Marxism.[2] Some acknowledge the persistence of dialectical language or categories into the Marx's mature writings, but insist it can be excluded from Marxism without loss,[3] and yet others see a basic conflict between the dialectical Marx and the scientific Marx - a tension unresolved by Marx himself.[4]

Evidence has already been presented (chapters two and three) to demonstrate the dialectical themes running throughout Marx's work. The weight of this evidence is such that the question is clearly not 'Did Marx accept or reject dialectics?' but rather, 'What was the nature of Marx's dialectics?' The defensibility or usefulness of dialectics is another question again, but that Marx believed his work to be dialectical cannot be denied. In this chapter Marx's dialectical approach will be explored and clarified, and its centrality and value defended.

The starting point of any examination of Marx's dialectics must be the thought of Hegel. Lenin's comment that "it is impossible to understand Marx's *Capital*, and especially its first chapter, without having understood the whole of Hegel's *Logic*"[5] may be an exaggeration, but the point is well made.

Hegel's Dialectic

Wherever there is movement, wherever there is life, wherever anything is carried into effect in the actual world, there dialectic is at work. It is also the soul of all knowledge which is truly scientific.[6]

Hegel puts dialectics at the heart of his philosophy. For him, dialectics characterises the nature, meaning and method of apprehending the world. His ontology, metaphysics and epistemology are dialectical.

Before dealing directly with Hegel's dialectics, something must be said of his overall philosophical system and outlook. Hegel's basic conception of reality is as the expression of *Geist*, or Spirit, and human history as the self-actualisation and self-realisation of Spirit. Hegel derives his entire system from first principles, or to be precise from first concept: 'pure being'. From 'pure being' Hegel derives a complete series of concepts ending with 'the absolute idea', the final and complete truth. Reason, and more specifically dialectical necessity link together the whole structure.

Spirit or Mind (*Geist*), while occupying a central place in Hegel's philosophy, remains an ambiguous term. It is, perhaps, best described as 'subject-writ-large',[7] i.e., that which has, or potentially has, self-consciousness/awareness. Rather than seeing consciousness or mind in individual terms, Hegel sees it as the property of (or identical with) a general, all-encompassing Spirit which expresses itself through the individual parts of reality. Spirit is God identified with its creation, not separate from it. For Hegel, Spirit is self-positing, that is, it expresses and manifests itself in different forms of reality, and through such embodiments it achieves ever greater self-realisation and self-knowledge. The dialectic of Spirit completes itself with comprehensive self-realisation and understanding.

Hegel's dialectics may usefully be separated out into two forms, the conceptual and the empirical.[8] This division, it must be emphasised, is for purposes of analysis only and does not conform to Hegel's treatment of dialectics.

Regarding the conceptual dialectic, Hegel discusses the development of concepts as a dialectical process. Each concept according to Hegel, is in some way incomplete, an inadequate expression of Spirit. For example, 'pure being' is inadequate because it is unintelligible without the concept of 'nothing', and this in turn necessitates the positing of a further concept 'becoming'. 'Being' without any characteristics or determinate form is not only unintelligible without its opposite 'nothing', it also is its opposite 'nothing'. This is dialectical contradiction: the unity of opposed concepts. 'Becoming' is arrived at by the realisation that 'being' and 'nothing' are both the same but different, and so are in constant flux into and apart from each other, i.e., they are in a state of 'becoming'.[9]   Each dialectical movement to the next concept is a movement towards a truer picture of reality, and is a necessary step derivable by reason. However, by reason

Hegel does not mean deductive logic, rather it is dialectical reason. The links between concepts are dialectically necessary, and form an ascending order of ever greater truth about reality.

The conceptual dialectic is a 'logical' process of development of concepts, whereby dialectical reasoning generates an ascending series of concepts, each necessarily connected with its predecessor, and each a closer approximation to the truth, a greater revelation of reality. The process is driven by contradiction, the essential, internal tension within every concept, which is the root of all movement. In its entirety the process constitutes a totality of interconnected concepts, of moments which are only truly understood when the totality is realised.

The empirical dialectic refers to dialectical change in the world. Hegel portrays history and philosophy as expressing stages of the development of Spirit or Reason in time. Indeed, Hegel identifies the unfolding of the temporal-empirical dialectic with that of the conceptual dialectic. Chronological development is also 'logical', conceptual development. The history of philosophy is the history of the development of Spirit, of Spirit's self-comprehension through human understanding.

Similarly, in history itself, Spirit gradually reveals and realises itself in a dialectical process where contradictions, or limited and inadequate manifestations of Spirit, are worked out through gradual but constant change. Each new and higher society is generated from its predecessor, and is progressively freer. The temporal dialectic like the conceptual dialectic expresses the self-realisation of Spirit.

Three features stand out in this account of Hegel's dialectic: change, connection and contradiction. These are the heart of dialectic and are retained by Marx. All three are fundamental to reality; they are the starting point and the focus of our understanding of the world.

Beginning with the notion of change, Hegel expresses its fundamental nature as follows:

> We are aware that everything finite, instead of being stable and ultimate, is rather changeable and transient.

> ...everything finite (such as existence) is subject to change...mutability lies in the notion of existence, and change is only the manifestation of what it implicitly is.[10]

In other words, change is constant and universal; it characterises existence. It is also internal to things, not a force from without. Change is in the nature of things; it is a part of their essence. But change cannot be understood or even described without reference to contradiction. For Hegel, "contradiction is the root of all movement and vitality; it is only in so far as something has a contradiction within it that it moves, has an urge and activity."[11]

It will be recalled that movement was introduced into Hegel's conceptual scheme out of a contradiction, that between 'being' and 'nothing'. The contradiction is an internal property and hence the movement it creates is of internal origin. The movement of concepts into and apart from one another, and the dialectical necessity that leads from one concept to the next is a constant process. For Hegel, concepts are in a continuous process of change and development, such that no concept can be understood in isolation.[12] Change and contradiction cannot be separated in reality, and like change, contradiction is fundamental to reality. Contradiction is no aberration:

> ...our consideration of the nature of contradiction has shown that it is not, so to speak, a blemish, an imperfection or a defect in something if a contradiction can be pointed out in it. On the contrary, every determination, every concrete thing, every Notion, is essentially a unity of distinguished and distinguishable moments, which, by virtue of the *determinate, essential difference*, pass over into contradictory moments.[13]

For Hegel, everything contains contradictions and everything is in a state of change. Paradoxically, the essence of a thing consists in contradictory moments, not in a single unchanging nature. The identity of a thing consists of essentially different moments, a unity of opposites, not of an exclusive and static oneness. Hence, "to comprehend an object is equivalent to being conscious of it as a concrete unity of opposed determinations" and, as Hegel comments on identity:

> It is important to come to a proper understanding on the true meaning of Identity: and, for that purpose, we must especially guard against taking it as abstract Identity, to the exclusion of all Difference. That is the touchstone for distinguishing all bad philosophy from what alone deserves the name of philosophy.[14]

Hegel distinguished his philosophical method by its aim of capturing in thought this change and contradiction found in everything:

It is in this dialectic... that is, in the grasping of opposites in their unity or of the positive in the negative, that speculative thought [Hegel's philosophy] consists. It is the most important aspect of dialectic, but for thinking which is as yet unpractised and unfree it is the most difficult.[15]

Speculative thought is dialectical and needs to be acquired and developed. It requires an effort of the human mind to practise it, and it also represents an innovation, "The old metaphysic... when it studied the objects of which it sought a metaphysical knowledge, went to work by applying categories abstractly and to the exclusion of opposites."[16] In other words, Hegel criticises older philosophy for failing to grasp things in their contradiction, for not grasping their unity of opposites, or, what is a different expression of the same thing, the things in motion. The old philosophy shares this fault with ordinary thinking:

...though ordinary thinking everywhere has contradiction for its content, it does not become aware of it, but remains an external reflection which passes from likeness to unlikeness, or from the negative relation to the reflection-into -self, of the distinct sides. It holds there two determinations over against one another and has in mind only them, but not their transition, which is the essential point and which contains the contradiction. Intelligent reflection...consists, on the contrary, in grasping and asserting contradiction.[17]

Ordinary thinking and the old philosophy share the error of viewing things statically, and so only seeing one side of a contradiction at any one time. Contradictions exist in motion; their unity lies in the transition from the one opposite to the other. Ordinary thinking and the old philosophy only perceives each opposite separately, as a distinct determination, not as a determination in constant transition to and from its opposite with which it constitutes a unity. To comprehend the world our thinking must incorporate change and contradiction, in other words, it must be dialectical:

We have to think pure change, or think antithesis within the antithesis itself, or contradiction. For in the difference which is an inner difference, the opposite is not merely one of two - if it were, it would simply be, without being an opposite - but it is the opposite of an opposite, or the other is itself immediately present in it.[18]

The third feature of Hegel's dialectics is connection, which is inextricably intertwined with change and contradiction. Like change and contradiction it is fundamental to reality: "A determinate, a finite, being is one that is in relation to an other; it is a content standing in a necessary relation to another content, to the whole world."[19] Everything is inter- and intra-connected. Nothing stands in isolation, but, rather, everything is related to another thing, and, ultimately, to every other thing, to the whole world.

This idea of connection entails the notion of system, or totality, or whole. Hegel believes that reality constitutes a coherent whole, and that complete truth is to be identified with the whole. In the conceptual dialectic 'the absolute idea' is the whole, and once reached it completes the jig-saw and finally allows the picture to be seen in its entirety and the meaning of the pieces to be known. Hegel writes: "The True is the whole. But the whole is nothing other than the essence consummating itself through its development."[20]

The idea of connection is also related to Hegel's conception of identity: "The subsistence or substance of anything that exists is its self-identity; for its want of identity, or oneness with itself, would be its dissolution. But self-identity is pure abstraction."[21] In other words, self-identity, or things considered in themselves and unconnected to other things, is an abstraction. Without self-identity a thing would not exist, but a thing is more than its self-identity, and to truly understand it we must go beyond this 'abstraction'. Hegel writes, "if we stick to the mere 'in-itself' of an object, we apprehend it not in its truth, but in the inadequate form of mere abstraction."[22] Things exist in relations and the truth about a thing contains these relations ('The True is the whole'). E.M. Forster's motto, "Only connect", may equally be applied to Hegel.

The whole is in one sense a system, i.e., a comprehensive and coherent set of concepts (and things) which are interconnected and whose interconnections are demonstrable. But it is also a process, the development of concepts and things. To view things statically is to view them abstractly, but a thing in reality is changing, and that change is part of it. The truth of a thing is the thing in its entirety, its past, present and future, which are all connected as moments in the same process. Process and system describe the same thing, and knowledge or complete truth is the culmination of process, or the totality in its entirety.[23]

Before moving on to Marx's dialectic, two aspects of Hegel's approach must be emphasised. First and foremost, Hegel's philosophy is idealist, conceiving of reality as but the expression of Spirit - the true active subject in the world. The primacy of the ideal is clearly stated by Hegel:

The procession of mind or spirit from Nature must not be understood as if Nature were the absolutely immediate and the *prius*, and the original positing agent, mind, on the contrary, were only something posited by Nature; rather it is Nature which is posited by mind, and the latter is the absolutely *prius*. Mind which exists in and for itself is not the mere result of Nature, but is in truth its own result.[24]

Hegel is equally direct in his definition of idealism: "The proposition that the finite is ideal constitutes idealism. The idealism of philosophy consists in nothing else than in recognizing that the finite has no veritable being."[25]

Secondly, dialectics is 'a thinking of necessity', that is, it aims to identify the necessity in things - their necessary connections and contradictions. According to Hegel:

...the aim of philosophy is to abolish indifference, and to ascertain the necessity of things. By that means the other is seen to stand over against its other. Thus, for example, inorganic nature is not to be considered merely something else than organic nature, but the necessary antithesis of it. Both are in essential relation to one another; and the one of the two is, only in so far as it excludes the other from it, and thus relates itself thereto. Nature in like manner is not without mind, nor mind without nature. An important step has been taken, when we cease in thinking to use phrases like: Of course something else is also possible. While we so speak, we are still tainted with contingency: and all true thinking...is a thinking of necessity.[26]

The banishing of contingency, or accident is part of Hegel's aim. The necessity of a thing is essential or inner necessity. Part of the essence of organic nature is inorganic nature; the latter is in essential relation to the former and *vice versa*. The connection between the two is not contingent or accidental, but necessary and essential. Hegel's 'scientific' project is to demonstrate the necessary connections between things, and this aspect of Hegel's dialectics is again a feature retained by Marx.

Marx's Dialectic

The mystification which the dialectic suffers in Hegel's hands by no means prevents him from being the first to present its general forms of motion in a comprehensive and conscious manner. With him it is standing on its head. It must be inverted, in order to discover the rational kernel within the mystical shell.[27]

Marx accepted the validity and importance of the dialectic, but rejected Hegel's treatment of it. Marx sought to be a dialectical thinker without being Hegelian. But, while this much is clear, Marx is not helpful in the matter of how exactly he perceived the dialectic disentangled from Hegel's philosophy. The metaphors of standing the dialectic 'on its head' and discovering 'the rational kernel within the mystical shell', are at best vague, at worst misleading. Comments on dialectics are few and far between, and scattered throughout Marx's works. Furthermore, these comments do not necessarily imply a single view of the dialectic. It is not unreasonable to assume a development in Marx's attitude towards dialectics over the course of time. In chapters one and two a movement from critical analysis of Hegelian dialectics in the early works, to stronger criticism in the transitional works and then a more explicitly favourable view of the dialectical approach in the later writings was suggested.[28] However, certain dialectical themes, principally those already identified in Hegel's dialectics - change, connection and contradiction - do recur throughout Marx's writings, and a coherent picture of his dialectics can be drawn by attention to these themes. These themes represent the 'rational kernel' of Hegel's dialectics, and the inversion consists in placing them in a materialist framework.

Looking a little more closely at the mixed metaphors Marx employs in discussing his debt to Hegel (turning a nut upside down - or right way up - is an odd way of getting to the kernel inside the shell), it seems apparent that the 'mystical shell' surrounding the 'rational kernel' of dialectics is a reference to Hegel's metaphysics. Marx rejects the entire idea of Spirit unfolding in history and of it attaining self-realisation in philosophy. He rejects Hegel's mystical view of Spirit as the creative subject and as the explanation of the nature of the world. Marx's rejection takes the form of an inversion of Hegel's view: it is human beings who are the creative subject, and the realm of ideas is derived from and explained by material reality - the finite has a 'veritable being'.

The term 'inversion' only approximately describes Marx's transformation of Hegel's dialectics though. Marx's materialism is not a straightforward inversion of idealism; he does not simply reverse the relationship of the material and the ideal, turning the material into active subject and the ideal into passive object. The dualism identified by Marx in Hegel would be reproduced if Marx simply inverted Hegel's idealist dialectics. The TOF is a denial of precisely this, and an assertion of the unity of theory and practice (of ideal and material) in praxis. Nevertheless, inversion does convey the basic sense of Marx's treatment of Hegelian dialectics: the source of change is now located in human practice, not the activity of Spirit, and contradictions exist in material reality and cannot be dissolved in the ideal realm; dialectics describes the nature and structure of material reality, but not a metaphysical theory based on Spirit. The focus and application of Marx's dialectics are entirely different. Marx's inversion of Hegel is an embracing of a dialectical ontology, but a rejection of dialectical metaphysics.[29] Marx endeavours to substitute the adjective 'materialist' for 'idealist' in his version of dialectics:

> ...my method of exposition is *not* Hegelian, since I am a materialist, and Hegel an idealist. Hegel's dialectic is the basic form of all dialectic, but only *after* being stripped of its mystical form, and it is precisely this which distinguishes *my* method.[30]

The three elements identified as characteristic of dialectics - change, connection, and contradiction - are themselves interlinked, indeed, inseparable, with each implying the others. Nevertheless, of the three one stands out as *primus inter pares*. There are three things that last forever (with apologies to St. Paul), change, connection, and contradiction, but the greatest of these is contradiction. The heart of dialectics, and the centre of much of the dispute surrounding it is the notion of contradiction. Indeed, ideas of change, inter-relatedness, system and process could all be accepted without embracing dialectics, because the key component of contradiction is missing. Contradiction, in a sense, contains the notions of connection and change, so examination of dialectical contradiction inevitably involves consideration of them also.

In clarifying Marx's version of dialectics, the notion of dialectical contradiction will be focussed on to see in what way it is distinctive, and what implications it has for our understanding of the world. By looking at the various issues and debates surrounding dialectics and the notion of dialectical contradiction in particular, a clearer understanding will be achieved of the 'rational kernel' Marx obtains from the mystical Hegelian shell.

(i) Dialectical Contradiction and Formal Logic

A dialectical contradiction involves a 'unity of opposites', that is to say, a combination of two contradictory notions or elements in the same concept or entity. This may be illustrated by looking at Hegel's account of the doctrine of being.[31] According to Hegel, the notion of 'being' in its purest, most indeterminate form, is 'nothing'. Stripped of all its determinate qualities 'being' is 'nothing'. These two opposite notions are, upon closer consideration, found to be bound together in a 'unity of opposites', co-existing inseparably in a unity, each presupposing the other, and neither conceivable without the other.

The question arises with this assertion of the unity of opposites, what is the relationship of dialectical contradiction to logical contradiction? Or, put another way, does dialectical contradiction involve logical contradiction, and if so does dialectical philosophy reject the formal logic law of non-contradiction?

One radical answer is put forward by Sayers who argues, "the philosophy of dialectics, properly understood, implies a profound and thorough-going critique of the law of non-contradiction and of the other traditional laws of logic."[32] In support of this interpretation Hegel's comments on formal logic and identity may be cited:

> It is asserted that the maxim of identity, though it cannot be proved, regulates the procedure of every consciousness, and that experience shows it to be accepted as soon as its terms are apprehended. To this alleged experience of the logic-books may be opposed the universal experience that no mind thinks or forms conceptions or speaks in accordance with this law, and that no existence of any kind whatever conforms to it. Utterances after the fashion of this pretended law (A planet is - a planet; Magnetism is - magnetism; Mind is - mind) are, as they deserve to be, reputed silly. That is certainly a matter of general experience. The logic which seriously propounds such laws and the scholastic world in which alone they are valid have long been discredited with practical common sense as well as with the philosophy of reason.[33]

The implication is that formal logic produces only tautology, and applies only in textbooks, not in 'real life'. As Sayers writes:

> The assurances that 'contradictions cannot be accepted as they stand' and that the law of non-contradiction governs all rational thought are commonplaces of traditional logic; but when we leave the realm of the logic books, as Hegel says, and look instead at the way real, concrete thought proceeds, it becomes clear that this law is far from being sovereign and supreme.[34]

Sayers' basic argument is that contradictions exist in all things, and this fact is recognised by dialectics, but is denied by formal logic. Whilst contradiction cannot occur in the abstract, it can and does in concrete reality. Using the example (pertinent to this thesis) of scientific theories he argues that they all, by necessity, contain contradictions, but, contrary to the law of non-contradiction, they are not rejected, and, indeed, the contradictions are fruitful and promote development in the theories. He concludes:

> [The] law of non-contradiction is not a necessary principle of rational and scientific thought...[D]ialectics, although it does indeed involve a questioning of the traditional principles of logic...neither embraces irrationalism nor involves any elementary logical errors.[35]

This view contrasts with that represented by Popper who writes, "if one were to accept contradictions then one would have to give up any kind of scientific activity."[36]

Sayers tries to turn the tables on such opponents as Popper, who argue that the law of non-contradiction is a prerequisite of rational argument, by suggesting that the law of non-contradiction if applied to concrete scientific theories would itself be irrational:

> ...contradictions do not lead the scientist to reject his theory on these grounds alone, as the law of non-contradiction suggests that he should. On the contrary, if a scientist really behaved as the law of non-contradiction says he should, and rejected his theory (or his observations) at the first sight of contradiction, so far from being in accordance with the laws of logic and the necessary principles of reason and so on, this behaviour would by the very epitome of irrationality and the abandonment of science. For no scientific theory provides a perfect account of reality, free of all problems and discrepancies...[37]

Formal logic only lives and breathes in the pure air of textbooks, and real theories about real life inevitably, and fruitfully, contain contradictions in defiance of the law of non-contradiction.

This radical interpretation of dialectical contradiction and its relation to formal logic is neither tenable nor required by dialectical philosophy. Beginning with Hegel's comment that assertions which follow the maxim of identity to the letter are 'reputed silly'. As Lawler points out, Hegel does not say that such assertions are false, only 'silly'.[38] Hegel does not reject formal logic, rather, he observes its limitations. In addition, Engels' apparently accepts both dialectics *and* formal logic in the following passage:

> Modern materialism is essentially dialectical, and no longer needs any philosophy standing above the other sciences. As soon as each separate science is required to get clarity as to its position in the great totality of things and of our knowledge of things, a special science dealing with this totality is superfluous. What still independently survives of all former philosophy is the science of thought and its laws - formal logic and dialectics. Everything else is merged in the positive science of Nature and history.[39]

If formal logic is rejected by dialectics, why the distinction between the two? Sayers seems to acknowledge this point at times, but the thrust and force of his argument lies in rejection of complete adherence to formal logic and the law of non-contradiction in particular.[40]

Regarding Sayers' comments on the irrationality of upholding the law of non-contradiction when assessing scientific (and other) theories, the law of non-contradiction does not *require* the rejection of a theory if an incompatible observation occurs. The law means that such an observation indicates a problem exists, that the theory may require modification, development and even abandonment eventually, but it does not entail the instant rejection of the theory. Similarly, if a theory maintains two contradictory propositions, for example, (a) the world is round, and (b) the world is flat, then the law of non-contradiction implies that the theory is unsatisfactory, but rejection of the theory depends on other factors (as Sayers notes). The point is that a theory may continue to be accepted and used despite containing contradictions, but this does not mean the law of non-contradiction has been suspended.

Sayers also criticises Lakatos because he accepts that inconsistencies inevitably arise within theories, and between theories and observations, but while he "recognizes that it is often rational to tolerate inconsistencies...he cannot bring himself...to call the logical principle of non-contradiction into question."[41]

But, again, tolerating inconsistencies does not require the questioning of the logical principle of non-contradiction, because it is precisely a *toleration* of the inconsistency, and not an acceptance of it as satisfactory. The inconsistency is only tolerated whilst the theory continues to be otherwise consistent, fruitful, simple, etc., and it still awaits resolution and reconciliation with the theory.

Sayers also asserts, contrary to the law of non-contradiction, that a contradictory proposition can be meaningful and true. As an illustration, according to Sayers, the river paradox of Heraclitus contains a meaningful contradictory proposition. The paradox states, 'We step and do not step into the same river twice,' meaning that the river into which we step twice both is the same and is not the same. By the time we step into the river a second time the flow of the water has brought different fresh water to the point where we placed our feet the first time, and the actual water which wetted our feet the first time has moved on. Hence, the contradictory proposition that 'we step and do not step into the same river twice' is both meaningful and true.

However, it is again not at all clear that acceptance of this proposition entails a rejection of the law of non-contradiction. The law states that it is impossible for both a proposition and its negation to be true of the same thing, at the same time, in the same respect. The river paradox does not contravene this law because it asserts the river to be the same in one respect (its basic course), and not the same in another respect (the water flowing through any given point in the river). The contradictory proposition is only true when it is elaborated further. This point is made by Norman, who also spells out the consequences of interpreting such a paradox as a denial of the law of non-contradiction:

> To accept that, without further elaboration, a self-contradictory proposition can be true is to accept that one and the same proposition can be both true and false. And to accept this (again without further elaboration) is to obliterate the distinction between truth and falsity, that is, to abandon the notion of 'truth' altogether. Similarly, to abandon the law of non-contradiction is to abandon the very idea of rational argument.[42]

It is clear that Marx did not abandon the law of non-contradiction in his criticisms of other thinkers. For example:

> Because Adam [Smith] makes what is in substance an analysis of surplus-value, but does not present it explicitly in the form of a definite category, distinct from its special forms; he subsequently mixes it up directly with the further developed form, profit. This error persists with Ricardo and all his disciples. Hence, arise (particularly with Ricardo, all the more strikingly because he works out the fundamental law of value in more systematic unity and consistency, so that the inconsistencies and contradictions stand out more strikingly) a series of inconsistencies, unresolved contradictions and fatuities...[43]

This is by no means an isolated example, and shows Marx using the presence of contradictions in the thought of various political economists as ground for criticism of them. Without the law of non-contradiction he would not be able to make this criticism.

(ii) Dialectical Contradictions in Reality

Hegel's conceptual dialectic describes opposed concepts, such as 'being' and 'nothing', united by their mutual interdependence. The one cannot be conceived without the other; the use of one presupposes the existence of the other. Translating such dialectical contradictions into empirical, material terms means for Hegel showing the empirical world to be an expression of the working out of such contradictions, the unfolding of the dialectic of Spirit. The material world is understood to be the manifestation of the conceptual dialectic, and concrete phenomena are seen as containing the dialectical contradictions of the ideal realm.

This understanding of dialectical contradictions in reality is not open to the materialist Marx. So what is involved in a real, concrete dialectical contradiction according to Marx? One example given by Marx is the contradiction between proletariat and wealth:

> Proletariat and wealth are opposites; as such they form a single whole. They are both creations of the world of private property. The question is exactly what place each occupies in the antithesis. It is not enough to declare them two sides of a single whole.
>
> Private property as private property, as wealth, is compelled to maintain *itself*, and thereby its opposite, the proletariat, in *existence*. That is the positive side of the antithesis, self-satisfied private property.
>
> The proletariat, on the contrary, is compelled as proletariat to abolish itself and thereby its opposite, private property, which determines its existence, and which makes it proletariat. It is the *negative* side of the antithesis, its restlessness within its very self, dissolved and self-dissolving.[44]

The first thing to note is that the 'opposites' are products of a part of the material world, private property, and not of a concept or Spirit.

The second thing to note is the sense of 'opposites' being used. 'Wealth' (or 'private property-owner' as Marx later terms it) and 'proletariat' are not strictly logical opposites, but they do display a mutual interdependence. The existence of private property implies the existence of owners and non-owners, i.e., 'wealth' and 'proletariat'. It makes no sense to talk of one without the other, as the meaning of each term presupposes the existence of the other. In this sense they are opposites and constitute a unity. They are also opposites in the sense of being opposed or antagonistic. They are opposed in that wealth has power that it exercises over the proletariat, and the proletariat, in order to further its own interests and to free itself, seeks to resist this power and to ultimately overthrow it. Wealth seeks to preserve the contradiction, and the proletariat to destroy it. This is a real opposition in the sense that it is manifest in the tangible form of the class struggle - disputes, strikes, lock-outs and the like.

Another example of contradictions in reality given by Marx is that between productive forces and relations of production. The opposites in this case, forces and relations of production, are again mutually interdependent. They cannot exist without each other; they each presuppose the other. Relations of production presuppose production and production entails productive forces. Furthermore, a productive force is only a productive force in a certain set of relations of production. Marx writes:

A Negro is a Negro. He only becomes a slave in certain relations. A cotton-spinning jenny is a machine for spinning cotton. It becomes *capital* only in certain relations. Torn from these relationships it is no more capital than gold itself is *money* or sugar the price of sugar.[45]

As Sayers comments on this passage:

Productive forces are productive forces only in the context of the necessary relations of production - in the absence of these they are mere useless objects. A spinning jenny, therefore, is a machine for spinning cotton only given certain relations of production. Transferred to a stone-age society it would be a mere physical object of no productive use. Likewise, a stone axe has no place in our society as a productive force but only as a museum exhibit.[46]

So forces and relations of production form a unity, but they are also opposites in contradiction with each other. Specifically, productive forces in capitalism are forced to expand as rapidly as possible in order to maximise production of surplus-value, but this expansion is limited (contradicted) by relations of production only appropriate for a certain level of productive forces. Marx writes:

The fact that bourgeois production is compelled by its own immanent laws, on the one hand, to develop the productive forces as if production did not take place on a narrow restricted social foundation, while, on the other hand, it can develop these forces only within these narrow limits, is the deepest and most hidden cause of crises, of the crying contradictions within which bourgeois production is carried on and which, even at a cursory glance, reveal it as only a transitional, historical form.[47]

Forces and relations of production, as opposites, inevitably come into conflict in the course of the development of the one beyond the confines of the other. The forces of production are not static, and it is this very changing which precipitates the expression of the latent contradiction between forces and relations of production. It is the process of production that contains and reveals the contradiction.

Furthermore, this basic contradiction is the root of other collisions and contradictions in reality, such as political and ideological conflicts. The basic contradiction between forces and relations of production is a necessary contradiction in that the opposites require each other, are bound together, and yet are also opposed and conflicting. The link to other conflicts means that they too cannot be seen as simply accidental or arbitrary. This does not mean that they are inevitable, but the potential for them is contained in the fundamental contradiction between forces and relations of production. Marx brings out this last point in a discussion of crises:

> The general, abstract possibility of crisis denotes no more than the *most abstract form* of crisis, without content, without a compelling motivating factor. Sale and purchase may fall apart. They thus represent potential *crisis* and their coincidence always remains a critical factor for the commodity. The transition from one to the other may, however, proceed smoothly. The *most abstract form of crisis* (and therefore the formal possibility of crisis) is thus the *metamorphosis of the commodity* itself; the contradiction of exchange-value and use-value, and furthermore of money and commodity, comprised within the unity of the commodity exists in metamorphosis only as an involved movement. The factors which turn this possibility of crisis into [an actual] crisis are not contained in this form itself; it only implies that *the framework* for a crisis exists.[48]

The unity of opposites points to mutually interdependent phenomena that are in a state of contradiction. But the manifestation of these contradictions in the material world, as real contradictions, conflicts, crises and so on, exists as potential in the abstract form of a unity of opposites, and requires other factors to be made actual. In identifying a unity of opposites, we identify the framework in which events take place, the possibilities and the impossibilities. Marx believed the contradictions in capitalism could not be preserved indefinitely, but their eruption into crisis or revolution could not be predicted.

The point that dialectical contradictions occur in material reality, and that they are distinguished by their necessary or essential character can be found in Marx's writings in a variety of places. For example:

> Production and consumption are *in their nature* inseparable. From this it follows that since in the system of capitalist production they are in fact separated, their unity is restored through their opposition - that if A must produce for B, B must consume for A.[49]

Marx here asserts essential unity of production and consumption, a unity paradoxically expressed through their opposition when separated. Elsewhere Marx describes economic crises in terms of unity and separation:

> The circulation process as a whole or the reproduction process of capital as a whole is the unity of its production phase and its circulation phase, so that it comprises both these processes or phases. Therein lies a further developed possibility or abstract form of crisis...If they were only separate, without being a unity, then their unity could not be established by force and there could be no crisis. If they were only a unity without being separate, then no violent separation would be possible implying a crisis. Crisis is the forcible establishment of unity between elements that have become independent and the enforced separation from one another of elements which are essentially one.[50]

According to Marx, there is an essential unity between circulation and production in the reproduction process, but these phases also become separated (and therefore opposed) ultimately inducing crisis.

These examples indicate both the nature and centrality of dialectical contradictions in Marx's analysis of the concrete social world. Dialectical contradictions permeate the whole of reality, and they are more than just conflicts. Their character is well described by Sayers:

> [I]t is crucial to see that dialectical contradiction is more than mere conflict and opposition: it is essential opposition; conflict within a unity; internal conflict - not mere external and accidental conflict. The dialectical law of contradiction asserts that conflict and opposition are necessary, essential and internal to things...[51]

(iii) Dialectics and Identity

In algebraic terms a dialectical contradiction may be represented as 'A' and 'not-A'. 'Not-A' is the negation of 'A', and similarly 'A' is the negation of 'not-A'. Formal logic and mainstream analytical philosophy assert that a thing cannot be both itself and its opposite: 'A=A' and 'B=B', and a thing is either one or the other. It has already been argued that dialectical contradiction does not involve logical contradiction, but it does, nevertheless, seek to go beyond the notion of identity contained in the formula 'A=A'.

The unity of opposites asserts the connectedness of things, that a thing (or concept) cannot be considered in isolation. 'Being' cannot be considered without also considering 'nothing', forces of production cannot be considered without considering relations of production. The unity of opposites also asserts the movement of things, that they exist in processes that contain and bring out their contradictions. The production process contains and reveals the contradictions between forces and relations of production, and between production and consumption, for example. In other words, where non-contradiction implies non-connection and non-change, the unity of opposites implies that the notion of identity must take account of precisely these factors. Sayers again puts this well:

> Everything has self-identity, being-in-itself, but the matter does not end there; for nothing is merely self-identical and self-contained, except what is abstract, isolated, static and unchanging. All real, concrete things are part of the world of interaction motion and change; and for them we must recognize that things are not merely self-subsistent, but exist essentially in relation to other things.[52]

An example from Marx is his account of capital and labour. On the one hand they constitute opposites, but they are also, "expressions of the same relation, only seen from opposite poles".[53] A thing viewed from a different perspective, looked at in a different sense, or considered at a different time (or phase of its development) may take a different form or even appear as its opposite. So, rent, profit and interest all have their own distinct identities, but as well as displaying these distinct self-identities, they are also all forms of surplus-value, i.e., in a certain sense they are the same.[54] Marx writes:

> It is characteristic of the entire crudeness of 'common sense,' which takes its rise from the 'full life' and does not cripple its natural features by philosophy or

other studies, that where it succeeds in seeing a distinction it fails to see a unity, and where it sees a unity it fails to see a distinction. If 'common sense' establishes distinction determinations, they immediately petrify surreptitiously and it is considered the most reprehensible sophistry to rub together these conceptual blocks in such a way that they catch fire.[55]

Ollman makes the point that our definition of a thing, the identity we attribute to it, depends on how it is abstracted, or, to put it another way, the level of abstraction employed.[56] At a certain level of abstraction capital and labour are distinct, at another level they are the same.

This expanded view of identity is helpful in countering the notion of 'things-in-themselves', unconnected to other things and unchanging. But it raises the issue of whether or not things are, at least in part, constituted by the relations in which they stand. The radical dialectical position, as espoused by Ollman and Sayers, advances the view that there is no absolute distinction between relations and things. Sayers writes, "concrete things exist in relations; and the essential point that dialectics makes is that these relations are not merely external, but internal to the things related."[57] For example, social relations are internal to productive forces, they are a part of what a productive force is. This philosophy of internal relations and view of identity is taken further by Ollman:

> In adhering to a philosophy of internal relations, the commitment to view parts as identical exists even before they have been abstracted from the whole, so that one can say that, in a sense, identity precedes difference, which only appears with the abstraction of parts based on some appreciation of their distinctiveness. Such differences, when found, do nothing to contradict the initial assumption of identity, that each part through internal relations can express the same whole.[58]

According to Ollman, a thing is always a part of a whole, and the relations that come together to make up the whole exist in the part. Ultimately, the identity of the part must include the whole, because of the inter(inner)-connectedness of everything, which entails the part expressing the whole. Priority is given to identity over difference. Connectedness here becomes expressed in terms of things belonging to wholes. This point is taken up by Lukács in his development of the notion of totality:

> It is not the primacy of economic motives in historical explanation that constitutes the decisive difference between Marxism and bourgeois thought, but

the point of view of the totality. The category of totality, the all-pervasive supremacy of the whole over the parts is the essence of the method which Marx took over from Hegel and brilliantly transformed into the foundations of a wholly new science...Proletarian science is revolutionary not just by virtue of its revolutionary ideas...but above all because of its method. The primacy of the category of totality is the bearer of the principle of revolution in science.[59]

Identity is understood in terms of totality. It is the totality that gives meaning to the individual part; understanding of individual things comes from understanding of the totality. This notion was described in the account of Hegel's dialectics earlier in the chapter, and the similarities are evident. In both cases the point is made that things do not exist in isolation, but are always parts (or moments) of larger totalities, and that when we consider them in isolation we must be aware that we are looking at them in abstraction. Abstraction carried out unthinkingly and in denial of totalities leads to a static, atomistic view of reality.

This account of identity and internal relations allows for change, connectedness and contradiction, but it carries with it a danger. It risks obliterating entirely the self-identity of things, their being-in-themselves. If identity precedes difference, if the point of view of the totality is supreme, and if all relations are internal, then the distinctions between things would appear to be subjective or arbitrary, imposed on material reality rather than stemming from it. In other words the philosophy of internal relations courts idealism and subjectivism. However, it is not necessary to assert that all relations are internal, just as it is not necessary to deny formal logic, in order to maintain a dialectical view of identity. The inclusion of change, connectedness and contradiction in the approach to identity requires only that relations be acknowledged as in part constituting the identity of a thing, and the notion of being-in-itself can be retained.

(iv) Dialectics and Teleology

Closely related to the issue of identity is that of teleology. It was noted in the chapter on materialism that a certain interpretation of Marx's materialism might be labelled teleological, despite the anti-teleology tenet associated with materialism. It is similarly the case with Marx's dialectics. The Ollman interpretation of dialectics, despite claims to the contrary, is teleological, and this teleology is rooted in his view of identity and internal relations.

Ollman's interpretation of dialectical identity runs into difficulties when he makes use of the Hegelian categories of 'potential' and 'becoming'. According to Ollman things have a potential which is a part of them; things are in a process of becoming, and what they are becoming is as much a part of them as what they already are. A thing's development or history includes its future development, its history that has yet to happen. So when Ollman says that the identity of a thing includes its history he includes its future as well as its past in that 'history'. Ollman writes:

> ...the probable future is an internally related part of the present, and exists there (here) as the point toward which real pressures are directing us. Grasped as 'becoming', it is the form assumed by the future within the present, and as such affects how we understand the present, how we should study it, and what we can do to help change it.[60]

An analysis of a thing's past and present will allow us to draw inferences about its future; we can identify the potential contained within it, and then include that projected future in its identity. Two objections come to mind: first, is it warranted to include a thing's possible future (one possible future) in our understanding of what that thing is; and secondly, is Ollman not introducing an element of teleology here?

Including the past of a thing can be justified on the grounds that it is not a matter of guesswork (more charitably 'projecting'), that it tells us something about the thing and it prevents an ahistorical view of the thing. For example, by including the notion of process, in the form of history, in our understanding of capitalism we are steered away from the danger of viewing it as something which has always existed (and, therefore, always will?), or from viewing it as just there, that is, static and unchanging (and, therefore, eternal?).

If the future could be deduced in *a priori* fashion then there would exist the warrant for including it as part of the identity of things existing now. But if that were the case then dialectical Marxism would be deterministic and teleological. The collapse of capitalism and advent of socialism would be inevitable and would be the end or goal towards which we are moving.

Ollman distances himself from all such charges. He explicitly states that the projected future is not inevitable, that dialectics is not teleological, and that Marxism is a materialist theory. However, it is not clear that his theory matches his explicit statements. For example, in looking at class consciousness Ollman describes it as, "a journey with an end, a goal established by the situation of the class as such and evoked by all the conditions and pressures that constitute that situation."[61] In other words class consciousness has an end or goal towards which it is moving, and which we can discern by a study of the objective situation of the workers. This end is contained in existing class consciousness as potential; it is what it is becoming and, hence, is part of what it is. Ollman writes:

> ...class (in all of its aspects), class struggle, and class consciousness all develop, mature, become over time, and only in late capitalist society do they realize their full potential...Moreover, viewed as historical processes, the mature form, of each can be taken as present in its earlier stages and vice versa. Such is the nature of becoming as a dialectical category. As regards class consciousness at the present time, rather than what any single person thinks, class consciousness refers to how, when, from, and toward what a whole class of people are changing their minds. [62]

Ollman puts great weight on the perceived potential or future development of a thing. The end or goal of class consciousness determines our understanding of present class consciousness. Ollman writes:

> Studying class consciousness has something in common with trying to catch a wave at the moment when it breaks. All movement toward this point is treated as development, as preliminary, as the unfolding of a potential. Everything that either contributes to or retards its movement is equally the object of study, but the constant point of repair, the perspective from which the whole process is viewed and interpreted, the event that gives everything that preceded it its distinctive meaning, is the moment at which the wave breaks. [63]

Here we see the strands of inevitability and teleology. Class consciousness has an end towards which it is moving like a wave moving towards its point of breaking (inevitability: breaking waves don't stop and turn around, they can only break). The realisation of the finished form of class consciousness is its goal (teleology) and it is from the perspective of fully realised class consciousness that we understand it now and as a whole. The echoes of Hegel are clear: class consciousness is like Hegel's view of history with a goal towards which it moving and which once arrived at allows the comprehension of the whole and reveals the meaning of history.

A similar use of the category 'potential' is made by Meikle in discussing accidental and necessary change:

> If a kitten gets run over before reaching maturity, then it meets with an accident; that is one kind of change. But a kitten that develops into a mature

cat does not thereby meet with an accident. That is another kind of change; not an accidental one, but one that is necessary. The potential for such a change is in the nature of a thing of that kind and anything lacking the potential for that change *is* not a thing of that kind and must be of another kind.[64]

Meikle openly embraces teleology and attributes it to Marx also. The teleology to which he subscribes, though, is not that of a goal or purpose set by a deity or Spirit. Meikle's teleology is the idea that an entity contains within its nature a *telos* in the sense of a state or form towards which it develops unless interrupted by external accident. So the kitten's *telos* is to develop into a cat. Capitalism, as an organic entity, has the *telos* of socialism, i.e., within its nature there is the potential to become socialism.

Again inevitability is denied, but as with Ollman there is a qualified form of determinism. Certainly, a kitten will not inevitably develop into a cat; it may well meet with a fatal accident and its potential remain unrealised. But the kitten will also never develop into a dog or a box of Maltesers, or, indeed, anything other than a cat. This understanding of potential when applied to capitalism entails that it can only ever develop into socialism, unless accidental change indefinitely defers this attainment of its telos.

Marx, as was noted earlier, talks of the possibility of crisis latent in various contradictions, and he clearly does not think the contradictions of capitalism can be sustained indefinitely. It is also evident that he sees the possibility of socialism residing in capitalism. However, this is by no means the same as the attributing of a single potential, which without the intervention of accident, will inevitably develop into its *telos* or goal. At any given moment in history there are certain possible immediate futures and certain impossible ones. Marx and Engels make this point in relation to the utopian socialists. But the notion of potential used by Ollman and Meikle narrows down the possibilities to an unjustifiable mere two: socialism or barbarism (Ollman), or socialism or accident (Meikle). Dialectics does not entail this teleology, but, as Ollman and Meikle show, it can be interpreted in this way.

*

The rational kernel of the Hegelian dialectic centres on the three elements change, connection and contradiction. In the sections above a radical interpretation of Marx's dialectics has been argued against, while putting the case for a dialectical dimension to Marx's understanding and investigation of the world. The radical interpretation, by its challenging of formal logic, espousal of comprehensive internal relations, and teleology presents an untenable picture, which is insufficiently distant from Hegel. Marx's dialectics is not so antithetical to analytical philosophy and formal logic, does not require that all relations be internal, and is opposed to teleology. It remains, though, a crucial element of Marx's approach and colours his entire thought.

In chapter two the distinction made by Marx between the method of inquiry and the method of presentation was noted. Both these forms of method have their dialectical aspect. The method of inquiry reflects the changing, interconnected and contradictory nature of reality insofar as it is alert to these characteristics of reality, and seeks to capture them in the descriptions and theories generated. Marx seeks to identify and analyse 'different forms of development' (change), to 'track down their inner connection' (connectedness), and, through the method of critique, to identify and analyse contradictions. The assumptions that guide investigation are dialectical giving Marx's method a sense of history and context, and stressing the need to identify contradictions (in contrast to the political economists who view things ahistorically, in isolation and with the aim of producing a harmonious description of society). But dialectics is only one aspect of Marx's method of inquiry, and should not be mistaken for a complete characterisation of it. The materialist-praxis side outlined in chapter four is equally important.

The method of presentation is also strongly influenced by dialectics, primarily in Marx's endeavours to demonstrate the necessity involved in his subject-matter. Hegel, as has been noted, sought to banish contingency from his presentation of reality, and to show the necessary, essential connections between things (or concepts). In investigation Marx seeks to identify necessary links between phenomena, and in presentation he seeks to portray the development of things as necessary rather than as accidental. In correspondence Marx distinguishes a dialectical method from a historical method of presentation, and he identifies the former with "the general scientific exposition."[65] Further illumination of this dialectical method of presentation is provided in the unpublished introduction to the CPE:

> [It] would be ...impractical and wrong to arrange the economic categories in the order in which they were the determining factors in the course of history. Their order of sequence is rather determined by the relation they bear to each other in modern bourgeois society, and which is the exact opposite of what seems to be their natural order or the order of their historical development.[66]

The relations between categories rather than their historical development is the crucial factor in their presentation. The debt to Hegel in Marx's exposition of economic categories in capitalism is suggested in a letter by Engels, "If you compare development from commodity to capital in Marx with development from Being to Essence in Hegel you will get quite a good parallel."[67] Marx's dialectical method of presentation, based on Hegel's method, aims to present things as they develop and are linked as categories, each category leading to the next and being deduced from the previous. Hence, Marx's comment in the preface to *Capital* I that a successful presentation may "appear as if we have before us an *a priori* construction."[68] Marx wishes to present the 'real movement' rather than the apparent or empirical movement.

The importance Marx attached to dialectics is beyond doubt. Both his ontology and his methodology display a dialectical character, and this has a significant bearing on his conception of science.

Notes

[1] See, for example, Ollman (1993), Norman and Sayers (1980), Lukács (1971), and Korsch (1970).
[2] See, for example, Cohen (1978), and Popper (1963) chapter 15.
[3] See, for example, Little (1986).
[4] See, for example, Acton (1955) and Gouldner (1980).
[5] Lenin quoted in Callinicos (1983) 2
[6] Hegel (1975) 116 [sec.81 Z]
[7] See Solomon (1983) 284
[8] Norman uses this division in Norman and Sayers (1980) chapter 2.
[9] Hegel (1975) sections 86-88
[10] Hegel (1975) 118 [sec. 81 Z]; ibid., 137 [sec. 92 Z]
[11] Hegel (1975) 439
[12] The importance of this is underlined by Norman: "This is what Hegel meant by saying that what we have to understand is, not static concepts, but a process, a constant change and transition from each concept to the next. Herein lies the essence of Hegel's philosophical method - the fact that we can start with one concept and from it generate a complete sequence." Norman and Sayers (1980) 32.
[13] Hegel (1969) 442
[14] Hegel (1975) 78 [sec. 48 Z]; ibid., 167 [sec. 115 Z]
[15] Hegel (1969) 56
[16] Hegel (1975) 78 [sec. 48 Z]
[17] Hegel (1969) 441
[18] Hegel (1977) 99
[19] Hegel (1969) 86

[20] Hegel (1977) 11

[21] ibid., 33

[22] Hegel (1975) 181 [sec. 124 Z]

[23] The interconnection of change and connection is noted by Norman: "...'system' or 'totality', and 'dialectical process', are the same thing considered from a static and from a dynamic point of view." Norman and Sayers (1980) 33.

[24] Hegel quoted in Norman and Sayers (1980) 88-89.

[25] Hegel (1969) 154

[26] Hegel (1975) 174 [sec. 119 Z]

[27] *Capital* I, 103

[28] A similar development of Marx's attitude to dialectics is suggested by Bhaskar (1989) 118.

[29] For a useful discussion of the inversion/rational kernel metaphor see Wood (1981) chapter 14.

[30] CW. 42. 544

[31] Hegel (1975) 124-161 [sec. 86-111]

[32] Norman and Sayers (1980) 110.

[33] Hegel (1975) 167 [sec. 115]

[34] Norman and Sayers (1980) 117.

[35] Sayers (1981) 410

[36] Popper (1965) 316

[37] Sayers (1981) 418

[38] Lawler (1982) 20

[39] Engels (1969) 31

[40] Sayers (1981) 125: Traditional laws of logic are "*genuine but limited*"; but the area in which Sayers wishes to suspend formal logic is larger and more significant than the area in which he considers it to apply.

[41] Sayers (1981) 420-21

[42] Norman and Sayers (1980) 49. This debate is conducted between Norman and Sayers at various points in the book, particularly essays 3 and 4.

[43] TSV I, 89

[44] CW. 4. 35-36 [HF]

[45] CW. 9. 211 [Wage, Labour and Capital]

[46] Sayers (1984) 7

[47] TSV III, 84

[48] TSV II, 509

[49] TSV I, 283

[50] TSV II, 513

[51] Norman and Sayers (1980) 16.

[52] ibid., 3

[53] TSV III, 491

[54] This account of identity draws on Ollman (1993) especially 42-44.

[55] Marx quoted in Ollman (1993) 42.

[56] Ollman (1993) 43, and chapter 2 more generally.

[57] Sayers (1984) 7-8

[58] Ollman (1993) 43

[59] Lukács (1971) 27

[60] Ollman (1993) 160

[61] ibid., 158

[62] ibid., 158

[63] ibid., 159

[64] Meikle (1985) 9-10

[65] Marx to Meyer 20 April 1867; other correspondence mentioning this distinction includes Engels to Marx 16 June 1867, Marx to Engels 2 April 1858, Marx to Engels 27 June 1867. See Evans (1967) especially 7-8 on this point, and for an account of Marx's dialectical presentation.

[66] CW.29.505 [CPE]

[67] Engels to Schmidt 1 November 1891.

[68] *Capital* I, 102

5   Conceptions of Science

Science has been characterised in various ways, nearly always with due deference to its perceived authoritative status. Its achievements have seemingly been prodigious and it has been held to be the 'royal road to truth'. If we want facts, certain knowledge, it is to science we turn. Science has been seen as objective, rational, methodical and, above all, true.

Philosophy of science has sought to characterise and understand science, and may be counted a relatively new branch of philosophy. If it was not actually born in the twentieth century it has come of age in it, and it is the principal conceptions of science developed this century which will be examined.

Four major conceptions of science may be discerned: scientific positivism, critical rationalism, conventionalism and scientific realism. These labels do not have a uniform use in philosophy of science and their meanings are often strongly contested. In this chapter I will briefly describe my view of them, suggest how they are related and offer some comments and criticisms. The first, scientific positivism, is of particular importance because of its very considerable influence, and the fact that the others may all be seen in relation to it, as both developments and critiques of it.

Scientific Positivism

Science and the philosophy of positivism are closely linked. Positivism has always held science to be of central importance, even to the extent of reducing philosophy to philosophy of science.

The founding figure of positivism, August Comte, believed it essential to apply a scientific approach to human affairs as the only way to obtain certain knowledge. He had great faith in the scientific approach, which he believed could meet the needs and solve the problems of society. Knowledge he saw as consisting of observable phenomena and the relations between them.   Facts he conceived as being accumulated primarily by observation and experimentation from which could be derived law-like regularities and relations between phenomena. He also adopted a criterion of meaningfulness based on whether or not a statement could be factually tested. Truth he believed lay at least in part in the utility of a theory; if it provided knowledge that allowed the control and manipulation of our physical and/or social conditions then it was true.

Comte's thought contains or points to many of the tenets associated with scientific positivism: primacy of science; unity of science; emphasis on observation and law-like regularities in explanation; testability criterion of meaning, and knowledge-control correlation. From the outset the centrality of science is established.

Positivism reached its zenith in the first half of the twentieth century with the rise of the logical positivists. It was then that the positivist conception of science was fully elaborated and was most influential.

In the 1920s the Vienna Circle, as it came to be known, established itself as a grouping of thinkers of considerable importance and influence. It defined its primary project as combating metaphysics and establishing a criterion of meaningfulness. They developed the verification principle by which they sought to distinguish between sense and nonsense, with the former being that which was empirically verifiable or a logical/mathematical tautology.   This distinction between sense and nonsense was seen as corresponding to a science-metaphysics distinction.

The themes identified in the work of Comte were here brought out more clearly and in a more developed form.   The respect for science seen in Comte's work became even more pronounced with the logical positivists. They sought 'to connect philosophy with science', believing that while not identical to science, philosophy 'ought to contribute in its own way to the advance of scientific knowledge'.[1]   As Hanfling puts it, "It was thought that all genuine questions must be capable of scientific treatment, and all genuine knowledge part of a single system of science."[2]

Furthermore, they embraced the unity of science viewpoint, arguing that the social sciences were no different from the natural sciences in principle, only in the complexity of the phenomena with which they dealt.

Already a strong sense of the positivist conception of science can be seen in the philosophies of Comte and the logical positivists, but more specific defining characteristics are required. Here we have to confront the inevitable problems encountered in any attempt to define a philosophy. Positivism and its conception of science is neither a single viewpoint nor a static one, and defining a common core or setting parameters to the philosophy is by no means straightforward. The problem is compounded by the fact that positivism, under the pressure of widespread attacks from many directions, has become all but a term of abuse. As Giddens writes:

> [T]he word 'positivist', like the word 'bourgeois', has become more of a derogatory epithet than a useful descriptive concept, and consequently has been largely stripped of whatever agreed meaning it may once have had.[3]

Nevertheless, despite these difficulties some kind of workable definition is necessary and possible.

One approach has been to restrict the term positivism to its original use, i.e., to refer just to the thought of Comte, and by implication to his conception of science.[4] However, this denies that positivism can be traced in the work of other thinkers since Comte, which seems contrary to the evidence and analytically unhelpful.

Another approach has been to identify positivism through the eyes of its critics.[5] So, for example, there is the positivism that Popper attacks, the positivism against which critical theory is set, and the positivism with which realism engages in battle. This method highlights the different perceptions of positivism, and in so doing indicates different facets of positivism. However, it does not offer a single definition and it is not clear that by adopting different perspectives of rival positions a coherent picture of positivism will emerge. Furthermore, to define something according to how its opponents view it seems unlikely to do it justice.

Perhaps the most common approach to the problem of defining positivism is to draw up a list of central tenets. Peter Halfpenny, summarising various commentators' views, gives the following list:[6]

1. Unity of science or scientific method.
2. Empiricism in some form.
3. Science is the only valid knowledge.
4. Philosophy is identical to the logic of science.
5. Science to be used for the benefit of mankind.
6. Mathematical physics as the ideal science.
7. Causal explanations as characteristic of science.
8. Sociological relativism with respect to norms.

The first two tenets are identified as central to positivism by Halfpenny and the commentators he surveys, but they diverge on which and how many of the other tenets they consider to be central to positivism. This illustrates the point that there is no agreed definition of positivism or its conception of science, and that even core tenets are contested.

Given the diversity of forms of positivism, and the changes it has undergone in its development, it is inevitable that any list of its characterising tenets must be either very general or very long. Halfpenny favours the very general, but in so doing he risks emptying the tenets of any specific content, and even with his minimal list not all of them apply to all forms of positivism.

I propose to offer a more extensive list of tenets wide enough to convey a full sense of what positivism and its conception of science are. In drawing up the list the intention is not to provide a list of tenets to which all positivists subscribe, or to provide a list of tenets which are exclusively positivist. Some positivists will subscribe to tenets not listed and not subscribe to some of the tenets on the list. Some tenets on the list may be found in other philosophies or be held by non-positivists. The list represents an abstraction, an analytical definition to which no position may exactly be matched, but which provides a means by which different positions may be compared to determine their degree of positivism or positivist tendencies within them.

What is being put forward, then, is a set of loosely associated tenets which are characteristically positivist. Caution should be exercised to avoid (i) branding a position as positivist because some of its tenets are on the positivist list; (ii) assuming that because a position embraces some of the positivist tenets it, therefore, embraces all of them; (iii) assuming that because a position does not embrace some positivist tenets that it, therefore, does not embrace any or is not a form of positivism; and (iv) believing that demolishing the arguments in favour of one/some of the positivist tenets demolishes all the others/positivism as such.

The list I propose is as follows:[7]

1. Emphasis on testability (e.g., verification, confirmation).
2. Observation or sense experience is basis of knowledge.
3. Observation is neutral, not theory-dependent.
4. Anti-theoretical entities, i.e., reality consists only of observables; the existence of theoretical entities cannot be inferred from causal effects.
5. Aim of science is to gain predictive and explanatory knowledge of world.
6. Deductive system is integral to prediction and explanation (e.g., the deductive-nomological model).

7. Explanation consists in showing an event is an instance of a regularity.

8. Cause is understood as the regularity of one event following another (no necessary connections).

9. Theories should consist of highly general statements expressing regular relationships (laws) in the world.

10. Science should be value-free, i.e., no values should intrude into the scientific method.

11. Unity of science (method, laws, and/or language).

12. Paradigm science is mathematical physics.

13. Science is the paradigm or only method of obtaining knowledge.

14. Anti-metaphysics - the scientifically ascertainable is superior to the groundless speculation of metaphysics.

15. Philosophy is the servant or logic of science.

16. Science is of benefit to the human race.

The list incorporates and expands Halfpenny's list. For example his point on empiricism is developed into three distinct and more specific points on observation and theoretical entities (tenets 2-4). Without this elaboration there is nothing to distinguish this empirical emphasis from that to be found in critical rationalism or scientific realism. Similarly, he mentions causal explanations, but insufficient development of the point leads to the distinctive nature of the positivist view of explanation not being made clear, i.e., the emphasis on law-like regularities (in contrast to the realist view, for example). Halfpenny also makes some important omissions, the main one being the emphasis on testability which is not even hinted at, and yet would be endorsed by all positivists.

In addition, Halfpenny's list warrants criticism for what it emphasises. There is undue emphasis on the unity of science tenet, which while advanced by many positivists should not be viewed as indispensable. For example, it is quite possible to endorse the positivist conception of science as a descriptive/prescriptive model for the natural sciences, but reject it entirely for the investigation of the social world.

The list of tenets associated with scientific positivism may be divided into groups with similar themes. Tenets 1-4 form a cluster on the theme of empiricism and testability; tenets 5-7: explanation and prediction; tenets 8-9: causation and laws; tenet 10: value-freedom; tenets 11 and 12: unity of science; and tenets 13-16: view of philosophy and science. These groupings will be utilised in looking at other models of science.

Positivism provided the first model of science, a model that dominated thinking about science through the nineteenth and first half of the twentieth century. It strongly influenced Marxist thinking on the subject. Other conceptions of science may all be seen as, in part, critiques of positivism, and in looking at them a comprehensive critique of positivism will be developed. Critical rationalism very much grew out of positivism, but has only provided a partial critique of it. Conventionalism has been more far-reaching in its critique, but ultimately does not escape its premises. Scientific realism suggests a more sustainable critique and a more viable alternative. Each conception will be looked at in turn.

Critical Rationalism

Critical rationalism is the name given to a conception of science propounded by Karl Popper and his followers. Popper developed his approach in opposition to logical positivism. He knew various members of the Vienna Circle, but never joined the group and became increasingly opposed to their views, particularly regarding science and metaphysics. Despite this the label 'positivist' has been applied to Popper, but his views diverge significantly from positivism as is argued by Popper himself:

> I have fought against the aping of the natural sciences by the social sciences, and I have fought for the doctrine that positivist epistemology is inadequate even in its analysis of the natural sciences which, in fact, are not 'careful generalizations from observation', as it is usually believed, but are essentially speculative and daring; moreover, I have taught ...that all observations are theory-impregnated, and that their main function is to check and refute, rather than to prove, our theories. Finally, I have not only stressed the meaningfulness of metaphysical assertions and the fact that I am myself a metaphysical realist, but I have also analysed the important historical role played by metaphysics in the formation of scientific theories.[8]

This quotation suggests some of the areas where Popper differs from logical positivism: epistemology, the unity of the sciences, the role of induction, the nature of observation, the role of refutation, the significance of metaphysics, and ontology. These areas will be discussed within the categories of features identified in the section on scientific positivism.

(i) Empiricism and Testability

A major difference between Popper and the positivists concerns his view of testing. Popper's views on testing largely stem from his views on induction. Induction is the reasoning from particular cases to general conclusions, and the validity of such reasoning has been questioned by various thinkers, most notably Hume who framed what became known as the logical problem of induction. This may be stated as follows:

(i) All known cases of 'A' have characteristic 'B'.
Therefore,
(ii) All 'A's have characteristic 'B'.

The above is an example of inductive reasoning, and reflection on it soon shows the logical problem to which it gives rise. While statement (i) is consistent with the truth of statement (ii), it does not logically entail it. Indeed, statement (i) is not only consistent with the truth of statement (ii) but also with its falsity, because there is no logical reason why a future case of 'A' should not have characteristic 'B'. That is to say, it is not a valid inference to make that because all known cases of 'A' have had characteristic 'B' then all 'A's have characteristic 'B'. It is logically possible that there are unknown cases of 'A' which do not have characteristic 'B'.

Despite this unresolved flaw in inductive reasoning it has been held (by the logical positivists for example) to be at the heart of the scientific method. However, for Popper inductive reasoning had to be rejected as inconsistent with the notion of science as a rational form of enquiry.

The problem for Popper may be represented as a trilemma, i.e., as a set of three statements only any two of which are mutually consistent:[9]

(i)   Science is a rational form of enquiry.
(ii) Inductive argument is not rationally justifiable.
(iii) Science uses inductive arguments.

For the positivists statements (i) and (iii) are true, while (ii) is rejected. For Hume, the sceptic, statement (i) is rejected, while for Popper statement (iii), that science uses inductive arguments, is rejected.

In place of induction Popper suggests deduction as a logically valid form of reasoning, which science both should and does use. This preference for deduction over induction leads to Popper's rejection of verification and acceptance of falsification in its stead. Popper argues that the logical problem of induction prevents inductive proof, i.e., verification, but falsification remains possible. For example, deductive reasoning may be applied to a speculative hypothesis to derive test implications, which can be upheld or not by experiment. If the implications are confirmed then the theory is open to further tests, although it is not proven or verified. If the implications are not upheld then the theory is falsified. As Popper writes, "Hume showed that it is not possible to infer a theory from observation statements; but this does not affect the possibility of refuting a theory by observation statements."[10]

For the logical positivists the verification principle demarcates science from metaphysics, For Popper the characterising feature of science is the falsification principle: "the criterion of the scientific status of theory is its falsifiability."[11]

For Popper the falsification principle does not demarcate science from metaphysics, but rather science from non-science. Popper, unlike the logical positivists, refuses to dismiss metaphysics. Indeed, he sees it as not only meaningful but as having played a key role in the history of science. Popper sees certain key beliefs of his own, for example, his ontological realism, as metaphysical, because they are not falsifiable in principle (and hence not scientific).

Testing or testability is at the heart of Popper's conception of science. Not only is it the criterion for demarcation between science and non-science, but it is also the measure of verisimilitude and a requirement of progress.

Popper's view of empiricism also draws on his arguments regarding inductivism. Popper attacks what may be termed epistemological empiricism, the idea that observation or sensory experience must be the ultimate source of knowledge. This view constitutes what Popper terms the commonsense theory of knowledge, that "there is nothing in our intellect which has not entered it through the senses".[12] Popper argues that this implies reliance on inductive reasoning, i.e., our knowledge is based on repeated observations leading us to infer the existence of regularities or laws in the world. Popper, as will be elaborated later in this section, rejects inductivism as irrational, which is another major divergence from positivism.

For Popper there is no ultimate source of knowledge; all such sources, including the senses, are liable to mislead, and the whole question of the origins of knowledge is misplaced. Our starting point is what we have, our existing scientific theories and common sense. The point is to subject these existing ideas to rigorous criticism and testing.

Furthermore, Popper rejects the positivist notion of theory-neutral observation: "there is nothing direct or immediate in our experience...It is all decoding, or interpretation."[13]

There is no such thing as an unprejudiced observation. All observation is an activity with an aim (to find, or to check, some regularity which is *at least* vaguely conjectured); an activity guided by problems, and by the context of expectations...There is no such thing as passive experience; no passively impressed association of impressed ideas. Experience is the result of active exploration by the organism, of the search for regularities or invariants. There is no such thing as a perception except in the context of interests and expectations, and hence of regularities or 'laws'.[14]

However, these criticisms of key aspects of empiricism do not mean Popper rejects empiricism in its entirety. Indeed, he wants to preserve what he terms the 'principle of empiricism', which, "asserts that in science, only observation and experiment may decide upon the acceptance or rejection of scientific statements, including laws and theories."[15] The point is that a theory or law cannot be inferred from empirical evidence, but they may be tested using observation.

(ii) Explanation and Prediction

Popper still retains much of the character of the positivist conception of explanation and prediction. For example, if we refer back to the list of tenets associated with scientific positivism (see previous section), tenets five and six could equally be used to describe Popper's views. Tenet five reads, "Aim of science is to gain predictive and explanatory knowledge of the world". In *Objective Knowledge* Popper writes, "The task of science is partly theoretical - *explanation* - and partly practical - *prediction and technical application*."[16]

Tenet six reads, "Deductive system is integral to prediction and explanation". Popper writes:

> ...the various methods of explanation all consist of a *logical deduction*; a deduction whose conclusion is the *explicandum* - a statement of the thing to be explained- and whose premises consist of the *explicans* [a statement of the explaining laws and conditions].[17]

He puts forward the following model:

Universal Law	(premiss)
Specific Initial Conditions	(premiss)
Explicandum	(conclusion)[18]

This model bears more than a passing resemblance to the deductive-nomological model utilised by scientific positivists. Prediction, for both Popper and the positivists, uses the same model as for explanation, or as Popper puts it, "there is no great difference between explanation, prediction and testing. The difference is not one of logical structure, but rather one of emphasis; it depends on *what we consider to be our problem.*"[19]

This brings us to the third positivist tenet concerning explanation: "Explanation consists in showing an event is an instance of a regularity." Popper's model of explanation requires that at least part of an explanation consists of reference to a universal law, i.e., to a regularity.

A further aspect of Popper's views on explanation is brought out in his attack on 'essentialism':

> The essentialist doctrine I am contesting is solely the doctrine that science aims at ultimate explanation; that is to say, an explanation which (essentially, or by its very nature) cannot be further explained, and which is in no need of any further explanation.[20]

Popper is opposed to the idea that there can be ultimate explanations and that the truth of a theory can ever be established beyond reasonable doubt. We cannot appeal to "essential properties inherent in each individual or singular thing"[21] to explain the behaviour of a thing. Theories can only ever be falsified and not proved, and, consequently, all theories (or explanations) are always provisional. Essentialism brings conjecture to a premature conclusion and prevents the raising of fruitful questions; it eliminates the crucial element of criticisability from science.

However, Popper does allow a modified essentialism:

> ...although I do not think that we can ever describe, by our universal laws, an *ultimate* essence of the world, I do not doubt that we may seek to probe deeper and deeper into the structure of our world or, as we might say, into properties of the world that are more and more essential, or of greater and greater depth.[22]

Popper, here, seems to allow the possibility of deeper structures and more essential properties in the world affording us better explanations.

(iii) Causation and Laws

For Popper to explain something in science is to show its cause. He puts it in the following way:

> In all sciences, the ordinary approach is from the effects to the causes. The effect raises the problem - the problem to be explained, the explicandum - and the scientist tries to solve it by constructing an explanatory hypothesis.[23]

On cause and effect Popper writes the following:

> Given some conjectured regularity and some initial conditions which permit us to deduce predictions from our conjecture, we can call the conditions the (conjectured) cause and the predicted event the (conjectured) effect. And the conjecture which links them by logical necessity is the long-searched-for (conjectural) necessary link between cause and effect. (The whole can be called a 'causal explanation'...).[24]

His notion of cause follows closely his account of explanation; the cause of an event will be a set of specific initial conditions plus relevant universal laws.

Laws, then, are integral to Popper's notions of testing and explanation. Laws are universal, conjectural and artificial according to Popper's model of science. They are universal in the sense that they have unlimited spatio-temporal applicability. Without this insistence falsification would be impossible, and Popper's conceptions of testing and explanation would collapse. Laws are conjectural in that they are provisional and cannot be proven or, for that matter, rated probable. They are artificial in the sense that they are not laws read from nature but imposed on it. Popper writes:

> The laws of nature are our invention...we try to impose them upon nature. Very often we fail, and perish with our mistaken conjectures. But sometimes we come near enough to the truth to survive with our conjectures.[25]

(iv) Value-Freedom

Popper believes in the objectivity of science, and in objective knowledge. For Popper "truth is beyond human authority,"[26] and the truth of a theory may be objectively tested. This does not mean that Popper believes scientists proceed in quite the value-free way that the positivists imagine. For example, he does not believe that they derive their hypotheses by an objective inductive method free from the intrusion of values and subjective bias. Indeed, he says that scientific objectivity does not rest "on the mental or psychological attitude of the individual scientist, on his training, care, and scientific detachment."[27]

The objectivity of science rests on its public character and the requirement that it be criticisable (falsifiable). That the proponents and opponents of a theory may be motivated by social prejudice, class bias or personal interest does not matter, so long as their views may be put to the test and we hold on to the notion of truth being beyond human authority.

(v) Unity of Science

Despite his claim (quoted earlier in this section) that he did not favour "the aping of the natural sciences by the social sciences," Popper clearly endorses a strong unity of science thesis:

> I do not intend to assert that there are no differences whatever between the methods of the theoretical sciences of nature and of society; such differences clearly exist, even between the various natural sciences themselves, as well as between the various social sciences...But...the methods in the two fields are fundamentally the same...The methods always consist in offering deductive causal explanations, and in testing them (by way of predictions). This has sometimes been called the hypothetical-deductive method...[28]

Popper sees social and natural sciences as being united in their method, a method based on the same view of explanation, prediction and testing. Popper applies the same demarcation principle to both natural and social science, i.e., the principle of falsifiability, and it is on the grounds of non-falsifiability that Popper rejects the claims to scientific status made for Marxism and Freudian psycho-analysis. Popper opposes views that sharply distinguish natural and social science and proffer an alternative method (such as hermeneutics) for the latter.

Popper allows for some variation in techniques to take into account the different subject-matter of social and natural sciences. Specifically, he endorses methodological individualism for the scientific study of society.

There is little here to distinguish critical rationalism from positivism except that the unity of method proposed by Popper is based on a different, though not entirely different, method of science.

(vi) View of Philosophy

Where the positivists are generally hostile to philosophy that goes beyond the logic of science, Popper is keen to assert both the meaningfulness and the importance of philosophy. The logical positivists distinguish science and metaphysics and assert the identity of this distinction with that between sense and nonsense. Popper comments on this:

> The repeated attempts...to show that the demarcation between science and metaphysics coincides with that between sense and nonsense have failed. The reason is that the positivistic concept of 'meaning' or 'sense' (or of verifiability, or of inductive confirmability, etc.) is inappropriate for achieving this demarcation - simply because metaphysics need not be meaningless even though it is not science.[29]

Indeed, Popper's own conception of science includes embracing philosophical realism, which he happily accepts is unfalsifiable and therefore metaphysical. Popper is against the view that the only genuine problems are scientific problems and that philosophical problems are 'pseudo-problems.[30] But he does insist that philosophy addresses practical problems and not indulge in 'scholasticism': *"Genuine philosophical problems are always rooted in urgent problems outside philosophy, and they die if these roots decay."*[31] He further insists that there be no "philosophising without knowledge of fact,"[32] so that overall his position may be viewed as less extreme than logical positivism, but still displaying a positivistic character.

*

Critical rationalism has had a tremendous influence, and since Popper advanced his views it has been developed in different directions. The most notable revision of critical rationalism has been by Imre Lakatos with his 'sophisticated methodological falsificationism'.[33] Lakatos retains the key element of falsificationism in his model of science, but he suggests that it should be placed in the context of a scientific research programme. He sees a research programme as consisting of a hard core of unchallengeable central principles and a surrounding 'protective belt' of theories and other aspects of the research programme which may, if necessary, be dispensed with. The hard core consists of principles that cannot be falsified even if evidence seems to challenge them. Rather anomalies and counter-evidence must be dealt with in the protective belt by devising ad hoc theories or assumptions, or by allowing some feature to be falsified. A positive heuristic guides research based on the principles in the hard core, and helps determine how the protective belt should be modified or elaborated. The positive heuristic identifies an agenda of research including which anomalies are pursued.

It should be clear by now how Popper and critical rationalism diverges from the logical positivists (and scientific positivism), and also why the label 'critical rationalism' is appropriate to his position. Popper views science as both critical and rational. For Popper, the rejection of induction and the utilisation of deduction are central to science's rationality, and falsifiability means criticisability.[34] Popper's critical rationalism differs from positivism in these views on rationality and falsification, and also in his denial of theory-neutral observation, his assertion of philosophical realism, and his generally more favourable view of philosophy. He concurs with positivism in his belief that science is a rational enterprise, his anti-essentialism, and broadly in his views on explanation, prediction, causality, laws, objectivity and unity of science.

Critical rationalism is both a departure from positivism and an extension of it. It involves a critique of important aspects of scientific positivism, but it is only a partial critique. A more radical critique is offered by conventionalism.

Conventionalism

Conventionalism as a conception of science is very much a twentieth century development.[35] Its founding fathers were Poincaré and Le Roy with Duhem also contributing to its early growth. These three wrote a number of pieces at the beginning of this century that elaborated various key features of conventionalism.[36] However, the real impact of conventionalism did not arrive until the ideas of Kuhn and Feyerabend began to take hold in the 1960s. Despite important differences between them

Kuhn and Feyerabend are united by the key characteristics of conventionalism which they share, and it is these two writers who still constitute the main conventionalist challenge to other conceptions of science today.

Kolakowski provides a useful definition of conventionalism that identifies various characterising features of it:

> The fundamental idea of conventionalism may be stated as follows: certain scientific propositions, erroneously taken for descriptions of the world based on the recording and generalization of experiments, are in fact artificial creations, and we regard them as true not because we are compelled to do so for empirical reasons, but because they are convenient, useful, or even because they gave aesthetic appeal. Conventionalists agree with the empiricists on the origin of knowledge, but reject empiricism as a norm that allows us to justify all accepted judgements by appealing to experience, conceived of as a sufficient criterion of their truth...the data of experience always leave scope for more than one explanatory hypothesis, and which one is to be chosen cannot be determined by experience.[37]

This definition suggests three distinctive features of conventionalism:

(1) scientific statements/theories are not descriptions of an external reality, and as such either true or false. Rather, they are 'artificial creations' or constructions devised by the scientist.
(2) theory acceptance or rejection is based on subjective considerations, not on any universal, rational criterion.
(3) theories are always under-determined by the empirical evidence; their truth or falsity cannot be determined by a straightforward appeal to the empirical data.

Kuhn and Feyerabend, while very different in some respects, would both broadly embrace the points highlighted by Kolakowski. Kuhn puts forward the view that science is characterised by periods of 'normal science' during which the scientific community engages in 'puzzle-solving' on the basis of a stable set of shared values, assumptions, standards and exemplars. The community has a shared paradigm that guides its activity. In the course of this activity anomalies or unsolved puzzles arise which, as they accumulate and continue to remain unresolved, lead to a crisis in the scientific community. The paradigm comes into question and an alternative paradigm is put forward that eventually replaces the old paradigm.

Feyerabend argues against the idea that science can be characterised as a rational and objective activity. Indeed, he argues that it cannot be characterised by any set of rules at all. Its method is varied and inconsistent, and the attempt to characterise it by a single method is both unworkable and undesirable.

The characterising features of conventionalism will be explored using the framework already applied to positivism and critical rationalism.

(i) Empiricism and Testability

Scientific conventionalism can, to a large extent, be characterised by its position regarding empiricism and testability. This is suggested by Keat and Urry:

> What unites conventionalists is their opposition to the view of science as providing true descriptions and explanations of an external reality, through theories which can be objectively tested and compared by observation and experiment.[38]

In other words, as the Kolakowski definition suggests, conventionalists reject the weight given to empirical data (observation) and testing (falsification) by positivism and critical rationalism respectively.

Conventionalists deny the 'purity' of empirical data, arguing that all observation (sensory data) is theory-impregnated. Indeed, theory is a pre-requisite of experience (as experience is a pre-requisite of theory!). Feyerabend writes:

> Experience arises together with theoretical assumptions not before them, and an experience without theory is just as incomprehensible as is (allegedly) a theory without experience: eliminate part of the theoretical knowledge of a sensing subject and you have a person who is completely disoriented and incapable of carrying out the simplest action. Eliminate further knowledge and his sensory world (his 'observation language') will start disintegrating, colours and other simple sensations will disappear until he is in a stage even more primitive than a small child.[39]

A similar point is made by Kuhn when he discusses his idea of 'paradigms' (loosely, a notion of a unifying conceptual or theoretical framework, which determines in some sense meanings and significance of concepts in a science) in relation to perception:

> ...something like a paradigm is a prerequisite to perception itself. What a man sees depends both upon what he looks at and also upon what his previous visual-conceptual experience has taught him to see. In the absence of such training there can only be, in William James' phrase, "a bloomin' buzzin' confusion."[40]

The fundamental point here is that there is no such thing as pure sensory data, the theory-neutral observation of positivism. All observation is theory-impregnated, and the very distinction between theory and observation is challenged by conventionalists.

The implications of this view of observation are quite profound for our understanding of testability. If what we observe is influenced or even determined by what we believe (our theories) then observation (empirical data) cannot be a basis for accepting or rejecting a theory. Observation can no longer be considered an independent test of our theories since it cannot be disentangled from our theories. Furthermore, empirical data cannot decide for us between competing theories, since the proponents of each theory will each view the world differently; their observations will be conditioned by their theories. Theories are rendered irrefutable and incommensurable. This does not mean that there is no role for empirical testing, but it does seriously qualify its importance. Some sense of this conventionalist qualification of the role of empirical testing is given by Kuhn:

> No process yet disclosed by the historical study of scientific development at all resembles the methodological stereotype of falsification by direct comparison with nature. That remark does not mean that scientists do not reject scientific theories, or that experience and experiment are not essential to the process in which they do so. But it does mean...that the act of judgement that leads scientists to reject a previously accepted theory is always based upon more than a comparison of that theory with the world.[41]

Feyerabend goes further, asserting that not only is observation an insufficient basis for theory testing, but also that theories should be developed even in the face of conflicting observations:

The idea that information concerning the external world travels undisturbed via the senses into the mind leads to the standard that all knowledge must be checked by observation: theories that agree with observation are preferable to theories that do not. This simple standard is in need of replacement the moment we discover that sensory information is distorted in many ways. We make the discovery when developing theories that conflict with observation and finding that they excel in many other respects.[42]

Kuhn also claims that much of what is taken to be testing of a theory is actually what he terms 'puzzle-solving'. That is to say, most of scientific work is not aimed at testing theories but at solving puzzles derived from the theories. Failure to solve such a puzzle is not a falsification of the theory, but, rather, a failure on the part of the scientist. Kuhn writes:

Normal science does and must continually strive to bring theory and fact into closer agreement, and that activity can easily be seen as testing or as a search for confirmation or falsification. Instead, its object is to solve a puzzle for whose very existence the validity of the paradigm must be assumed. Failure to achieve a solution discredits only the scientist and not the theory.[43]

Testability is a quality of paradigms, but the form it takes is not the (relatively) straightforward confirmation or falsification through direct comparison with nature that positivism and critical rationalism assume. Rather, paradigm testing involves comparison of different and competing paradigms, and the result is both confirmation and falsification: confirmation of the new paradigm and falsification of the old.

(ii) Explanation and Prediction

The conventionalist view of explanation and prediction tends towards pluralism and pragmatism. Standards governing what constitutes a good explanation vary between paradigms or traditions and are internal to them. In other words what is valued in an explanation in one tradition may not be the same as that which is valued in another.

For Kuhn the main indicator of progress in normal science is the solving of puzzles. But what these puzzles are and what counts as a satisfactory solution are determined by the paradigm in which they fall. Kuhn writes:

In learning a paradigm the scientist acquires theory, methods, and standards together, usually in an inextricable mixture. Therefore, when paradigms change, there are usually significant shifts in the criteria determining the legitimacy both of problems and of proposed solutions.[44]

The nature and role of explanation and prediction in scientific theory are determined by the relevant paradigm. However, in broad terms, to explain something is to reconcile it with the prevailing paradigm, to fit it into the paradigm. Kuhn writes, "in physics new canons of explanation are born with new theories on which they are, to a considerable extent, parasitic," and, "what was once an explanation is an explanation no longer".[45] Similarly, the role and significance of predictions is paradigm-dependent, and the prominence given to prediction in the positivist model is not reflected in the history of science.[46]

The narrow and rigid positivist view of explanation and prediction, as exemplified by the deductive-nomological model, is rejected as a universal standard by conventionalists. Feyerabend specifically targets the positivist view, and in particular the hypothetico-deductive (deductive-nomological) model, for criticism, concluding that "a formal and 'objective' account of explanation cannot be given," and, "it seems perhaps advisable to eliminate altogether considerations of explanations from the domain of scientific method."[47]

(iii) Causation and Laws

Again the paradigm in which a scientist is operating will determine exactly what role and form cause and laws take. Having said that, laws are an integral part of science for Kuhn given his views on anomalies. An anomaly is an event that cannot be assimilated under existing scientific laws. Part of the claims in favour of a new paradigm will focus on its ability to subsume anomalies under new laws such that they cease to be anomalous.

Kuhn adopts a historical approach to demonstrate the changes in the notion of cause utilised in science, identifying four main stages in the evolution of causal notions in physics. The understanding of causality and explanation adopted will clearly also affect the understanding and role of laws in science.[48]

(iv) Value-Freedom

The conventionalist position takes a very different view of values from that of positivism. The role of values in scientific practice is emphasised if not embraced, and Kuhn describes science as "a value-based enterprise."[49] Conventionalists reject the idea of universal standards of rationality and see theory acceptance (theory choice) as based on the shared criteria (values) of the scientific community, with more idiosyncratic subjective factors playing a part in any given individual's assessment. Scientific practice is suffused with values; in conventionalist writing 'objectivity' forever appears in quotation marks. Beyond denying value-freedom and objectivity as either characterising or even possible in science, Feyerabend puts the case for a humanitarian liberal-anarchism against what passes for objectivity in the sciences:

> For is it not possible that science as we know it today...will create a monster? Is it not possible that an objective approach that frowns upon personal connections between the entities examined will harm people, turn them into miserable, unfriendly, self-righteous mechanisms without charm and humour? 'Is it not possible,' asks Kiekegaard, 'that my activity as an objective [or critico-rational] observer of nature will weaken my strength as a human being?' I suspect the answer to all these questions must be affirmative and I believe that a reform of the sciences that makes them more anarchic and more subjective (in Kiekegaard's sense) is urgently needed.[50]

(v) Unity of Science

For the conventionalist the naturalism debate is largely misplaced. The boundaries of science have shifted through history and their existence is dependent on convention rather than being something that can be objectively determined. Kuhn suggests that the term science has been equated with progress, and so the debates about unity of science are really debates about various social sciences being recognised as progressive.

To a very great extent the term 'science' is reserved for fields that do progress in obvious ways. Nowhere does this show more clearly than in the recurrent debates about whether one or another of the contemporary social sciences is really a science.[51]

Indeed, Kuhn goes so far as to ask, "Can very much depend upon a definition of 'science'?".[52] Conventionalism is compatible with both naturalism and anti-naturalism, and the issue is largely seen as a socio-historical question: what in the history of science has united science and what has been considered scientific? The unity of science thesis itself is considered by Kuhn to be part of scientists' values.[53]

(vi) View of Philosophy

As suggested by the last quotation Kuhn is not concerned to establish a hard and fast distinction between science and philosophy. Clearly philosophy has an important part to play in any paradigm, in constituting values and standards, ontology and epistemology. It assumes a prominent role in conventionalism, being seen as continuous with, rather than radically separate from, or even opposed to, science. Where positivism excluded metaphysics and critical rationalism kept it in the background, conventionalism brings it forward, directly involving philosophy in scientific practice. Feyerabend argues that the method Galileo used in advancing Copernican ideas actually involved increasing the metaphysical content and decreasing the empirical content of the theory of motion:

> ...a comprehensive empirical theory of motion is replaced by a much narrower theory plus a metaphysics of motion, just as an 'empirical' experience is replaced by an experience that contains speculative elements. This, I suggest, was the actual procedure followed by Galileo.[54]

Feyerabend argues against the restrictive empiricist science of the logical positivists that "if a theory is to be meaningful at all, its interpretation must go beyond whatever counts as its 'empirical content': *the interpretation of any physical theory contains metaphysical elements.*"[55]

Instrumentalism, Conventionalism and Positivism

Instrumentalism may be considered a variant of conventionalism. Keat and Urry suggest the following definition:

> First, 'instrumentalism' may refer to a view about the general purpose of scientific enquiry, that it should aim to give us predictive and manipulative power over our physical environment...Second, the term may denote a view about the logical status of scientific theories, that they are computational devices which generate testable predictions. Theories are instruments, and, as such, only their utility can be assessed, and not their truth or falsity. They do

not provide any knowledge of the physical world over and above the predictions that can be derived from them.[56]

The similarities with conventionalism as just described are evident. The view of theories as instruments is but a more specific rendering of the conventionalist view of theories as constructs. The idea that truth or falsity of a theory cannot be directly assessed by an appeal to empirical data is common to both positions. Similarly, the idea that theory assessment is based on utility is a more specific form of the view that subjective, non-universal considerations are the basis for theory evaluation. In addition, instrumentalism entails the features of irrefutability and of knowledge being 'produced' as in conventionalism.

The aim of science, according to instrumentalism, is to provide 'useful' knowledge, i.e., knowledge that affords predictive and manipulative power. This is not a necessary feature of conventionalism, but it is compatible with it.

Instrumentalism is the bridge between conventionalism and positivism. There is very little difference between the positivist view of explanation as but the other side of the coin to prediction, and the instrumentalist view of theories as tools for prediction. Prediction and control lie at the heart of each view of theories.

The link between conventionalism and positivism also extends to their shared aim of establishing a model of justification for knowledge. For the positivists the final justification is experience, while for conventionalists the final justification is provided by convention.[57] There is an empiricist element in the conventionalist view of the origin of knowledge, but the stronger empiricism of positivism is rejected in the critique of 'the given'.

They also both favour an anti-realist viewpoint. Both positivism and conventionalism reject the ontological status accorded unobservable entities by realism. Where realism holds that in referring to an unobservable entity the scientist is positing its existence, positivism and conventionalism consider such a claim to be unwarranted.

But the link between the two is yet stronger, as Kolakowski suggests in his comment that conventionalism is the "expression of a self-destructive tendency inherent in [positivism]."[58] Positivism, through its own contradictions, has an inevitable tendency to move towards conventionalism. In seeking to ground knowledge in experience positivism is led to an infinite regress which can only be broken by the introduction of the idea of conventions. Eliminating all produced knowledge is impossible for the positivists, which leads to the acceptance of an *a priori* element, i.e., conventions. The inherent tendency of positivism to self-destruction is an inherent tendency towards conventionalism.

This tendency of positivism to turn into conventionalism is echoed by a mirror opposite tendency of some forms of conventionalism (those wishing to avoid relativism) to turn to positivism. Just as positivism's search for a final basis of experience for knowledge must fail and end up in the adoption of conventions, so the flaws of conventions, principally their lack of a secure basis, lead conventionalism back into the arms of positivism. Positivism offers a model from which to draw conventions.[59]

The relationship of conventionalism to positivism bears similarities with that of critical rationalism to positivism. Both, while seeking to criticise positivism and to distance themselves from it, share certain characteristics of positivism, and, ultimately, only offer a partial critique of it. Conventionalism, despite offering a more radical alternative to positivism, still remains linked to it.

Scientific Realism

'Realism' is a term that like 'positivism' has been applied to diverse and divergent viewpoints. In general philosophy realism stands for a perspective which asserts the existence of something in opposition to viewpoints which seek to deny its existence. For example, the notion that universals do exist is a realist one.

It is but a short step from this to the more specific 'scientific realism', which is a conception of science that elaborates and evolves the basic philosophical realist position. A useful starting definition is provided by Jerrold Aronson:

> Scientific realism maintains a commonsensical view that there is a world that exists independently of our perception of it, and that our theories inform us about the existence and nature of this realm, even if the things of which our theories are about are not directly observed or, in some cases, not even observable. The realist holds that the truth or success of a theory in some sense entails the existence of the theoretical entities mentioned by the theoretical terms in its language.[60]

This definition suggests the following characteristics of scientific realism:

(1) a commitment to what Roy Bhaskar calls 'perceptual realism', i.e., material objects exist in space and time independently of their being perceived.
(2) theories are intended to give us a literally true picture of the world, to inform us about the existence and nature of objective reality.
(3) a theory is successful or fruitful because, and to the extent that, it reflects independent reality.
(4) a commitment to the possibility of the actual existence of unobservable or theoretical entities.

These features immediately begin to distinguish realism as a model of science, but they are not comprehensive. A fuller picture will be given using the framework established at the start of this chapter, and drawing principally on the writings of the leading contemporary scientific realist, Roy Bhaskar.

(i) Empiricism and Testability

Scientific realism upholds a model of science that, like positivism, has a commitment to empirical testing. However, both its understanding of empiricism and its notion of testing differ in important respects from positivism. In the first place, the realist view of empiricism is informed by its commitment to the existence of unobservable or theoretical entities. Where the positivist denies the existence of unobservable things, the realist accepts their existence. As Ian Hacking writes, "scientific realism says that the entities, states and processes described by correct theories really do exist."[61]

The positivist, at the very least, will leave a question mark hanging over such things as electrons and other sub-atomic particles that cannot be observed and are theoretical postulates. They will argue: how can a term like 'electron' refer to an actual existing entity, or even be meaningful when it is unobserved and never directly experienced? The realist, on the other hand, derives no such ontological implications from the observability or otherwise of an entity. That an entity features in a correct theory is grounds for asserting its existence, and any empiricism which denies this is rejected by realists.

Bhaskar identifies an ideology of empiricism that accords with the positivist model of science, and from which he wishes to distance scientific realism. He writes:

In the ideology of empiricism the world is regarded as flat, uniform, unstructured and undifferentiated: it consists essentially of atomistic events or states of affairs which are constantly conjoined, so occurring in closed systems. Such events and their constant conjunctions are known by asocial, atomistic individuals who passively sense (or apprehend) these given facts and register their constant conjunctions. Underpinning and necessary for the reified facts and fetishized systems of empiricism are thus dehumanised beings in desocialised relationships. Facts usurp the place of things, conjunctions that of causal laws and automata those of people, as reality is defined in terms of the cosmic contingency of human sense-experience (as conceived by empiricism).[62]

Bhaskar sees the empiricist emphasis on sense-data as leading to an entire, and mistaken, ideology. The ontological criterion of perceptibility applied by empiricism leads to the view of reality Bhaskar outlines above, with the reification of facts, causal laws viewed as conjunctions of events, and prediction elevated above explanation in significance. This is entirely at odds with the position of scientific realism, just as it is entirely in keeping with scientific positivism.

The realist view of testing suggests an asymmetry between explanation and prediction in contrast to the mirror image view of these put forward by positivism (which in practice privileges prediction). Bhaskar writes: "because social systems are intrinsically open and cannot be artificially closed, our criteria for the empirical testing of social theories cannot be predictive and so must be exclusively explanatory."[63] The realist notions of prediction and explanation will be explored further in the next section.

(ii) Explanation and Prediction

In contrast to positivism the realist privileges explanation over prediction, and asserts that there is an important distinction between the two. A description of the realist notion of explanation is provided by Keat and Urry:

> To explain phenomena is not merely to show they are instances of well-established regularities. Instead we must discover the necessary connections between phenomena, by acquiring knowledge of the underlying structures and mechanisms at work. Often this will mean entities and processes that are unfamiliar to us: but it is only by doing this that we get beyond the 'mere appearances' of things, to their natures and essences.[64]

The passage suggests three aspects to the realist view of explanation. First, it is based on a critique of the Humean theory of causality, i.e., the basis for the positivist conception of explanation. For the modern Humean (positivists):

> To say that one event is the cause of another is to say that the first is temporally prior to the second, and that whenever an event of the same type as the first occurs, it is always followed by one of the same type as the second.[65]

Such a view is inadequate from the realist perspective, because it fails to tell us why an event occurred, i.e., what the necessary connections between phenomena are. Instead it treats explanation as a form of logical argument with causation as but a regularity of events. At best such a regularity may be a *necessary* condition of explanation (although Bhaskar denies even this), but for the realist it is certainly not *sufficient*. It provides us with no means of distinguishing a true explanatory law from a 'purely accidental concomitance'. What is required in addition is the identification of an underlying structure or mechanism, i.e., a natural mechanism that links the phenomena being explained.

The second aspect of the realist notion of explanation suggested in the passage is the assertion of the existence of unobservable entities and processes. For the realist the denial of their existence is not only unwarranted (observability being a poor criterion of existence), but must also impoverish scientific explanation. If we are to go beyond the identification of instances of well-supported regularities then inevitably unobservable structures and entities will be postulated. These are not only justified, but also vital to many explanations if they are to be complete and true.

This leads to the third aspect of realist explanations highlighted by Keat: the necessity of going beyond appearance to discover the underlying mechanisms connecting phenomena, to identify the essences of things. This aspect of realism reintroduces the notions of powers, natures and generation, which positivism eschews. For realists scientific explanation must attempt to identify the intrinsic nature of things where the powers that generate the effects to be explained may be found. So explanation does not merely refer to, or consist of, descriptions of the regular succession of kinds of events, but instead involves the notion of the generation of one event by another. Realism rejects Humean based accounts of causality and explanation. In going beyond appearance to identify essences and underlying mechanisms, science frequently goes beyond the observable and the regularity of successive events to the theoretically postulated and to necessary connections and generative powers of phenomena.

(iii) Causation and Laws

The realist view of causal laws contrasts with that of positivism. Bhaskar writes:

> ...causal laws must be analysed as tendencies, which may be possessed unexercised and exercised unrealized, just as they may of course be realized unperceived (or undetected by anyone). Thus in citing a law we are referring to the transfactual activity of mechanisms, that is, to their activity as such, not making a claim about the actual outcome (which will in general be co-determined by the effects of other mechanisms too). And a constant conjunction, or empirical invariance is no more a necessary, than it is a sufficient condition for the operation of a causal law.[66]

The positivist idea that a causal law requires the constant conjunction of the phenomena concerned is rejected. Because realism focuses on the underlying mechanisms and structures it applies laws at this deeper level rather than at the level of surface phenomena, which, particularly in an open system (a characteristic of the subject matter of the social sciences), may not display constant conjunctions. The error of positivism is to treat constant conjunctions as causal laws rather than as the empirical manifestations of underlying structures, or as Bhaskar puts it, "the tendencies of mechanisms ontologically irreducible to them."[67]

According to scientific realism, a causal relationship entails natural necessity, or as Bhaskar describes it, "a necessity in nature quite independent of humans and their activity."[68] Natural necessity is not reducible to constant conjunctions, and it is not imposed on nature by our minds. Nor is it the necessity of logic: "Logic connects statements, not events, actions and the like, which are connected, when they are, by relations of natural necessity."[69]

(iv) Value-Freedom

Bhaskar rejects the idea of value-free social science. He writes:

> ...critical realism suggests that social theory is non-neutral in two ways. It always consists in a practical intervention in social life and sometimes (other

things being equal) it logically entails values and actions. In these circumstances, the standard fact/value and theory/practice distinctions break down. Thus if we accept Marx's critique of political economy, which is also a critique of the illusory or false consciousness which capitalist society generates, we may - indeed must - pass immediately to a negative evaluation of those structures and to a positive evaluation of action rationally directed to changing them.[70]

What Bhaskar is saying here is that social science must act upon and change its subject matter in the course of its activity as science. Its subject matter is society and so it has an effect on society. In addition, the knowledge derived from social scientific investigation entails action to change society in certain ways. However, this does not mean that scientific standards are rejected, that scientific theories cannot be tested and assessed on rational grounds.

(v) Unity of Science

An important aspect of scientific realism has been its insistence on the unity of the sciences. The scientific realists see anti-naturalism as based on a mistaken conception of the scientific method, namely the positivist conception. Once the positivist model is dispensed with it becomes entirely possible to assert a unity of the sciences, with both natural and social science sharing the same fundamental scientific method and standards. However, this does not preclude an acknowledgement of the differences between natural and social science based on their different subject matter. Bhaskar writes:

> ...I want to argue for a qualified anti-positivist naturalism. Such a naturalism holds that it is possible to give an account of science under which the proper and more or less specific methods of both the natural and social sciences can fall. But it does not deny that there are important differences in these methods grounded in the real differences in the real differences that exist in their subject matters.[71]

In other words, while whole-heartedly embracing naturalism, Bhaskar accepts there are certain limits to naturalism. These include the fact that society and many of the entities within it are theoretical, that social science forms part of its own field of enquiry, and that society is characterised by open rather than closed systems.

(vi) View of Philosophy

The scientific realist view of philosophy is a positive (rather than a positivist) one. Science neither stands in opposition to philosophy nor supplants it. Indeed, science requires philosophy, and philosophy stands as a distinct practice with its own role and method. Bhaskar writes:

> Philosophy...does not consider a world apart from that of the various sciences. Rather it considers just that world, but from the perspective of what can be established about it by *a priori* argument, where it takes as its premises scientific activities as conceptualized in experience (or in a theoretical redescription of it). As such philosophy is dependent upon the form of scientific practices, but irreducible to the content of scientific beliefs. Thus philosophy can tell us that, if experimental activity is to be intelligible, the world must be structured and differentiated, But it cannot tell us what structures the world contains or the ways in which they are different, which are entirely matters for substantive scientific investigation.[72]

While upholding the importance of philosophy, the scientific realists have tended to view it as in some sense subservient to science. This attitude is suggested by Bhaskar's description of philosophy as "an underlabourer for science".[73] This is perhaps in part a reaction to the anti-naturalist position maintained by hermeneutic and interpretative social theorists,[74] who, particularly regarding social theory, place philosophy above science.

*

Scientific realism stands opposed to positivism in all the areas identified: empiricism and testing, explanation and prediction, cause and laws, value-freedom, the nature of scientific unity, and the view of philosophy. In particular, it offers a critique of empiricism, stresses the reality and importance of underlying, unobservable structures, processes and essences, and posits natural necessity.

*

All of these models of science have at one time or another been applied to Marxism in the debate over its scientific status. In the next chapter the scientific standing of Marx's method will be discussed with reference to these different conceptions.

Notes

[1] Ayer (1959) 17
[2] Hanfling (1982) 2
[3] Giddens (1974) preface
[4] See Simon (1972) for example.
[5] See Stockman (1983)
[6] ibid., 7
[7] Accounts of positivist models of science incorporating many of these tenets may be found in Nagel (1961), Hempel (1966) and Van Fraasen (1980).
[8] Stockman (1983) 19
[9] This trilemma was suggested by R. Keat in an unpublished lecture.
[10] Popper (1963) 55
[11] ibid., 37
[12] Popper (1972) 3
[13] Popper (1963) 36
[14] Popper (1992) 51-52
[15] Popper (1963)55
[16] Popper (1972) 349
[17] ibid., 349
[18] ibid., 351
[19] Popper (1957) 133
[20] Popper (1963) 105
[21] Popper (1972) 195
[22] ibid., 196
[23] ibid., 115
[24] ibid., 91
[25] ibid., 92
[26] Popper (1963) 30
[27] Popper (1957) 155
[28] ibid., 131
[29] Popper (1963) 253
[30] ibid., 68
[31] ibid., 72
[32] ibid., 69
[33] See, for example, Lakatos (1981).
[34] O'Hear writes with regard to Popper's attitude to the demarcation criterion: "Popper's ultimate concern was not to distinguish between science and non-science, but to distinguish between criticizable and non-criticizable attitudes to theories of all types." O'Hear (1980) 147
[35] Although essentially twentieth century some have traced its history back to the nineteenth century. See Wisdom (1987) 29.
[36] See for example, Le Roy (1900); Poincare (1902); and Duhem (1904).
[37] Kolakowski (1972) 158-59

[38] Keat and Urry (1975) 5
[39] Feyerabend (1988) 155
[40] Kuhn (1962) 113
[41] Kuhn (1970) 77
[42] Feyerabend (1988) 252-53
[43] Kuhn (1970) 80
[44] ibid., 109
[45] Kuhn (1977) 29; ibid., 28
[46] Kuhn (1977) 188, notes how few predictions Newton's three laws of motion and Einstein's general theory of relativity yielded (particularly when the theories were first put forward).
[47] Feyerabend (1981a) 94; ibid., 91. See chapter 4 of Feyerabend (1981a) for his critique of formal accounts of explanation, and chapter 3 of Feyerabend (1981b) for his critique of the hypothetico-deductive model.
[48] See chapter 2, Kuhn (1977) on the evolving concepts of cause and explanation in physics.
[49] Kuhn (1977) 332
[50] Feyerabend (1988) 160
[51] Kuhn (1970) 160
[52] ibid., 160
[53] See chapter 3, Kuhn (1977).
[54] Feyerabend (1990) 126
[55] Feyerabend (1981a) 42
[56] Keat and Urry (1975) 63
[57] ibid., 38-39
[58] Quoted in Stockman (1983) 35
[59] This point is made by Schnädelbach in Stockman (1983) chapter 3.
[60] Aronson (1984) 6
[61] Hacking (1983) 21
[62] Bhaskar (1989) 8-9
[63] ibid., 5
[64] Keat and Urry (1975) 5
[65] ibid., 28
[66] Bhaskar (1989) 16
[67] ibid., 9
[68] ibid., 17
[69] Bhaskar (1979a) 85
[70] Bhaskar (1989) 5
[71] ibid., 67
[72] ibid., 14
[73] ibid., 2
[74] See, for example, Winch (1958).

6   Marx and Science

Attempts to portray Marxist method as scientific have utilised different conceptions of science - usually the dominant model of the time.   At different times Marxism has been interpreted to fit the models of science put forward by scientific positivism, critical rationalism, conventionalism and scientific realism. In each case the philosophy of science embraced has been taken to be the true account of science and Marxism has been taken to exemplify the particular conception of science. Thus Marxism has been 'proved' to be scientific.

In this chapter Marx's method will be compared with the four models of science noted above, and the various attempts to match Marxism with the conceptions of science will be assessed.   The six categories used to describe the characterising tenets of the different conceptions of science in the previous chapter will also be employed in this chapter.

Marx and Scientific Positivism

The most prevalent interpretation of Marxism's scientificity has been the positivist one.[1]   The case for Marxism being a science in the positivist mould (or of Marxists considering it as such) finds support in the writings of 'orthodox' Marxists such as Kautsky, Plekhanov and (for all his revising still at heart orthodox) Bernstein. These writers very much emphasise the scientific character of Marxism ('scientific socialism'), and their views of science appear akin to scientific positivism. Scientific positivism was the dominant model of science at the end of the nineteenth century and in the first half of the twentieth century, and continues to exert a strong influence. Interpretations of Marxism's scientificity have tended to reflect this.

(i) Empiricism and Testability

Empiricism, or some form of it, is central to positivism, and testability is very closely linked to it. To be is to be perceived and to know is to test.

Verification is always by empirical means. The ontological and epistemological aspects of positivism meet in this cluster of tenets.

H.B. Acton draws attention to the empirical strand in Marxism, which he believes signifies the positivist character of Marxism, "the fundamental Marxist thesis is identical with that of positivism, namely, that nothing can be known but what sense perception and the methods of science reveal."[2]

There is much evidence in Marx's writings to support this claim, particularly in the early and transitional works, most notably the GI. As Callinicos notes, "There is an almost Comtean ring to the passages of The German Ideology which denounce idealist metaphysics in the name of positive science."[3]

In the GI Marx and Engels set out to criticise the speculative philosophy of the Hegelians, particularly the 'Young Hegelians'. Marx and Engels repeatedly counter-pose their own empirically based approach to the abstract, metaphysical method of the Hegelians:

> The premises from which we begin are not arbitrary ones, not dogmas, but real premises from which abstraction can only be made in the imagination...These premises can thus be verified in a purely empirical way.[4]

> This method of approach [that used by Marx and Engels] is not devoid of premises. It starts out from the real premises and does not abandon them for a moment. Its premises are men, not in any fantastic isolation and rigidity, but in their actual empirically perceptible process of development under definite conditions.[5]

This empirical theme is also found in the EPM:

> ...I arrived at my conclusions though an entirely empirical analysis based on an exhaustive critical study of political economy.[6]

> Sense perception must be the basis of all science...[7]

The two quotations from the GI also suggest the close link between the empiricism and testability tenets; verification is understood to be by empirical means. This link between empiricism and testability is brought out further by Engels in the introduction to *Socialism: Utopian and Scientific*:

> The proof of the pudding is in the eating. From the moment we turn to our own use these objects, according to the qualities we perceive in them, we put to an

infallible test the correctness or otherwise of our sense-perceptions. If these perceptions have been wrong, them our estimate of the use to which an object can be turned must also be wrong, and our attempt must fail. But if we succeed in accomplishing our aim, if we find that the object does agree with our idea of it, and does answer the purpose we intend it for, then that is positive proof that our perceptions of it and of its qualities so *far*, agree with reality outside ourselves.[8]

However, before jumping to the conclusion that Marx embraced positivist empiricism and testability tenets, the context of the quotations must be appreciated. In the GI Marx and Engels are attacking the speculative, idealist philosophising of the Hegelians. They, therefore, emphasise that aspect of their approach which most contrasts with that of the Hegelians, i.e., the empirical component. This does not mean they are empiricists in the strong sense of believing all knowledge to be rooted in sense-perception, or that they accept all aspects of positivist empiricism, such as the ontological claim that only observable entities can be held to exist. It should be noted in this regard that Marx criticises Hegel in the EPM not only for 'uncritical idealism', but also for 'uncritical positivism',[9] and in the GI he criticises 'empiricists' for collecting 'dead facts' and being abstract.[10]

Furthermore, there are good grounds for suggesting that Marx did not embrace the positivist theses regarding empiricism and testing. While it is clear that Marx favoured an empirical approach as opposed to a purely deductive, rationalist approach, it is also clear that he did not favour a naive, uncritical empiricism. As Farr points out, Marx, like Comte, Mill and many others "shared the general view that science was an empirical, factual, and observational form of human inquiry",[11] but this did not make him an empiricist or positivist who believed that science could be based on sense-data or sense-certainty. Farr develops his argument suggesting that Marx maintained at least three beliefs that are incompatible with positivist empiricism:

(i) important terms in theories often refer to non-observable entities, processes or relations.
(ii) real causal agents are often unobservable essences underlying appearances.
(iii) observation is theory-dependent.

Many of Marx's key concepts, such as value (or surplus-value) and abstract labour, refer to hypothetical entities or qualities of observable phenomena which are not themselves observable. This links in with Marx's essentialism, i.e., his distinction between appearance and essence, which is central to his notion of science. He writes, "But all science would be superfluous if the outward appearance and the essence of things directly coincided."[12] The point is also made in a letter from Marx to Engels:

> The philistine's and vulgar economists way of looking at things stems from...the fact that it is only the direct form of manifestation of relations that is reflected in their brains and not their inner connection. Incidentally, if the latter were the case what need would there be of science?[13]

The use of the essence-appearance distinction[14] and postulating of unobservable entities as real causal mechanisms is incompatible with positivist empiricism's hostility to theoretical/unobservable entities. Furthermore, Marx seems to clearly challenge the theory-neutrality of observation on which positivism puts so much weight. For example, in the EPM Marx writes, "The *senses* have therefore become *theoreticians* in their immediate praxis," [15] implying the theory-dependency of observation. In the GR he writes:

> Carey absorbs from all directions the massive material furnished him by the old world...Hence his strayings and wanderings through all countries, massive and uncritical use of statistics, a catalogue-like erudition.[16]

Marx is clearly eschewing a simple empiricism here. It should also be evident that Marx's and Engels' comments on verification and testing do not entail the positivist view. They again have to be considered against a background of combating speculative philosophy where 'verification' is obtainable by abstract reason alone. Marx believed his theories to be supported by empirical evidence, and that their truth could be shown empirically or in practice rather than such truth being a question of philosophical or *a priori* demonstration. Certainly, he did not subscribe to the kind of testability entailed by the hypothetico-deductive model of explanation and prediction favoured by positivists, which will be discussed in the next section.

(ii) Explanation and Prediction

As noted in the previous chapter, positivism places great weight on explanation and prediction as the aim of science, and at the same time offers a very narrow view of them. The classic positivist model of prediction and explanation is the deductive-nomological model, which assumes a logical identity of the two, and as the name suggests is centred around deductive reasoning and the formulation of laws:

Universal law
Specific Initial Conditions
Explicandum/Prediction

If we assume we have something to be explained (the *explicandum*), then its explanation will consist of the specific conditions of the event and a universal law. The explanation will show the event to be an instance of a regularity (universal law). With a prediction we start with the universal law and the specific initial conditions from which the prediction is logically deduced. Both explanation and prediction involve logical deduction and the same formal structure. Testing of theories will have certain test implications (predictions), and so the same model is utilised.

Marx made a number of apparent predictions in *Capital* based on the laws he claimed to have discovered. Various Marxists have defended the scientific status and accuracy of these in such a way as to make them broadly accord with the positivist model. For example Mandel writes:

> It is precisely because of Marx's capacity to discover the long-term laws of motion of the capitalist mode of production...that his long-term predictions - the laws of accumulation of capital, stepped-up technological progress, accelerated increase in the productivity and intensity of labour, growing concentration and centralization of capital, transformation of the great majority of economically active people into sellers of labour-power, declining rate of profit, increased rate of surplus-value, periodically recurrent recessions, inevitable class struggle between Capital and Labour, increasing revolutionary attempts to overthrow capitalism - have been strikingly confirmed by history.[17]

The important thing to note here is that a predictive model akin to the positivist one is assumed involving the key components of general laws, specific conditions and a prediction. Such a model also implies a notion of explanation holding something in common with positivism.

However, Marx's predictions have been criticised, most notably by Popper, for being vague and unconditional. The laws of tendency Marx posits do not lend themselves to precise predictions, and Marx specifies countervailing factors that give an 'unpositivist' latitude to them. In the positivist scheme predictions are tests of hypotheses, and it is difficult to see Marx's predictions fulfilling this role. The law of the tendency of the rate of profit to fall cannot be used to deduce an exact prediction that would act as a test of the hypothesis embodied in the law. Actual movements of the rate of profit cannot be predicted on the basis of the law, even over an extended period, because of the counteracting influences specified by Marx. The law is more of an abstract tendency than an empirical one; it is abstracted away from the counteracting influences, and as such not a guide to the actual movement of the rate of profit.[18]

If Marx's notion of prediction diverges from the positivist norm, the Marxian idea of explanation does so even more drastically. In common with positivist requirements Marx's explanations often make reference to laws, but, as is shown in the next section, Marx's laws differ from the positivist type. Furthermore, Marx does not halt explanation at demonstration of an event being an instance of a regularity. Sayer gives the example of ground-rent variations that can be correlated, *ceteris paribus*, to variations in natural conditions of production like soil fertility. But such regularities do not constitute an explanation for Marx. Sayer writes:

> Marx saw empirical correlations as needing to be explained, and for him to explain them meant above all to unearth the mechanism through which they are brought about, and behind them their conditions. Explanation thus ultimately proceeds from the properties of these latter entities an, unlike in the Humean [positivist] tradition, causal propositions are understood as referring to these properties.[19]

Just as Marx's essentialism positing hidden unobservable entities as real, causal mechanisms is incompatible with positivist empiricism, so it is incompatible with the positivist concept of explanation.

(iii) Causation and Laws

The basic positivist view of cause draws its inspiration from Hume's analysis of causality as merely constant conjunction. This view is expressed by the logical positivist, Moritz Schlick:

> The difference between a mere temporal sequence and a causal sequence is the regularity, the uniformity of the latter. If C is *regularly* followed by E then C is the cause of E; if E only 'happens' to follow C now and then, the sequence is

called mere chance...The word 'cause', as used in everyday life, implies *nothing but* regularity of sequence, because *nothing else* is used to verify the propositions in which it occurs.[20]

In other words, cause is understood as the regularity of one event following another and this view is embodied in the notion of a law as a statement expressing a regular relationship. Laws are held to be universal; they apply at all times and in all places. The laws of natural science or of nature, as exemplified by Newtonian physics, are the model.

That causal explanation and the formulation of laws were important in Marx's work is evident. On laws, for example, Marx states in the preface to *Capital*, "it is the ultimate aim of this work to reveal the economic law of motion of modern society."[21] Marx also quotes with approval a review of *Capital* in which the reviewer emphasises Marx's concern with laws: "The one thing which is important for Marx is to find the law of the phenomena with whose investigation he is concerned."[22]

Engels speech at Marx's graveside also emphasises Marx's discovery of laws in his work:

Just as Darwin discovered the law of development of organic nature, so Marx discovered the law of development of human history...

But that is not all. Marx also discovered the special law of motion governing the present-day capitalist mode of production.[23]

Such quotations are in keeping with the central aim of identifying scientific laws and the suggestion of a natural science model, but are the laws truly positivist in character? There is certainly a strand of interpretation within Marxism that does see a positivist character to Marx's laws:

[T]he general laws which govern the movement of society are of the same pattern as the laws of the external world. These laws which hold good universally, both for men and things, make up what may be called the Marxist philosophy or view of the world.[24]

This is a view of laws entirely in keeping with the positivist view of them as universal, exceptionless and natural. However, it is apparent that Marx did not see all laws as natural and immutable:

> The aim [of the political economists]...is to present production...as encased in eternal natural laws independent of history, at which opportunity bourgeois relations are then quietly smuggled in as the inviolable natural laws on which society in the abstract is founded.[25]

Or again, he criticises Proudhon and bourgeois economists for viewing, "economic categories as eternal and not as historical laws which are only laws for a particular historical development."[26] This is a recurrent theme in Marx's critique of political economists that they are ahistorical in outlook, and this is shown by their portrayal of historically specific laws as natural and eternal. This does not mean that Marx denied the existence of transhistorical, natural laws, merely that his principal concern was with those specific to capitalism.

Another feature of Marx's laws that may distance them from the positivist model is their tendential character. In the preface to *Capital* Marx writes:

> Intrinsically, it is not a question of the higher or lower degree of the development of the social antagonisms that spring from the natural laws of capitalist production. It is a question of these laws themselves, of these tendencies winning their way through and working themselves out with iron necessity.[27]

The phrasing is ambiguous, but at the very least it suggests a notion of laws which does not conform to the universal and deterministic exemplar of positivist laws. Laws of tendency do not permit the kind of predictive capability that the positivist model demands. Precise predictions cannot be derived from them.

Marx also employs the essence-appearance distinction that again influences the nature of his laws away from the positivist model. Marx is critical of other political economists for failing to go beyond the merely visible, the immediate appearance to the underlying structures and causal mechanisms. He himself seeks the 'real laws' behind the 'merely external movement':

> If, as the reader will have realised to his great dismay, the analysis of the actual intrinsic relations of capitalist production is a very complicated matter and very extensive; if it is a work of science to resolve the visible, merely external movement into the true intrinsic movement, it is self-evident that conceptions which arise about the laws of production in the minds of agents of

capitalist production and circulation will diverge drastically from these real laws and will merely be the conscious expression of the visible movements.[28]

The classic positivist notion of causal laws stops precisely at the visible external movement, the level of constant conjunction.

(iv) Value-Freedom

According to scientific positivism science must be conducted in a neutral, value-free way, always impartial and objective.

Marxists such as Kautsky, Bernstein, Plekhanov and the Second International took the view that Marx provided an objective analysis and account of capitalism, describing what would happen (its decline and collapse) rather than what should happen. Marx and Engels themselves were scathing of ethically inspired socialism and contrasted their own scientific approach with the study of capitalism and its consequences with that of the 'utopian socialists', who could only reject capitalism as bad. The implication is clearly that the utopian socialists only put forward moral condemnations of capitalism, while Marx and Engels scientifically (and objectively) explained capitalism. Mandel takes this view of Marx:

> Marx strove...to analyse capitalism in an objective and scientific way...he did not simply give vent to an aggressive hostility towards a particular form of economic organization, for reasons of revolutionary passion and compassion for the downtrodden and oppressed...Marx sought to discover objective laws of motion. There was nobody...whom he despised more than the man with scientific pretensions who nevertheless deliberately twists empirical data or falsifies research results to suit some subjective purpose.[29]

Marx's comments on the impact of the bourgeoisie coming to power in France and England on 'scientific bourgeois economics' seem to offer further support for this view:

> It was thenceforth no longer a question whether this or that theorem was true, but whether it was useful to capital or harmful...In place of disinterested inquirers there stepped hired prize-fighters; in place of genuine scientific research, the bad conscience and evil intent of apologetics.[30]

In *Theories of Surplus Value* Marx commends Ricardo for his 'scientific honesty', his 'scientific impartiality' and for being 'stoic, objective, scientific'. Malthus, on the other hand, he condemns because his scientific conclusions are 'considerate towards the ruling classes' and he 'falsifies science for those interests [of the ruling classes]'.[31]

However, it is also clear that Marx subjected capitalism to the most savage critique and indictment. His work seems to incorporate moral judgements throughout. This would still be compatible with the positivist idea of value-freedom if the scientific enquiry could be clearly separated from the moral judgements. If Marx's account of capitalism could be shown to be neutral, value-free and entirely distinct from his moral judgements then the positivist standard of objectivity would be preserved. However, it is not at all clear that this is the case, or that Marx saw his work in this way. The very language Marx uses belies a value-free account. For example, with reference to the extraction of surplus-value, he talks of "the total surplus-value extorted...the common booty", and "the loot of other people's labour." Elsewhere he talks of "the theft of alien labour time," and "all progress in capitalist agriculture is a progress in the art, not only of robbing the worker, but of robbing the soil."[32]

Capital is not just an account of capitalist political economy; it is, in the words of its sub-title, a 'critique of political economy'. Marx sets out to be critical and he clearly has a political agenda that informs all his work. This critical approach does not uphold the fact-value and theory-practice distinctions entailed by positivist objectivity. Bhaskar writes of Marxism (and other social theory):

> [It] is non-neutral in two ways. It always consists in a practical intervention in social life and sometimes (other things being equal) it logically entails values and actions. In these circumstances, the standard fact/value and theory/practice distinctions break down. Thus if we accept Marx's critique of political economy, which is also a critique of the illusory or false consciousness which capitalist society generates, we may - indeed must - pass immediately to a negative evaluation of those structures and to a positive evaluation of action rationally directed to changing them.[33]

In other words, Marx's scientific approach is clearly at odds with scientific positivism's understanding of value-freedom. He insists on the highest standards of scientific integrity, but also insists on a fierce, critical perspective.

(v) Unity of Science

The unity of science thesis is held by many commentators to be central to the positivist conception of science.[34] Its place in Marx's method has been the subject of some debate by commentators wishing to prove or disprove Marxism's scientificity/positivism.[35] Early evidence that Marx did subscribe to a unity of science thesis can be found in the EPM:

> History itself is a real part of natural history and of nature's becoming man. Natural science will in time subsume the science of man just as the science of man will subsume natural science: there will be one science.[36]

This extract, on the face of it, suggests Marx embraced a form of unity of science based on a unified subject matter, and is consistent with a unity of method and of laws. The passage lends itself to a strong unity of science interpretation.

Moving forward to *Capital* there appears to be further support for this position in an explicit paralleling of social and natural science:

> ...a scientific analysis of competition is possible only if we grasp the inner nature of capital, just as the apparent motions of the heavenly bodies are intelligible only to someone who is acquainted with their real motions, which are not perceptible to the senses.[37]

Further examples of Marx comparing his project with that undertaken in natural science can be found elsewhere in his work[38] and are supported by comments made by Engels. For example Engels speech at Marx's graveside: "Just as Darwin discovered the law of development of organic nature, so Marx discovered the law of development of human history."[39]

In *Capital* there can also be found an echo of the unity of subject-matter suggested by the passage from the EPM quoted above: "the development of the economic formation of society is viewed as a process of natural history."[40] Marx seems here to be linking social and natural history in a single process, and thereby opening the way for a comprehensive unity of science involving unity of method, laws and language.

Engels in *Anti-Duhring* puts forward an account of dialectics which seems to validate the unity of laws construction put upon Marx's writings above: "...in nature, amid the welter of innumerable changes, the same dialectical laws of motion impose themselves as those which in history govern the apparent fortuitousness of events..." [41] Engels seems to be describing a unity of laws thesis where the same laws of motion and development apply to both society and nature.

The Leninist stamp of approval for the unity of science thesis is implied by Lenin when he writes, "Historical Materialism made it possible for the first time to study with the accuracy of the natural sciences the social conditions of the life of the masses and the changes in these conditions."[42]

However, a battery of commentators rejects this interpretation arguing that Marx did not and could not have held a unity of science thesis.[43]   In general their motivation has been to prove Marx was not a positivist and they have taken the unity of science thesis to be a litmus test of this.   To assess the arguments a closer examination of the unity of science thesis is required.

Farr distinguishes three aspects of the positivist unity of science theses: unity of language, of laws and of method.   The first of these is the proposition that all scientific terms should be reducible in principle to a single universal language, namely the language of observation or physics. Unity of laws refers to the view that all scientific laws are reducible to the laws of physics, that there is a hierarchy of connected laws that are ultimately derivable from the basic laws of physics.   Unity of method is the idea that all sciences can and should utilise the same basic method, the same model of testing , explanation, prediction and laws.

Farr argues that Marx's view was 'methodological relationism', that is he emphasised social relations as providing the context of meaning for things.   For example, Marx writes:

> The special difficulty in grasping money... is that a social relation, a definite relation between individuals, here appears as a metal, a stone, as a purely physical, external thing which can be found, as such, in nature, and which is indistinguishable in form from its natural existence...Nature does not produce money, any more than it produces a rate of exchange or a banker...To be money is not a natural attribute of gold and silver, and is therefore quite unknown to the physicist, chemist, etc., as such.[44]

Social relations give money its economic existence, and without them money only has a metallic or physical existence.   The language of social relations is not reducible to the language of physical observation.   Indeed, as Farr writes:

> Physical thing terms cannot provide the bedrock of a unified scientific vocabulary because they misdescribe the very reality a social science attempts to capture.   As thing terms, they fall through the language of social relations that make the social sciences possible.[45]

If social relations are the distinctive characteristic of society and crucial in any science of society, then Marx could not have embraced a unity of language or unity of laws thesis. Each requires social science to be a derivative of physics.

Farr also argues against anything but a very weak unity of method thesis. For him Marx's method reflects the subject matter, so explanations, predictions, testing and laws are different in the social sciences compared with the natural sciences. In physics laws are universal and ahistorical, and predictions and test implications can be derived from them. In social science the dynamic nature of social relations gives a different character to all these: laws are tendencies, explanations are limited and particular, predictions are contingent and tests non-conclusive.

A similar 'unpacking' of the unity of science thesis is undertaken by Callinicos,[46] who analyses it into five separate theses, which may be summarised as follows:

(i) man is a dependent part of nature.
(ii) the methodological principles are the same in the natural and social sciences.
(iii) the concepts and propositions are the same in the natural and social sciences.
(iv) social science is reducible to natural science.
(v) social behaviour can be explained as a manifestation of human nature.

Callinicos wants to argue that Marx does subscribe to a unity of science thesis, but his understanding of Marx is actually very similar to Farr's on this issue. He asserts that Marx endorses (i) and (ii) of the above, but rejects the rest. In other words there is unity of subject matter to the extent that human beings are a part of and dependent on nature, and the basic methodological principles are the same for social as for natural science. However, the concepts and propositions of social science, according to Callinicos' reading of Marx, are neither identical to nor modelled upon those of natural science. Social scientific explanations are independent and adequate in themselves, and do not require translation into a more fundamental scientific language even if it were possible. In addition, human nature is no basis for explanation of social behaviour, the social is not reducible to the biological.

There is no substantive point of difference between Farr and Callinicos even though they are ostensibly in opposed camps. Farr acknowledges a weak unity of method thesis whilst maintaining that this does not entail an acceptance of a form of unity of science. The additional thesis which Callinicos claims Marx endorses does not conflict with Farr's general position. The difference seems to lie in intention: where Farr is concerned to distance Marx from positivism and views unity of science as integral to positivism, Callinicos is more concerned, if anything, to demonstrate Marxism's scientific credentials,[47] and does not see a qualified unity of science thesis as committing Marx to positivism.

The disassociating of the unity of science thesis from positivism is a view supported by scientific realists willing to endorse a form of it based on their conception of science. There seems to be no reason why the unity of science thesis cannot be interpreted in such a way as to be released from its positivist framework and to allow difference as well as unity between the social and natural sciences.

Given the interpretations of Marx put forward by Farr and Callinicos, the evidence of Marx's writings must now be reviewed. The broad parallels drawn by both Marx and Engels between Marxism and natural science, whilst implying some basic similarity between social and natural science, do not entail any strong positivist unity of science. The generality of the phrasing precludes any inference of a unity of language or laws, and unity of method is suggested in no more than a weak sense. Furthermore, the unity of method implied by Marx when he compares analysis of competition with astronomy is based on a method that goes beyond perception to 'grasp the inner nature', in other words, it has the flavour of scientific realism rather than scientific positivism.

When Marx talks of natural science subsuming the science of man, and vice versa, resulting in one science he is clearly putting forward some version of a unity of science thesis. However, it is a very idiosyncratic one based on the end of the separation of human beings and nature, the over-coming of alienation which has estranged human beings from nature. As Farr writes:

> This unity is not to be a result of the internal unification of scientific language, laws or method.   Rather, science becomes more and more unified.   A humanized nature and a naturalized humanity make possible the unity of science in the peculiarly nonpositivistic Marxist sense.[48]

The dialectical laws that Engels identifies as operating both in nature and society are less easily disposed of, and Engels whole outlook seems to lend itself more readily to a strong unity of science interpretation. However, the well-known dialectical laws which Engels enunciates are very general in their formulation and it is not at all clear how they can be held to be the basic laws of the world (of physics), to which all other physical and social laws are connected in a great hierarchical structure.

The evidence suggests that Marx was not committed to a unity of science thesis in any strong or positivistic sense. That such a unity of science thesis does not fit Marx's method does not mean that Marx's method was not scientific, or that he conducted his social science in an entirely different way and according to different standards from natural science. It is clear that Marx saw himself as engaged in a scientific enterprise that was in some ways akin to that of natural science, but this does not preclude the possibility of differences in the method of social science he employed.

(vi) View of Science and Philosophy

Positivism has always tended to try to restrict what is meaningful, important or valid to that which can be readily established. Logical positivism rejected that which could not be empirically verified as meaningless; scientific positivism denies the existence of the unobservable, and asserts the necessity of testability based on sensory experience for truly scientific theories and for the validation and verification of knowledge.

Marx and Engels expressed a hostility to speculative philosophy which at times seemed to extend to a rejection of all philosophy in favour of science:

> ...one has to "leave philosophy aside"...one has to leap out of it and devote oneself like an ordinary man to the study of actuality.

> Where speculation ends - in real life - there real, positive science begins...When reality is depicted philosophy as an independent branch of activity loses its medium of existence.[49]

The view suggested in these quotations casts philosophy as pre-scientific and speculative. Philosophy is superseded by science, which replaces the speculations of philosophy with a true and attested picture of reality. Engels seems to give further expression to this perspective in *Anti-Dühring*:

> As soon as each separate science is required to clarify its position in the great totality of things and of our knowledge of things, a special science dealing with this totality is superfluous. All that remains in an independent state from all earlier philosophy is the science of thought and its laws - formal logic and

dialectics. Everything else merges into the positive science of nature and history.[50]

Engels seems to suggest here that philosophy loses its separate identity and is (sub)merged into science. In a comparison of philosophy and utopian socialism the thought is continued: "The natural philosophers stand in the same relation to consciously dialectical natural science as the Utopians to modern communism."[51] Engels is saying here that just as pre-scientific utopian socialism contrasts with the scientific socialism of Marx, so natural philosophy contrasts with 'dialectical natural science'; 'theoretical natural science' will make philosophy superfluous.

This apparent hostility to philosophy shown by both Marx and Engels is the other side of the coin to their views on empiricism and testability. Their emphasis on the scientific and empirical nature of their work and their negative comments on philosophy are efforts to distance themselves from much of the philosophy of their time. However, this perspective should not be construed as an outright rejection of all philosophy. At various times Marx criticised Hegelian idealist philosophy, speculative metaphysics, passive contemplative philosophy, bourgeois philosophy and plain bad philosophy, but he did not dismiss philosophy as such. In fact, he continued to utilise philosophical concepts throughout his work (for example, alienation and essence and appearance), and he acknowledged his debt to Hegel even in *Capital*, where he proclaimed himself "the pupil of that mighty thinker". His entire scientific approach is underwritten by a dialectical and materialist philosophy, which he largely worked out in his early works. He then moved on to focus more on political economy, but he did not leave behind his philosophy, he merely no longer needed to fight the philosophical battles of the earlier works; he had resolved those philosophical disputes to his own satisfaction. The GR in particular shows the extent to which he integrated his philosophical thinking into his later work.[52]

It is also worth noting that Marx was frequently scathing about some science, notably the "bourgeois science of economics."[53] That is to say, it is not tenable to portray Marx as having rejected philosophy for science, when it is clear that he was critical of certain kinds of scientific practice as well as certain philosophical approaches and arguments. It is also notable that Marx in endorsing one reviewer's opinion of *Capital* stated that the reviewer was describing none other than the dialectical method. He did not seek to distinguish his scientific method from dialectics, but rather identified the two.

As much as anything, Marx was critical of a philosophical tradition that privileged philosophy over science. Marx wished to assert the claims of the latter, but not to the extent of extinguishing the former.

*

The positivist Marxists have emphasised the later writings as Marx's most scientific (and therefore most positivist) work, downgrading the more 'philosophical' earlier writings. However, the evidence against the positivist interpretation is largely to be found in the later work, while, on the other hand, evidence supporting the positivist case, where it can be found, is in the earlier works, particularly the EPM and the GI. McCarthy suggests a period of 'positivistic experiments' coinciding with the anti-speculative philosophy polemics of the transitional works.[54] In other words, Marx is at his most 'positivist' in a transitional period before his science has reached its maturity. Even this view of Marx as having gone through a positivist period relies on an out of context interpretation of his writings, and it is certainly the case that his most developed work does not display any positivist leanings.

The evidence for a positivist Marxism does not stand up to scrutiny. The common ground between Marx and the positivists is, as Farr notes, "...the general view that science was an empirical, factual, and observational form of human enquiry."[55] But this does not entail a subscription to any of the positivist tenets. Indeed, the evidence suggests that Marx's method diverged from positivism in almost every respect. That Marx's method does contrast so greatly with scientific positivism in the various particulars described suggests a fundamental difference of outlook. This difference may lie in the philosophy that underlies each. Absent from the philosophy of positivism is any dialectical dimension, whereas Marx's approach is strongly influenced by dialectics.

Marx and Critical Rationalism

The critical rationalist philosophy of science is represented principally by the works of Karl Popper and Imre Lakatos. Its key features are a critical element based on a falsification principle, and a rational element based on a belief in the rationality of the logical-deductive core of the scientific method.

Various Marxists and writers on Marxism have explicitly sought to match Marxism with critical rationalism, to prove Marxism's scientific status by demonstrating its compatibility with critical rationalist criteria of science. Popper and Lakatos themselves have expressly denied that Marxism is scientific, but their views have been challenged by critical rationalist Marxists on the grounds that (a) they misrepresent Marxism, and (b) their appraisals are influenced by their anti-Marxist political views.

The main views to be discussed will be those of Maurice Cornforth and Mark Cowling, who both argue for a scientific Marxism on Popperian lines.

(i) Empiricism and Testability

This is a crucial area of difference between positivism and critical rationalism, and the criticisms levelled against positivism by Popper suggest, at least on the face of it, a closer resemblance between Marxist method and critical rationalism.

Cowling argues that Marx and Popper concur in their anti-empiricism; they both reject the view that science is built up by careful observation (the inductivist view), and they both take observation to be theory-impregnated.[56] Popper like Marx is not a straightforward empiricist and he abjures much of the empiricism embraced by the positivists.

On the related issue of testing, Popper makes his profound departure from positivist verificationism and asserts instead his falsifiability principle. This follows from his solution to the problem of induction which denies the possibility of inductive inference, thus making verification of a theory (or test statement) impossible. Only the possibility of falsification based on deductive reasoning is left open. Science, contrary to the positivist view, proceeds by conjecture and refutation; the advancing of a hypothesis followed by attempts to falsify it. For Popper, it is precisely this falsifying activity which distinguishes science from non-science, or, to put it another way, a theory is scientific if it is falsifiable in principle.

Falsificationism is taken very seriously by both Cornforth and Cowling. They both see Marxism's scientific status as standing or falling on this issue. Popper's specific claim that Marxism is unfalsifiable and, hence, unscientific is rejected by them both on the grounds that it is based on a hostile misreading of Marx.

Cornforth endorses the Popperian view that "every 'good' scientific theory is a prohibition: it forbids certain things to happen."[57] He then proceeds to argue that Marxism conforms to this maxim:

The fundamental laws which Marx formulated as governing social development..."forbid certain things to happen". They say that there must always be a certain kind of correspondence between forces of production and relations of production. This allows all manner of things to done within the bounds of such correspondence, but denies the possibility of going outside those bounds...If uninterrupted economic development were to be combined with capitalist enterprise and capitalist profit, them Marx's theory would be falsified - just as if a perpetual motion machine were built the laws of thermodynamics would be falsified.[58]

Cornforth continues:

Certain things would assuredly falsify it [Marxism], only they do not happen - for example, a Stone Age community managing its affairs by parliamentary government and conducting controversies about the rights of man...[59]

Cornforth also seeks to demonstrate that Marxism does not depart from the principle of falsifiability by succumbing to *ad hoc* revisions to save itself from refutation (the 'weakest link' theory advanced to explain the advent of revolution in the industrially backward Russia is just such an *ad hoc* revision according to Popper). Cornforth writes:

...the Marxist procedure has never been to invent supplementary hypotheses. For example, to account for full employment in Britain [Cornforth was writing a number of years ago!] we do not invent a supplementary hypothesis - a kind of economic epicycle. We simply examine what has actually happened, which has by no means exceeded the bounds of possibility allowed by the general theory of Marxism, and find that it has led to consequences predictable and accountable within the theory. And similarly with the Russian Revolution.[60]

Cornforth's defence of Marxism's falsifiability cannot be counted a success. His example of the combination of uninterrupted economic development and capitalist enterprise and profit being an eventuality which would falsify Marxism is couched in the vague terms which Popper criticises as the 'soothsayer's trick'. It would be quite possible to argue that this eventuality has occurred in that economic growth and capitalism have gone hand in hand without major interruption since the beginning of capitalism. On the other hand if the slumps and depressions are to count as interruptions then there is no theory which predicts uninterrupted economic development in combination with capitalist enterprise and profit. The formulation of this possible falsification defies testability.

Cornforth's second example of a falsifying event, the retro-diction that we will not discover evidence of a Stone Age community with a parliamentary government, aside from bordering on the absurd, also fails to meet basic requirements of Popper's falsifiability principle. It is neither a bold conjecture, nor a serious attempt at refutation.

His defence of alleged *ad hoc* revisions of Marxism is equally flawed. It seems to rest on the argument that the 'weakest link' theory is an elaboration of the existing general theory of Marxism and, therefore, not an *ad hoc* supplementary theory. The problem with this is that it leaves Marxism with very few possible falsifying circumstances, since so much can be explained by an elaboration of the general theory. Cornforth's whole approach is one of defending Marxism rather than the critical approach advocated by Popper.

Cowling's argument for the Popperian character of Marxism also lacks force on the central point of the principle of falsifiability. He writes:

> On the crucial question of falsifiability, Marx never fully expressed his views. The idea of testing theories in practice is similar to falsifiability, as are some of Engels' ideas. I think we are justified in regarding these as hints of a falsificationist conception of science because of Marx's scientific practice: it is clear in his major works that the criterion of truth or falsity to which Marx is working is testing against reality, and the discarding of falsified theories.[61]

Cowling acknowledges that Marx did not make any explicit comments to suggest that he was a falsificationist, so Marx's practice is turned to for support of the thesis. However, 'testing theories in practice', 'testing against reality' and 'discarding of falsified theories' do not mark out Marx as a critical rationalist or even a proto one. These descriptive phrases of Marx's scientific practice are as applicable to positivism as to critical rationalism. Cowling fails to produce the evidence that Marx can convincingly be portrayed as following the principle of falsifiability.

(ii) Explanation and Prediction

Popper still retains the basic character of the positivist conception of explanation and prediction. Prediction and explanation, for both Popper and the positivists, are based on the same model, a variation on the deductive-nomological model, or as Popper puts it, "there is no great difference between explanation, prediction and testing. The difference is not one of logical structure, but rather one of emphasis; it depends on *what we consider to be our problem*."[62]

Therefore the same points made regarding the inapplicability of the positivist notion of explanation and prediction to Marx's approach apply to Popper's position. Indeed, Popper himself directly criticises Marxism for failing to produce predictions in keeping with the standards of the deductive-nomological model. Marx's 'predictions' are vague and unconditional, and his explanations do not aim to subsume a phenomenon under a general law.

In addition, Popper criticises Marxism for the 'essentialist' nature of its explanations. According to Popper the essentialist holds two doctrines in particular: (i) scientists can establish the truth of theories beyond reasonable doubt; and (ii) the best scientific theories describe the 'essences' of things which lie behind appearances. Popper argues that all theories are conjectures and can never become indubitable knowledge, and that the very idea of essences implies ultimate explanations which must effectively end scientific enquiry at the point when an essence is deemed to have been grasped. There is no reason to assume the existence of essences, and where they are assumed they are not helpful to scientific enquiry. Popper writes:

> The essentialist doctrine I am contesting is solely the doctrine that science aims at ultimate explanation; that is to say, an explanation which (essentially, or by its very nature) cannot be further explained, and which is in no need of any further explanation.[63]

Cowling accepts Popper's arguments against essentialism, but rejects the view that Marx was an essentialist. He seems to argue that Marx was not an essentialist because, first, essentialism doesn't make sense, and, secondly, the logic of Marx's position is anti-essentialist.[64] It is not clear why Marx's position is logically anti-essentialist, or why he could not have embraced a position that does not make sense. Moreover, Cowling is unable to explain the essentialist language used by Marx.[65] Cowling's only comment on this is to suggest that all such use of essence terms can be re-written in nominalist terms, but he gives no examples of such 'translating'.

A better response is provided by Keat and Urry, who, in putting the case for Marx being a scientific realist, see Marx's essentialism as supporting their interpretation. They reject Popper's understanding of essentialism arguing that it does not entail either of the doctrines he attributes to it.[66] There is no requirement in Marx's use of the essence-appearance distinction that any essence posited be taken to be an ultimate explanation. The use of essences in explanations need not preclude further investigation of the phenomenon concerned, or imply that the 'Truth' has been arrived at once an essence is identified.   Marx's method is, like Popper's, characterised by its critical attitude, an attitude Marx applies to precisely the kind of essentialist explanations objected to by Popper, i.e., those which deny further enquiry, most notably various notions of human essence Marx encounters.

(iii) Causation and Laws

Again, Popper's views on this aspect of science display a strong overlap with the positivist position. His notion of cause follows directly from his views on explanation: to explain something is to show its cause, and cause consists of a universal law and the a set of specific conditions. In other words, Popper takes the positivist line on cause and laws, just as he does on explanation and prediction. It has already been shown how Marx diverges from this line in the tendential, non-universal nature of his laws, and his use of a form of essentialism in his causal explanations.

(iv) Value-Freedom

Popper does not argue that the whole of the scientific enterprise is value-free, but he does insist that objectivity must enter in at the stage of testing. He also maintains that facts and values are distinct.

Marx has a committed stance in his investigations, but, as instanced by the virtues of Ricardo's scientific work that he cites - 'objective', 'honest', 'impartial' - Marx believes in some form of objectivity. He fumes against Malthus for falsifying science in the interests of the ruling classes and bemoans the superseding of 'genuine scientific research' by biased research with the aim not of achieving truth, but of producing results 'useful' to capitalism. In other words, Marx would appear to agree with Popper's contention that "truth is beyond human authority."   With both Popper and Marx, this is combined with a general critical approach to the study of other theories.

(v) Unity of Science

Popper puts forward a unity of science thesis based on a unity of method (see previous chapter). His formulation of the unity of science thesis very much resembles that of scientific positivism, albeit with the important and distinctive conjectural element in Popper's method. The same points made in relation to the positivist unity of method thesis apply: Marx endorsed a weak unity of method thesis, and the character of the method differs from that laid down by Popper. It is significant that Popper, when elaborating the details of the method of social science in accordance with the outline given above, labels it 'methodological individualism'.[67] This conflicts with the dialectical approach, which shapes Marx's method.

(vi) View of Philosophy

Popper was critical of the logical positivists for their rejection of metaphysics and their efforts to join philosophy ever more closely to science. Here again he comes closer to Marx, who, as was noted in the section on positivism in this chapter, adopts a more positive attitude to philosophy than the positivists. In addition, both Popper and Marx subscribe to philosophical realism, and insist on the importance of philosophy being related to practice. For example Popper writes, *"Genuine philosophical problems are always rooted in urgent problems outside philosophy, and they die if these roots decay."*[68] Popper argues specifically against the positivist view that there are no philosophical problems as such, while maintaining that philosophical problems are never 'pure' in the sense of being unrelated to 'real' problems, i.e., problems arising from human activity such as science.

However, to say philosophical problems are always rooted in the outside world is not the same as saying that their resolution ultimately lies in the outside world. In other words, for Popper there are genuine philosophical problems which can be resolved at the level of philosophy; for Marx philosophical problems are ultimately resolved in practice.

*

Popper's objections to Marxism being a science are, as Cornforth and Cowling argue, often misplaced. Popper sees Marxism as a form of dogmatic thinking which he contrasts with the critical thinking he believes to be the hallmark of science. However, the dogma Popper identifies lies not in Marx's method, but is primarily the contribution of the Second International and Soviet Marxism. Critical thinking is one thing Popper and Marx have in common. But it is also the case that the efforts of Cornforth and Cowling to portray Marxism as in keeping with critical rationalism are misplaced and unsuccessful. On the crucial issue of testing Marx and Popper diverge, and the efforts of Cowling and Cornforth to reconcile the two are unconvincing. On value-freedom and philosophy Popper and Marx are closer, but still differ to some extent, and on explanation and prediction, cause and laws, and unity of science, Popper remains too close to scientific positivism for a fit with Marx's method.

Several writers have suggested that Lakatos' account of science better describes Marx's method.[69] For example, Callinicos writes:

> Imre Lakatos distinguished between a scientific research programme's heuristic, the set of privileged propositions forming its 'hard core' and specifying procedures for resolving problems, and the 'protective belt' of revisable and empirically falsifiable auxiliary hypotheses surrounding the heuristic. One could say, in the case of Marxism, that its heuristic consists in the basic concepts and propositions of historical materialism, while the auxiliary hypotheses are analyses of specific modes of production, social formations and conjunctures. Much of the point of auxiliary hypotheses is to account for phenomena that apparently contradict the factual claims made in the heuristic. An example of such recalcitrant phenomena in the case of Marxism are the pre-capitalist societies in which authoritative rather than allocative domination seems to prevail.[70]

Lakatos' account has the advantage of neutralising Popper's arguments concerning the unfalsifiability of Marxism. Alleged falsifications can be held to apply only to aspects of the 'protective belt', and the unfalsifiable features of Marxism can be held to be justifiably irrefutable since they constitute the 'hard core' of the research programme.

The problem with this position is that there is still much of Popper in Lakatos. For example, prediction is still to the fore in Lakatos' view, albeit in evaluating a research programme rather than an individual theory. Lakatos writes:

> ...I inject some hard Popperian elements into the appraisal of whether a programme progresses or degenerates...I give criteria of progress and stagnation within a programme and also rules for the 'elimination' of whole research programmes. A research programme is said to be progressing as long as its theoretical growth anticipates its empirical growth, that is as long as it keeps predicting novel facts with some success ('progressive problemshift'); it is stagnating of its theoretical growth lags behind its empirical growth, that is , as long as it gives only post hoc explanations either of chance discoveries or of facts anticipated by, and discovered in, a rival programme ('degenerating problemshift').[71]

According to this criterion, it is doubtful whether Marxism could be considered a 'progressive' research programme as the prediction of novel facts is a marginal activity within Marxism at best. This is even assuming that this is the intention of Marxism, and doubts on the centrality of prediction to Marx's work have already been expressed. The problem of testing is shifted to another level with Lakatos, but it remains an obstacle to a match between Marxism and critical rationalism.

Marx and Conventionalism

Conventionalism embraces a diversity of views on science, but common to all is the use of conventions in scientific theories and their assessment, and opposition to objectivist, realist or empiricist based models of science.

Louis Althusser in seeking to portray Marxism as science puts forward a view of science that falls into the category of conventionalism. Although not explicit in embracing scientific conventionalism, his conception of science has sufficient in common with it to be included under its rubric. In this section I will show how Althusser's Marxism matches up to scientific conventionalism, before criticising his understanding of Marx. The divergence between Marx's views and the conventionalist position will also be shown.

(i) Empiricism and Testability

Althusser's conventionalism principally lies in his anti-empiricism.[72] The conventionalist challenging of the empirical as a theory-neutral basis for the development of knowledge is shared by Althusser, along with the conventionalist rejection of empirical data as the final court of appeal in assessing truth and the acceptance or rejection of a theory.

Kolakowski writes, "What conventionalism sets out to criticize was [sic] this notion of 'the given.'"[73] By 'the given' is meant the idea of a pure unmediated experience or sense data, which can provide the ultimate foundation of knowledge, its source and validation. The notion of scientific theories as containing or being based on conventions implies that knowledge is, at least in part, 'produced', that scientific theories in some sense construct knowledge. Thought or theories in some way determine our perception of reality, all perception being 'theory-loaded'. Conventionalism opposes itself to all forms of empiricism where knowledge is understood to be empirically based, obtained by theory-neutral observation, and where theories are understood to be confirmed or falsified by the empirical facts.

Althusser writes of science (and hence of Marxism) as being anti-empiricist in like manner:

> Contrary to the ideological illusions...of empiricism and sensualism, a science never works on an existence whose essence is pure immediacy and singularity ('sensations' or 'individuals')...a science always works on existing concepts...It does not 'work' on a purely objective 'given', that of pure and absolute 'facts'.[74]

For Althusser, the scientific production of knowledge takes place in thought, and concepts and abstractions rather than pure sense-experience constitute the raw material of science.

The notion of theory-loaded perception is contained in Althusser's concept of the 'problematic' (which bears strong parallels with Kuhn's 'paradigms'[75]). A problematic is a theoretical framework which gives terms and concepts their meaning, and determines the problems raised, the questions posed and the things seen. As Brewster writes, "A word or concept cannot be considered in isolation; it only exists in the theoretical or ideological framework in which it is used: its problematic."[76] While Althusser writes:

> [Science] can only pose problems on the terrain and within the horizon of a definite theoretical structure, its problematic, which constitutes its absolute and definite condition of possibility, and hence the absolute determination of *the forms in which all problems must be posed*, at any given moment in the science.[77]

Perception is dependent on the problematic:

> Any object or problem situated on the terrain and within the horizon, i.e., in the definite structured field of the theoretical problematic of a given theoretical discipline, is visible. We must take these words literally. The sighting is thus no longer the act of an individual subject, endowed with the faculty of 'vision' which he exercises either attentively or distractedly; the sighting is the act of its structural conditions, it is the relation of immanent reflection between the field of the problematic and *its* objects and *its* problems.[78]

Althusser, like the conventionalists, also sees science as rejecting sense-experience as the criterion of the truth of a theory:

...for *theoretical practice* is indeed its own criterion, and contains in itself definite protocols with which to *validate* the quality of its product, i.e., the criteria of the scientificity of the products of scientific practice. This is exactly what happens in the real practice of the sciences: once they are truly constituted and developed they have no need for verification from *external* practices to declare the knowledges they produce to be 'true', i.e., to be *knowledges*.[79]

The similarities between Althusser and Kuhn here are evident: for Kuhn standards of assessment are internal to the paradigm, for Althusser they are internal to the scientific problematic. Empirical data cannot validate or invalidate a theory because it is theory-loaded, embedded in an existing paradigm (Kuhn) or in an existing ideological problematic (Althusser). Brewster represents Althusser's viewpoint as follows:

Ideological conceptions of knowledge are dominated by the 'problem' of the criteria by which a knowledge can be judged, the guarantee of its truth. These criteria may be pragmatic (practical or experimental verification) or *a priori*. Marxist theory replaces the problem of guarantees by the problem of the mechanisms producing a knowledge effect, the 'criteria' are defined within the science by it scientificity, its axiomatics.[80]

Althusser's interpretation of Marx on the problem of knowledge involves the rejection of a search for external guarantees, and the adoption of internal mechanisms or axiomatics as the criteria of scientificity and 'truth'. There can be no appeal to empirical data outside of a theory to judge its truth.

The opposition to external criteria for judging truth or guaranteeing knowledge includes the rejection of what Althusser terms pragmatism:

...pragmatism sets out in search of a *de facto* guarantee: *success* in practice, which often constitutes the sole content assignable to what is called the 'practice criterion'. At any rate, we are served with a *guarantee* which is the irrefutable index of an *ideological* question and answer, whereas we are in search of a *mechanism*! The proof of the pudding is in the eating! So what! We are interested in the *mechanism* that ensures that it really is a pudding we are eating and not a poached baby elephant, though we *think* we are eating our daily pudding![81]

Pragmatism for Althusser encompasses experimental science where experimental results are taken as proof of the truth or falsity of a theory.

For Althusser, the truth of a scientific theory cannot be proven by observation or experiment. That our observations concur with a theory is no proof since our observations are not theory-neutral; that the theory is experimentally successful or 'works' in practice is again no guarantee of truth, because practical success and truth are not the same - a theory may be of practical value and yet be untrue. Althusser explicitly distances Marxism from this 'pragmatist' view of science:

> It has been possible to apply Marx's theory with success because it is 'true'; it is not true because it has been applied with success. The pragmatist criterion may suit a technique which has no other horizon than the field in which it is applied - but it does not suit scientific knowledges. To be consistent we must go further and reject the more or less indirect assimilation of the Marxist theory of history to the empiricist model of a chance 'hypothesis' whose *verification* must be provided by the political practice of history *before* we can affirm its 'truth'. Later historical practice cannot give the *knowledge* that Marx produced its status as knowledge: the criterion of the 'truth' of the knowledges produced by Marx's theoretical practice is provided by his theoretical practice itself, i.e., by the proof-value, by the scientific status of the *forms* which ensured the production of those knowledges.[82]

The rejection of the positivist-pragmatist model of science could not be clearer. Empiricism and empirical based testing are rejected in favour of internal criteria produced by Marx's scientific theoretical practice itself.

(ii) Explanation and Prediction

Following on from his views on empiricism and testability, Althusser represents Marx as opposed to any empiricist notions of explanation and prediction. Prediction does not fulfil the role of verification or falsification assigned to it by positivism or critical rationalism, and standards for explanations are internal to the problematic. Althusser's Marxism is, again, very close to conventionalism in the view of explanation and prediction.

(iii) Causaton and Laws

Althusser ascribes to Marx the notion of multiple causality or 'overdetermination'. Causal determination is never simple, but always complex and multiple. So in place of a one way linear determination Althusser interprets Marx as using a structural causality where the structure determines the parts, but parts act upon each other. The economic structure is determinant in the last instance, but the superstructure has relative autonomy, and it, or parts of it, may at times dominate.

Such a notion of causality does not lend itself to the notion of universal laws, since any tendencies must always be qualified by the multiple causes operating and the relative autonomy of aspects of society. This interpretation of Marx prevents a match between Marxism and positivism or critical rationalism, but it is acceptable within conventionalism.

(iv) Value-Freedom

In one sense Althusser's scientific Marxism is very much value-free and objective. Scientific practice is autonomous, according to Althusser, not part of the super structure or social formation, and as such it follows its own course of development, independently of the social and economic factors that influence other practices and ideologies. Where ideology is governed by interests beyond those of knowledge ("the practico-social predominates in it over knowledge"),[83] science's interest is solely truth and knowledge.

In this Althusser distinguishes Marx's science from conventionalism, and, notably, from Kuhn's view that science is suffused with values and very much a part of society. The historical and social context is a key consideration for Kuhn, but Althusser extrudes science (non-ideological science) from social history.

(v) Unity of Science

There is a unity of science to be inferred from Althusser's definition of science as a practice in which the sole and paramount interest is knowledge, and given his 'theoretical anti-humanism' which denies human beings to be the active subject in history, the obstacle of different subject-matter would appear to be minimised.

From a conventionalist perspective the unity of science is not a crucial tenet, and Althusser's Marxism does not conflict with conventionalism in adopting this general unity of science thesis.

(vi) View of Philosophy

Althusser follows the conventionalist line in ascribing great importance to philosophy. Indeed, Althusser's abiding purpose is to investigate and elaborate Marx's philosophy.[84]

This project he closely links to Marxism as a science. In the course of establishing the science of historical materialism, and in making his scientific discoveries, Marx created, largely implicitly, a new philosophy: "By founding the theory of history (historical materialism), Marx simultaneously broke with his erstwhile ideological philosophy and established a new philosophy (dialectical materialism)."[85] It is Althusser's aim to develop this philosophy from its largely untheorised state into a robust and comprehensive philosophy underpinning Marx's science. In particular, the anti-empiricist epistemology constitutes an important part of this philosophical elaboration.

The content of Althusser's Marxist philosophy is opposed to positivism and critical rationalism, and, as already noted in this section, it conforms to the general thrust of conventionalism.

*

In Althusser's Marxism there are strong echoes of conventionalism. Most notable is the strong anti-empiricism of Althusser's Marxism, which colours the position taken on explanation, prediction, and laws. The only significant divergence noted from the conventionalist account of science is on value-freedom, where Althusser insists on the objective truth of Marxist science.

However, even if Althusser can be portrayed as a conventionalist, there must be major reservations as to whether Marx conforms in his method to the conventionalist model. Althusser's interpretation of Marx is highly questionable. To highlight just two aspects of his view of Marx, the epistemological break and the theoretical anti-humanism are not supported by the evidence of Marx's works. The case for a basic continuity between Marx's early and later works has already been argued, and Althusser himself had considerable difficulty in drawing a line between the old and the new philosophy of Marx, or his pre-science and science, and in explaining the persistence of elements of the pre-science in the science. The theoretical anti-humanism runs contrary to the praxis-based materialism of Marx, which makes human beings active subjects and not just the 'bearers' of social relations. Althusser asserts that the relations of production are the true active subject.

In addition, Althusser shares with the conventionalists certain contradictions, which in his case lead to idealism, clearly not in accord with Marx. These shared contradictions stem from the initial rejection of empiricism. Without an empirical basis for knowledge the problem arises of what to put in its place. Even if the project of establishing a sure foundation for knowledge is abandoned, it is still necessary to provide some warrant for the acceptance of a theory. Two options are instrumentalism/pragmatism and relativism.

The first of these options involves accepting scientific theories as instruments to be judged according to their utility, which is usually measured in terms of ability to generate predictions and provide the means to manipulate and control phenomena in the world. This position may either hold that a theory is true if it 'works' and false if it does not, or simply maintain that truth and falsity are not assessable or applicable.

The second option is to accept that it is not possible to decide between competing theories, that the different theoretical frameworks in which they are embedded preclude commensurability, and that the notion of objective knowledge must be abandoned. In other words, theories are relative, and the external world cannot be used to verify one rather than another. At times both Kuhn and Feyerabend seem to favour the relativism option, Feyerabend explicitly and Kuhn implicitly.[86]

Althusser repudiates both these options, insulating science from them by denying the title of science to any practice in which "the practico-social predominates over knowledge,"[87] and placing scientific practice outside of the social formation. Having rejected empiricism and pragmatism as foundations for knowledge, Althusser is faced with the danger of relativism, which he wishes to avoid at all costs, because Marxism is objectively true. If truth cannot be guaranteed externally, and it is not relative, then the only option left is to ground it internally. Hence, his definition of science which gives it an independence from the external, from society and history, from the empirical and concrete world. The truth of the knowledge produced by Marxism is assured by the internal mechanism of its scientific practice, by protocols developed within the problematic. Althusser's approach may be described as an attempt at creating objective conventions, or a conventionalism that retains the notion of objective knowledge. The conventions used by Althusser have to be given an objective status if they are to validate the objective truth of knowledge produced by Marxism. The problem is that there is no clear reason why these 'mechanisms' or 'protocols' should be viewed as objective, or as proof of the truth and scientificity of Marxism. The conventionalist problem of validating theories is not satisfactorily solved by Althusser.

Furthermore, Althusser's 'solution' to the problem leads directly to a form of idealism. In trying to avoid relativism by ensuring the production of knowledge is not a part of the social process and not subject to the influences of interests and forces in the social formation, Althusser abstracts scientific practice from all other practices, and separates knowledge from the material world. Knowledge is idealised, purified, and located in its own conceptual realm.[88]

This idealism is reinforced by Althusser's distinction between the 'real object' and the 'object of knowledge'. The 'real object' is the actual concrete reality that constitutes the material world. The 'object of knowledge' is internal to thought, and the 'real object' is only known via the 'object of knowledge'. Althusser writes:

> ...the object of knowledge...[is] in itself absolutely distinct and different from the real object...the idea of the circle, which is the object of knowledge must not be confused with the circle, which is the real object.[89]

We can never have direct knowledge of the 'real object', only of the 'object of knowledge', and this cuts us off from material reality by interposing a conceptual realm between us and it. Benton notes the Kantian idealism of this:

> The 'real object' as an epistemological device has the same defect as the kantian notion of a 'thing-in-itself' - it is a 'something' of which, by definition, nothing can be said, but if which something must be said if it is to have a place in a theoretical system. The distinction between the 'real object' and the 'object of knowledge' in Althusser's thought is...[a] source for the charge of idealism.[90]

Conventionalism is susceptible to idealist tendencies in some form or other, due to its anti-empiricism. Such idealism is incompatible with the materialism that characterises Marx's thought, and casts further doubt on Althusser's depiction of Marxist science as a form of conventionalism.

Marx and Scientific Realism

In recent years a number of writers have endeavoured to portray Marxism as an example of scientific realism.[91] This has coincided with the development of scientific realism to a position of pre-eminence among philosophies of science. Realism asserts the possibility of social science based on a model that is less exclusive than the positivist unity of science, allowing such theories as psychoanalysis and Marxism to claim scientific status more plausibly.

(i) Empiricism and Testability

The realist position has an empirical commitment, but a qualified one. It does not place the same weight on sense data as positivism, or draw the same ontological conclusions from the observability or non-observability of a thing. Realist ontology does not insist on observability before asserting the existence of an entity, but posits its existence if it features in a correct theory.

Realist testing again takes the empirical to be a key element, but, again, with reservations. Realism accepts that there is a theory component in observation, and stresses the importance of going beyond appearance to hidden structures and mechanisms in the search for causal explanations. Realism also prioritises explanation over prediction, particularly in the social sciences where open social systems are the norm, and do not allow accurate prediction. A theory is assessed primarily on the explanations it provides rather than on the predictions it generates.

The realist view fits Marx's method well with regard to empiricism and testing. In the section on Marx and positivism evidence was put forward to suggest that Marx views observation as in some sense theory-dependent, and that non-observable entities, processes, structures and relations perform a key role in his explanatory theories, for example, 'surplus value', 'abstract labour' and 'class'. In the case of class, the term is one that is used in a distinctive way by Marx that is clearly realist rather than, for example, positivist. For Marx, class refers to entities not directly observable, but which nevertheless exist and generate observable features such as inequalities of income and status. The positivist identifies the entity class with the observable features.[92]

Contrary to the Althusserian interpretation of Marx, Marx himself assumes an empirical starting point rather than an abstract one, and proceeds, in the first instance, from the concrete to the abstract.[93] Marx does not share the anti-empiricism of Althusser, but is committed to an approach that incorporates an empirical dimension.

However, Marx is critical of the same kind of empiricism objected to by the scientific realists. Marx repeatedly criticises political economists for only reflecting appearance and not penetrating to the essence that generates the phenomenal form. His use of the essence-appearance distinction carries with it his rejection of uncritical empiricism that generalises from appearances. He reproaches Smith, who at times does seek the intrinsic connection or essence of phenomena, because he also:

> ...sets forth the connection as it appears in the phenomena of competition and thus as it presents itself to the unscientific observer...[he] takes the external phenomena of life, as they seem and appear and merely describes, catalogues, recounts and arranges them under formal definitions.[94]

Marx is critical of unreflective empiricism, as is apparent from his notion of explanation.

(ii) Explanation and Prediction

The privileging of explanation over prediction meets many of the objections made against Marxist science concerning the nature and success of Marx's predictions. Once these 'predictions' are seen not as attempts to forecast actual future events, but rather as abstract tendencies, then their apparent lack of success is no longer an issue. If predictions have no great role in the social sciences then it is no failing for a theory not to generate specific testable predictions.

Marx's explanations conform to the realist model by seeking to identify the necessary connections between events, the often hidden mechanisms that generate the phenomena to be explained. In general terms he seeks to identify and describe the hidden internal structure of capitalism that accounts for its visible features. Important in this is the fact that social reality does not appear as it is, and, therefore, the merely observable is likely to mislead if the hidden structure is not investigated. Profit may appear to arise from capital, but the hidden structure of exploitation shows profit to be actually derived from surplus-value.

For Marx and the realists explanation requires the use of abstractions, but not abstractions which merely generalise from appearance, for example, separating out general features common to all societies or forms of production. Rather the Marxist and realist approach is to abstract out the essence, or essential relations, or structure that underlies the appearance.

(iii) Causation and Laws

Marx's causal laws readily fit the realist model by their reference to the intrinsic movement behind visible phenomena. Marx's causal laws do not seek to identify constant conjunctions as in the positivist model, but rather to identify deeper laws pertaining to often unobservable entities or processes, that may not generate the kind of visible regularities which constitute positivist laws. This implies that criticisms of Marx's laws for failing to describe observable regularities or trends are misplaced.

(iv) Value-Freedom

The idea of value-free science is challenged by many scientific realists, notably Bhaskar, but this does not mean the abandonment of objectivity. Rooted in Marx's dialectical approach is his notion of immanent critique, which in identifying internal contradictions may entail action. Hence, Bhaskar's example:

> ...if we accept Marx's critique of political economy, which is also a critique of the illusory or false consciousness which capitalist society generates, we may - indeed must - pass immediately to a negative evaluation of those structures and to a positive evaluation of action rationally directed to changing them.[95]

Any social theory stands in contradiction with other social theories offering alternative, rival accounts and explanations. A materialist approach seeks to explain the rival accounts, to show how they have arisen and what aspect of material reality they reflect in their error. For example, the shortcomings of the political economists identified by Marx are, in part, reflections of shortcomings or contradictions of that which they seek to describe. Distorted descriptions of capitalism reflect the fact that the appearance of reality is distorted ('inverted'); contradictions in theories often reflect contradictions in reality. Marx moves from criticisms of other theories to criticisms of material reality, of the system that generates the distorted ideas or false consciousness.[96]

In other words, social science, by virtue of the fact that it has for its subject matter, not just the social world, but also theories about the social world, cannot be entirely neutral and value-free. Marx seeks objective truth, i.e., to reflect accurately the social world, and he criticises other theories not for the values they embody, but for their errors and distortions. Marx seeks to combine critique and objectivity.

(v) Unity of Science

The unity of science thesis propounded by the realists opposes itself to, on the one hand, positivist unity of science, and, on the other hand, to anti-naturalism that accepts the positivist conception of science as accurate and appropriate for the natural sciences. The discussion in the section on positivism and Marx suggested that Marx holds to a general, non-positivist unity of science. Given the overlap between Marx's method and the other aspects of the realist conception of science, it is now clearer that Marx's unity of science converges with that of realism. That Marx has some form of realist unity thesis in mind is suggested by his comment that:

> ...a scientific analysis of competition is possible only if we grasp the inner nature of capital, just as the apparent motions of the heavenly bodies are intelligible only to someone who is acquainted with their real motions, which are not perceptible to the senses.[97]

For Marx both natural and social science have to identify the 'inner nature' or 'real motions' of phenomena, and this inner nature may well not be perceptible. This quotation clearly implies a realist view.

(vi) View of Science and Philosophy

The realists view philosophy as important, but, ultimately, subservient to science. This is precisely Marx's view. Marx opposes the Hegelian tradition that privileges philosophy over science, and the realists oppose the anti-naturalist schools of hermeneutics and interpretive social theory, that also place philosophy above science.

Marx's philosophy, which underpins his scientific method, is composed of dialectics and materialism. In developing his method, his criticisms of other approaches are often on a philosophical level, for example, his objections to analytical philosophy from the standpoint of dialectics.

*

There is much common ground between Marx and scientific realism, suggesting that the model for Marx's scientific method is the realist one. The realist model accommodates Marx's distinctive explanations, and finds no fault with the nature of his predictions or laws. His critical commitment to an empirical approach is echoed by realism as is his emphasis on explanations rather than predictions in theory assessment. His view of causation is in keeping with that of realism, and unity of science to be found in Marx converges with that in the realist model. On value-freedom and philosophy there is also no conflict between Marx and scientific realism. In addition, the overlap extends beyond the categories identified above to include a commitment to philosophical realism in the sense of an independently existing world - one of the tenets of materialism.

Notes

[1] See, for example, Acton (1955); Wetter (1958); Jordan (1967); McMurtry (1978); and Masaryk (1972).
[2] Acton (1955) 109
[3] Callinicos (1983) 47
[4] CW. 5. 31 (GI)
[5] ibid., 37 (GI)
[6] Marx (1975) 281 (EPM)
[7] ibid., 355 (EPM)
[8] CW. 27. 287 (*Socialism: Utopian and Scientific*)
[9] Marx (1975) 385 (EPM)
[10] CW. 5. 37 (GI)
[11] Farr (1991) 110
[12] *Capital* III, 817
[13] CW. 42. 390 (Correspondence)
[14] The importance of the essence-appearance distinction in the work of Marx is discussed by a number of authors including Keat and Urry (1970), Sayer (1979), Wilson (1991), Meikle (1985), Murray (1988) and McCarthy (1988). Sayer identifies seven different synonyms for essence-appearance used by Marx.
[15] Marx (1975) 352 (EPM)
[16] GR 888
[17] *Capital* I, 23
[18] See Fine and Harris (1979) 58-65 for discussion of 'abstract tendency' in Marx.
[19] Sayer (1979) 114
[20] Quoted in Hospers (1967) 288-289
[21] *Capital* I, 90-91
[22] ibid., 100-102
[23] CW. 24. 467-68 (*Speech at Graveside*)
[24] Burns (1966) 4
[25] GR 87
[26] CW. 38. 100 (Correspondence)
[27] *Capital* I, 90-91
[28] TSV III, 312-313
[29] *Capital* I, 17
[30] ibid., 97
[31] TSV II, 118, 125, 119 (on Ricardo); 120 (on Malthus).
[32] *Capital* III, 312-313; TSV II, 29; GR 705; *Capital* I, 638. See Geras (1986) especially 17-18 for more examples of this kind of language.
[33] Bhaskar (1989) 5
[34] See Stockman (1983) 7 ff., and Farr (1984) 218-219.

[35] See, for example, Farr (1984); Carver (1984); and Ball (1984).

[36] Marx (1975) 355 (EPM)

[37] K. Marx, *Capital* I, 433

[38] For example, the Preface to the first German edition of *Capital*.

[39] CW. 24. 467 (*Speech at Graveside*)

[40] K. Marx, *Capital* I, 92

[41] Engels (1969) 16 (*Anti-Dühring*)

[42] Quoted in Little (1986) 11.

[43] See, for example, Farr (1984); Carver (1984); Ball (1984); and Little (1986).

[44] GR 239

[45] Farr (1984) 223

[46] See Callinicos (1983) chapter 4.

[47] A basic thesis of his book is that historical materialism is the 'scientific theory of working -class self-emancipation'. Callinicos (1983) 8.

[48] Farr (1984) 230

[49] CW. 5. 236; CW. 5. 37 (GI)

[50] Engels (1969) 36 (*Anti-Dühring*)

[51] ibid., 17

[52] See McLellan (1980), especially 12-15. It is also interesting to note that the Comtean positivist journal, *La Philosophie Positive*, criticised Marx for "treating economics metaphysically." *Capital* I, 99. It appears the positivists of Marx's day found him too philosophical and not one of their own.

[53] *Capital* I, 96-98

[54] McCarthy (1988) 9

[55] Farr (1991)110

[56] Cowling (1972) chapter 14, especially 393-94

[57] Cornforth (1968) 20

[58] ibid., 20

[59] ibid., 27

[60] ibid.,.23

[61] Cowling (1972) 394

[62] Popper (1957) 133

[63] Popper (1963) 105

[64] Cowling (1972) 389

[65] See, for example, *Capital* I, 102; *Capital* II, 220; *Capital* III, 43, 313 and 817; and CW. 42. 390 (Correspondence). These examples by no means exhaust Marx's use of 'essentialist' language.

[66] Keat and Urry (1975) 42-43

[67] Popper (1957) 136

[68] Popper (1963) 72

[69] See, for example, Chalmers (1982) and Little (1986).

[70] Callinicos (1989) 133-34

[71] Lakatos (1981) 117

[72] Althusser's definition of empiricism, while encompassing the usual understanding, is broader and idiosyncratic: "Althusser uses the concept of empiricism in a very wide sense to include all 'epistemologies' that oppose a given subject to a given object and call knowledge the abstraction by the subject of the essence of the object. Hence the knowledge of the object is part of the object itself." Brewster in Althusser (1970) 313.

[73] ibid., 35

[74] Althusser (1977) 183-84

[75] See Keat and Urry (1982) 132-33 for a comparison of the two.
[76] Brewster in Althusser (1977) 253
[77] Althusser (1970) 25
[78] ibid. (1970) 25
[79] Althusser (1970) 59
[80] Brewster in Althusser (1970) 314
[81] Althusser (1970) 57
[82] Althusser (1970) 59
[83] Brewster in Althusser (1970) 314
[84] See Althusser (1977) 21-38, and Althusser (1970) 75-78
[85] Althusser (1977) 33
[86] Feyerabend (1988) 230
[87] Brewster in Althusser (1970) 314
[88] See Benton (1977) 184.
[89] Althusser (1970) 40
[90] Benton (1977) 186
[91] See, for example, Keat and Urry (1975), Benton (1977), and Bhaskar (1978).
[92] Keat and Urry (1982) 94-95 raise this point.
[93] See Sayer (1979) 94-95 on the Althusserian misreading of GR in relation to this point.
[94] TSV II, 165-66
[95] Bhaskar (1989) 5
[96] This argument is also put forward in Edgley (1979).
[97] *Capital* I, 433

Conclusion

> Let us assume for the sale of argument that recent research had disproved once and for all every one of Marx's individual theses...every serious 'orthodox' Marxist would still be able to accept all such modern findings without reservation and hence dismiss all of Marx's theses *in toto* - without having to renounce his orthodoxy...Orthodox Marxism...does not imply the uncritical acceptance of the results of Marx's investigations. It is not the 'belief' in this or that thesis, nor the exegesis of a 'sacred' book. On the contrary, orthodoxy refers exclusively to method.[1]

For Lukács Marxism is first and foremost a method. Lukács goes as far as to suggest that the orthodox Marxist could accept the disproving of all Marx's individual theses and yet remain true to Marxism by maintaining a belief in the method.

Insofar as Lukács is asserting the crucial importance of method in Marxism and the rejection of uncritical adherence to dogma his words are to be welcomed. To the extent that the statement is a rejection of rigid positivist criteria of theory assessment, which would dismiss a theory on the basis of limited counter-examples, it is to be endorsed. However, Lukács goes beyond these points. He claims that the method is so distinct from the theses that the latter could all turn out to be wrong and yet the method still be valid. But if a method consistently produces incorrect theses then the method is surely in some way flawed. Paradoxically, Lukács' position, while intended to be critical, leads him into a form of dogmatism. In effect he puts method beyond criticism since he apparently does not permit falsified theses (however many) to reflect badly on the method. In trying to avoid the dogma of clinging to theses regardless of evidence to the contrary simply because Marx advanced them, Lukács instead falls into the dogmatic position of isolating method from all criticism.

Furthermore, as has been shown in the course of this book, the dividing line between method and theses is not so clear-cut. The thesis of historical materialism may in one sense be a result of Marx's investigations, but in another sense it guides his work and informs his method. In addition, characterising Marxism solely in terms of method puts too great a burden on method. The identity of Marxism is more than its method, it is also embodied in a range of theses about class struggle, alienation, exploitation and so on. Nevertheless, Lukács is right to emphasise the centrality of method.

Science is largely defined in terms of its method, which might lead us to expect an emphasis on method by proponents of scientific Marxism in similar fashion to Lukács. However, it is Lukács who denies the scientific status of Marxism, and the scientific Marxists who pay little attention to method. Soviet and 'orthodox' Marxists have been insufficiently mindful of method, and this has resulted in a more or less uncritical acceptance of an orthodox conception of science along positivist lines. In other words, scientific Marxists have all too readily embraced a conception of science which is at odds with much in Marxism. This has led to various distortions of Marxism, notably a deterministic and mechanical interpretation of Marx's scientific laws.

The term 'method' can be understood in a variety of ways. In its loosest sense it may refer to a basic disposition or orientation suggesting some broad approach. For example, a general philosophical position, such as a dialectical ontology or metaphysics, which gives some general sense of the nature of the world and points to some general methodology. By contrast, method may also be understood as a technique, such as the Feuerbachian inversion technique, which may be applied at a very specific level to particular cases. Between these lie the notions of method as heuristic or procedure, that is to say, a set of broad guidelines for investigation or a set of stricter rules or steps to be followed, such as the method of immanent critique (outlined in chapter two).

Any methodology will address all of these different senses of 'method'. It will incorporate a general philosophical position, a broad heuristic, and certain procedures and techniques. These senses may be seen as different levels of method linked together, although not necessarily entailing each other. A particular method at one level may preclude certain positions on other levels, while being consistent with others. An analytical philosophy, which sees things as distinct, self-existing entities only related to other things externally by mechanical causal relations, lends itself to, for example, methodological individualism and the deductive-nomological model. A dialectical philosophy, on the other hand, is consistent with the method of immanent critique and a scientific realist model of cause and explanation.

It is partly because of a failure to appreciate the general philosophical position of Marx (dialectical and materialist), that it has been possible to mistake his method on other levels for that of scientific positivism, critical rationalism or conventionalism. Marx's underlying philosophy informs his method and precludes various aspects of these models of science, but is compatible with scientific realism.

Dialectics as a basic philosophical outlook points to three fundamental characteristics of the world: change, connection and contradiction. Any approach that neglects these categories will be incompatible with dialectics. The dialectician is not going to approach the investigation of reality by looking to explain it in terms of static phenomena and purely external laws. Marx criticises various methodological approaches that fail to incorporate an appreciation of these elements, for example, by assuming unchanging laws, natures or systems (the political economists who view laws of bourgeois economy, human nature under capitalism, and capitalism itself as eternal and unchanging), or assuming no intrinsic connections (the vulgar economists who fail to see inner connections between various elements of capitalism, such as, capital-interest, land-rent and labour-wages), or assuming no contradictions (the harmonious capitalism described by bourgeois economists). Since connections and contradictions often occur beneath the surface and beyond the apparent, any satisfactory dialectical method must look to pierce through appearances and to grasp the underlying essences of phenomena. In addition, abstractions must be of essential natures, relations and structures, and not mere generalisations from appearances.

If we move to the level of heuristic, dialectics may be presented as a set of guidelines for research. Implicit in Ollman's account of the dialectical method is such a heuristic which may be stated in the form of rules:[2]

(i) Think about the world in terms of processes and relations.
(ii) Incorporate change and interaction in abstractions.
(iii) Proceed from study of the whole to study of the part.
(iv) Study system before history.
(v) Look for and trace relations of contradiction, identity and difference, interpenetration of opposites, and quantity and quality.
(vi) Do not treat things as isolated, static and unchanging.

This heuristic guides research and ensures the research approach is appropriate to the nature of reality as expressed in the general philosophical outlook. This heuristic, it should be stressed, is based on Ollman's rendering of the dialectical method, but conveys a sense of what method at the level of heuristic means in a dialectical methodology (broadly speaking the heuristic matches the interpretation of Marx's dialectic given in this thesis, although points (iii) and (iv) would require further elaboration before they could be accepted as true to Marx).

Dialectical method at the level of procedure may be illustrated by the method of immanent critique. This procedure begins from within the subject matter. For example, Hegel is criticised initially on the basis of internal contradictions in his philosophy, which are irresolvable in the contest of his philosophical approach. Marx does not adopt an archimedean point outside of his subject as a viewpoint from which to judge it. He uses contradiction as the basic tool of an immanent critique from within, which directs the procedure to the next stage of transcendent critique. At this stage, the subject matter has to be transcended in the sense of going beyond it to grasp it by its roots. The root of the contradiction in concrete reality must be located, for example, the contradictions of religious consciousness lie in the dehumanised condition of reality. The final stage of this procedure is practical critique where the original contradiction in thought is finally resolved through practical activity which transforms the material conditions that gave rise to it. This procedure uses the dialectical notion of contradiction and blends it with the materialist theses of material primacy (or historical materialism) and praxis.

Finally, at the level of technique the inversion technique points to materialist explanations for contradictions in thought. Ideological representations of reality invert that reality, so the simple technique of inversion provides a starting point for a true understanding of reality. The technique may help identify the root of a contradiction. For example, the religious view suggests that 'God created Man', implying that any contradictions require a theological resolution, whereas the inversion technique gives the result 'Man created God' pointing to a material source of contradictions.

Method, then, operates at various levels which are loosely linked, and the above is a sketch of what a dialectical materialist method might look like on those different levels.

On the question of scientificity, evidence has been given that Marx thought of his method as scientific, and, even allowing for the broader meaning of the German word *Wissenschaft*, it is clear that Marx understood his work to be scientific in the stronger English sense of the term. By failing to reflect on the nature of science, Marxists have misconstrued (and some continue to misconstrue) Marx's method as a version of positivism. By assuming the positivist model of science to be the only (and therefore correct) model of science, and believing Marxism to be a science, Marxism and positivism became entangled. The desire to attach the status and authority of science to Marxism has fuelled distortions of Marx's method as proponents and sympathetic commentators have sought to match it to the dominant model of science of the time (chiefly positivism).

Once science itself comes under scrutiny, it becomes possible to allow for the scientific status of Marx's method without having to re-write Marx and ignore inconvenient features of his approach. Scientific realism not only offers a persuasive account of science, but is also able to accommodate Marx's method without compromise on either side. The merits of scientific realism have not been explicitly argued for in this book, but they have achieved widespread recognition within philosophy of science. The point is that those who would still wish to deny the scientific status of Marx's method must now either show that Marx's method does not conform to scientific realism, or that scientific realism does not accurately depict the scientific method. So far, the objections to Marx's credentials as a scientist have all been based on a positivist or critical rationalist model of science (objections to Althusser's portrayal of Marx as a conventionalist come from the direction of Marxists denying Althusser's interpretation of Marx).

Methodology has received too little attention from Marxists, particularly those who wish to take the scientificity claim seriously. In this book the question of the exact nature of Marx's method and the plausibility of the claim to scientific status have been directly addressed. Marx's method has been broken down into its component parts, and the key elements of critique, abstraction, essence and appearance, inversion, and empiricism have been detailed. In addition, the dialectical and materialist character of his method has been emphasised. Marx's dialectic has been elaborated and its relation to Hegel's dialectic discussed. A view of what Marx meant by the 'rational kernel' contained in the 'mystical shell' has been offered, and the elements of a Marxist (non-Hegelian) dialectic have been outlined. Marx's materialism has been analysed into its core theses and its centrality to his overall thought defended. Four distinct philosophies of science have been identified, described and analysed. Attempts to portray Marxism as conforming to scientific positivism, critical rationalism and conventionalism have been criticised and rejected.

Finally, the casting of Marx's method in scientific realist terms has been endorsed as a credible account of a scientific Marxism true to Marx's method.

Marx's comments on methodology and his own approach to the investigation of history and society may usefully be studied by historians and social scientists today. It is not necessary to be a Marxist to appreciate the validity and continuing relevance of much of what he has to say, and the convergence of the scientific realist model and Marx's approach suggests as much. His overall dialectical approach offers a convincing critique of methods grounded in positivism, empiricism and analytical philosophy, for example methodological individualism. The dialectical philosophy adopted by Marx also provides an interesting and potentially fruitful heuristic for guiding research, and informs his discussions of abstraction and critique, which are both balanced and insightful. Marx's materialism has a useful methodological dimension, providing as it does a framework for understanding history and society and a direction and focus for research. At a time when there are serious doubts about many of Marx's substantive theses, it may be that his view of social science method is his most lasting contribution.

Notes

1 Lukács (1971) 1
2 This heuristic is drawn from Ollman (1993) part II.

Bibliography

Main Texts

Most of the texts cited are in:

Marx, K., and F. Engels. *Collected Works*. (London: Lawrence and Wishart, 1975 ff.).

In addition, the following editions were used [composition dates in square brackets]:

Marx, K. [1843-44] *Early Writings*. Translated by R. Livingstone and G. Benton. (Harmondsworth: Penguin, 1975).

___ . [1857-58] *Grundrisse: Foundations of the Critique of Political Economy*. Translated by M. Nicolaus. (Penguin: London, 1973).

___ . [1862-63] *Theories of Surplus Value*.
Volume I. Translated by E. Burns. (London: Lawrence and Wishart, 1969).
Volume II. Translated by R. Simpson. (London: Lawrence and Wishart, 1969).
Volume III. Translated by J. Cohen and S. Ryazanskaya. (London: Lawrence and Wishart, 1971).

___ . [1863] *Capital*, Volume II. Edited by F. Engels. (London: Lawrence and Wishart, 1974).

___ . [1864] *Capital*, Volume III. Edited by F. Engels. (London: Lawrence and Wishart, 1974).

___ . [1867] *Capital*, Volume I. Translated by B. Fowkes. (Harmondsworth: Penguin, 1976).

___ . [1879-80] *Notes on Adolph Wagner*, in *Texts on Method*, translated and edited by T. Carver. (Oxford: Basil Blackwell,1975).

Engels, F. [1876-78] *Anti-Dühring*. (London: Lawrence and Wishart, 1969).

For a full list of the principal works consulted see 'Abbreviations' at beginning of book.

Other Texts

Acton, H.B. *The Illusion of the Epoch: Marxism-Leninism as a Philosophical Creed.* (London: Routledge and Kegan Paul, 1955).

Agger, Ben. *Western Marxism: An Introduction.* (Santa Monica, California: Goodyear Publishing Co. Incorporated, 1979).

Ajdukiewicz, K. *Problems and Theories of Philosophy.* Translated by H Skolimowski and A. Quinton. (London: Cambridge University Press, 1973).

Althusser, L. *For Marx.* Translated by B. Brewster. (London: New Left Books, 1977).

Althusser, L. and E. Balibar. *Reading "Capital".* Translated by B. Brewster. (London: New Left Books, 1970).

Aronson, J.L. *A Realist Philosophy of Science.* (London: Macmillan, 1984).

Arthur, C.J. "Editor's Introduction" to Karl Marx *The German Ideology.* (London: Lawrence and Wishart, second edition 1974).

___ . "Dialectic and Labour," in *Issues in Marxist Philosophy*, Volume I, *Dialectics and Method*, edited by J. Mepham and D.-H. Ruben. (Brighton: Harvester, 1979).

___ . *Dialectic of Labour: Marx and his Relation to Hegel.* (Oxford: Blackwell, 1986).

Avineri, S. *The Social and Political Thought of Karl Marx.* (Cambridge and New York: Cambridge University Press, 1968).

Ayer, A.J., editor. *Logical Positivism.* (Glencoe, Illinois: The Free Press, 1959).

___ . *The Central Questions of Philosophy.* (Harmondsworth: Penguin, 1976).

Ball, T. "Marx and Darwin: A Reconsideration," in *Political Theory*, Volume 7, Number 4 (November 1979).

___ . "Marxian Science and Positivist Politics," in *After Marx*, edited by T. Ball and J. Farr. (Cambridge: Cambridge University Press, 1984).

Ball, T. and J. Farr, editors. *After Marx.* (Cambridge: Cambridge University Press, 1984).

Beiser, F.C, editor. *The Cambridge Companion To Hegel.* (Cambridge: Cambridge University Press, 1993).

Benjamin, A.C. *An Introduction to the Philosophy of Science.* (New York: Macmillan, 1937).

Benton, T. *Philosophical Foundations of the Three Sociologies.* (London and Boston: Routledge and Kegan Paul, 1977).

Berlin, I. "The Concept of Scientific History," in *Concepts and Categories.* (Oxford: Oxford University Press, 1980).

Bernstein, E. *Evolutionary Socialism.* Translated by E.C. Harvey. (New York: Schocken, 1961).

Bernstein, Richard J. *Beyond Objectivism and Relativism: Science, Hermeneutics and Praxis.* (Oxford: Basil Blackwell, 1983).

Bhaskar, R. *A Realist Theory of Science.* (Brighton: Harvester, 1978).

___ . *The Possibility of Naturalism.* (Brighton: Harvester, 1979a).

___ ."On the Possibility of Social Scientific Knowledge and the Limits of Naturalism," in *Issues in Marxist Philosophy*, Volume III, *Epistemology, Science and Ideology*, edited by J. Mepham and D.-H. Ruben. (Brighton: Harvester Press, 1979b).

___ . *Scientific Realism and Human Emancipation.* (London: Verso, 1986).

___ . *Reclaiming Reality: A Critical Introduction to Contemporary Philosophy.* (London: Verso, 1989).

___ . *Dialectic: The Pulse of Freedom.* (London: Verso, 1993).

Boeselager, W.F. *The Soviet Critique of Neopositivism.* (Dordrecht: D. Riedel, 1975).

Bologh, R.W. *Dialectical Phenomenology: Marx's Method.* (London and Boston: Routledge and Kegan Paul, 1979).

Bottomore, T.B.,editor. *Modern Interpretations of Marx.* (Oxford: Basil Blackwell, 1981).

Bromberger, S., A. Grünbaum and E. Nagel. *Observation and Theory in Science.* (London: John Hopkins Press, 1971).

Burns, E. *Introduction to Marxism.* (London: Lawrence and Wishart, 1966).

Bukharin, Nikolai. *Historical Materialism: A System of Sociology.* (New York: International Publishers, 1925).

Callinicos, A. *Althusser's Marxism.* (London: Pluto, 1976).

___ . *Marxism and Philosophy.* (London: Oxford University Press, 1983).

___ . "Critical Realism and Beyond: Roy Bhaskar's Dialectic," University of York, Department of Politics Working Paper, Number 7, 1994.

Carver, T. "Commentary"on Karl Marx, *Texts on Method.* (Oxford: Basil Blackwell, 1975).

___ . "On Warren's Response to 'Marx and Darwin: A Reconsideration," in *Political Theory*, Volume 10, Number 2 (May 1982).

___ . *Marx and Engels: The Intellectual Relationship.* (Brighton: Harvester, 1983).

___ . "Marxism as Method," in *After Marx*, edited by T. Ball and J. Farr. (Cambridge: Cambridge University Press, 1984).

___ ., editor. *The Cambridge Companion to Marx.* (Cambridge: Cambridge University Press, 1991).

Chalmers, A.F. *What is this thing called Science?* (Milton Keynes: Open University Press, second edition 1982).

Cohen, G.A. *Karl Marx's Theory of History: A Defence.* (Oxford: Clarendon Press, 1978).

Cohen, R.S., P.K. Feyerabend and M.W. Wartofsky, editors. *Boston Studies in the Philosophy of Science, Volume 39, Essays in memory of Imre Lakatos.* (Boston: D. Reidel, 1976).

Colletti, Lucio. *From Rousseau to Lenin: Studies in Ideology and Society.* (London: New Left Books, 1972).

___ . *Marxism and Hegel.* Translated by Lawrence Garner. (London: New Left Books, 1973).

___ . "Introduction" to Karl Marx *Early Writings.* Translated by T. Nairn. (Harmondsworth: Penguin, 1975a).

___ . "Marxism and the Dialectic." *New Left Review*, 93 (September/October 1975b).

Collier, A. "Materialism and Explanation in the Human Sciences," in *Issues in Marxist Philosophy*, Volume II, *Materialism*, edited by J. Mepham and D.-H. Ruben. (Brighton: Harvester Press, 1979).

___ . "In Defence of Epistemology," in *Issues in Marxist Philosophy*, Volume III, *Epistemology, Science and Ideology*, edited by J. Mepham and D.-H. Ruben. (Brighton: Harvester Press, 1979).

___ . "Scientific Socialism and the Question of Socialist Values," in *Issues in Marxist Philosophy*, Volume IV, *Social and Political Philosophy*, edited by J. Mepham and D.-H. Ruben. (Brighton: Harvester Press, 1979).

___ . *Critical Realism: An Introduction to Roy Bhaskar's Philosophy.* (London: Verso 1994).

Copleston, F. *A History of Philosophy.* Nine volumes. (London: Search Press, 1966 ff).

Cornforth, M. *Dialectical Materialism: An Introduction,* Volume one, *Materialism and the Dialectical Method.* (London: Lawrence and Wishart, 1952; fourth edition, 1968).

___ . *The Open Philosophy and the Open Society: A Reply to Karl Popper's Refutations of Marxism.* (London: Lawrence and Wishart, 1968).

Cowling, C.M. "The Dialectic in the Later Works of Marx and its Relation to Hegel." Ph.D Thesis, University of Manchester, 1975.

Dunayevskaya, R. *Philosophy and Revolution: From Hegel to Sartre and from Marx to Mao.* (Atlantic Highlands, New Jersey: Harvester, 1982).

Dupré, L. *The Philosophical Foundations of Marxism.* (New York: Harcourt, Brace and World Incorporated, 1966).

Duhem, P. *The Aim and Structure of Physical Theory.* Translated by P. Weiner. (Princeton: Princeton University Press, 1954).

Edgley, R. "Marx's Revolutionary Science," in *Issues in Marxist Philosophy:Volume III, Epistemology, Science and Ideology*, edited by J. Mepham and D.H. Ruben. (Brighton: Harvester Press, 1979).

___ . "Philosophy," in *Marx: The First Hundred Years*, edited by D. McLellan. (London: Frances Pinter Publishers, 1983).

Evans, M. "Marx and the Dialectic." Political Studies Association Conference Paper, 1967. (Unpublished).

Farr, J. "Marx and Positivism," in *After Marx,* edited by T. Ball and J. Farr. (Cambridge: Cambridge University Press, 1984).

___ . "Science: Realism, Criticism, History," in *The Cambridge Companion to Marx,* edited by T. Carver. (Cambridge: Cambridge University Press, 1991).

Fay, B. *Social Theory and Political Practice.* (London: George Allen and Unwin, 1975).

Feyerabend, P.K. "How to Defend Society against Science." *Radical Philosophy,* 11 (Summer 1975).

___ . "Marxist Fairytales from Australia." *Inquiry,* Volume 20 (1977).

___ . *Against Method.* (London: Verso, 1978; revised edition 1988).

___ . *Science in a Free Society.* (London: New Left Books, 1978).

___ . *Philosophical Papers:*
 Volume 1, Realism, Rationalism and Scientific Method. (Cambridge: Cambridge University Press, 1981).
 Volume 2, Problems of Empiricism. (Cambridge: Cambridge University Press, 1981).

Fine, B. *Marx's "Capital".* (London: Macmillan, 1975).

Fine, B. and L. Harris, *Rereading "Capital".* (New York: Columbia University Press, 1979).

Fisk, M. "Dialectic and Ontology," in *Issues in Marxist Philosophy: Volume I, Dialectics and Method,* edited by J. Mepham and D.H. Ruben. (Brighton: Harvester Press, 1979).

Fromm, E. *Marx's Concept of Man.* (New York: Frederick Ungar, 1961).

George, M. "Marx's Hegelianism: An Exposition," in *Hegel and Modern Philosophy,* edited by D. Lamb. (Beckenham: Croom Helm Limited, 1987).

Geras, N. *Marx and Human Nature: Refutation of a Legend.* (London: Verso, 1983).

___ . *Literature of Revolution: Essays on Marxism.* (London: Verso, 1986).

Giddens, A., editor. *Positivism and Sociology.* (London: Heinemann, 1974).

Giedyman, J. "Antipositivism in Contemporary Philosophy of Social Sciences and Humanities." *British Journal of Philosophy and Science,* 26 (1975).

___ . *Science and Convention.* (Oxford: Pergamon Press, 1982).

Gjertsen, Derek. *Science and Philosophy.* (London: Penguin, 1989).

Gould, C. *Marx's Social Ontology: Individuality and Community in Marx's Theory of Social Reality.* (Cambridge, Massachussetts and London: MIT Press, 1978).

Gouldner, A.W. *The Two Marxisms: Contradictions and Anomalies in the Development of Theory.* (London: Macmillan, 1980).

Gramsci, A. *Selections from the Prison Notebooks.* Edited by Quinton Hoare and Geoffrey Nowell Smith. (London: Lawrence and Wishart, 1971).

Guest, D. *A Textbook of Dialectical Materialism.* (New York: International Publishers, 1939).

Hacking, Ian. *Representing and Intervening: Introductory Topics in the Philosophy of Natural Science.* (Cambridge: Cambridge University Press, 1983).

___ . editor. *Scientific Revolutions.* (Oxford: Oxford University Press, 1981).

Hanfling, O. *Logical Positivism.* (Oxford: Basil Blackwell, 1981).

Hanson, N.R. *Patterns of Discovery.* (Cambridge: Cambridge University Press, 1958).

Harding, S., editor. *Can Theories Be Refuted?* (Dordrecht: D. Reidel, 1976).

Harré, R. *The Philosophies of Science: An Introductory Survey.* (London: Oxford University Press, 1972).

Hegel, G.W.F. (first published 1807) T*he Phenomenology of Spirit.* Translated by A.V. Miller. (Oxford: Oxford University Press, 1977).

___ . (1812) *The Science of Logic.* Translated by A.V. Miller. (London: George Allen and Unwin, 1969).

___ . (1821) *Philosophy of Right.* Translated by T.M. Knox. (Oxford: Oxford University Press, 1952).

___ . (1830) *Encyclopaedia of the Philosophical Sciences*:
Volume I, *The Logic of Hegel.* Translated by W. Wallace. (London: Oxford University Press, third edition 1975).
Volume II, *Philosophy of Nature.* Translated by A.V. Miller. (Oxford: Oxford University Press, 1970).
Volume III, *Philosophy of Mind.* Translated by W. Wallace and A.V. Miller. (Oxford: Oxford University Press, 1971).

___ . *Philosophy of History.* Translated by J. Sibree. (New York: Dover Publications Incorporated, 1956).

Heilbronner, R.L. *Marxism: For and Against.* (New York and London: W.W. Norton and Company, 1980).

Hellman, G. "Historical Materialism," in *Issues in Marxist Philosophy*, Volume II, *Materialism*, edited by J. Mepham and D.-H. Ruben. (Brighton: Harvester Press, 1979).

Hempel, C.G. *Philosophy of Natural Science.* (Englewood Cliffs, New Jersey: Prentice Hall, 1966).

Hesse, Mary. *Revolutions and Reconstructions in the Philosophy of Science.* (Brighton: Harvester Press, 1980).

Hoffman, J. *Marxism and the Theory of Praxis.* (London: Lawrence and Wishart, 1975).

Hook, S. *From Hegel to Marx.* (London: Victor Gollancz, 1936).

Hospers, J. *An Introduction to Philosophical Analysis*. (Englewood Cliffs, New Jersey: Prentice-Hall, 1967).

Howard, D. *The Development of the Marxian Dialectic*. (Carbondale and Eduardsville: Southern Illinois University Press, 1972).

Ilyenkov, E.V. *Dialectical Logic: Essays on its History and Theory*. Translated by H.C. Creighton. (Moscow: Progress Publishers, 1977).

Jordan, Z.A. *Philosophy and Ideology*. (Dordrecht: D. Reidel Publishing Company, 1963).

___ . *The Evolution of Dialectical Materialism*. (London: Macmillan, 1967).

Keat, R., and J. Urry. *Social Theory as Science*. (London: Routledge and Kegan Paul, 1975).

Keat, Russell. *The Politics of Social Theory*. (Oxford: Blackwell, 1981).

Kitching, G. *Karl Marx and The Theory of Praxis*. (London: Lawrence and Wishart, 1975).

Kolakowski, L. "Karl Marx and the Classical Definition of Truth," in *Marxism and Beyond*, translated by J.Z. Peel. (London: Pall Mall Press, 1969).

___ . *Positivist Philosophy*. (Harmondsworth: Penguin, 1972).

___ . *Main Currents of Marxism: Its Origin, Growth and Dissolution*. Three volumes. Translated by P.S. Falla. (Oxford: Clarendon Press, 1978).

Korsch, K. *Marxism and Philosophy*. Translated by F. Halliday. (London: New Left Books,1970).

Krige, John. *Science, Revolution and Discontinuity*. (Brighton: Harvester Press, 1980).

Kuhn, T.S. *The Structure of Scientific Revolutions*. (Chicago and London: University of Chicago Press, second edition 1970).

___ . *The Essential Tension: Selected Studies in Scientific Tradition and Change*. (Chicago and London: The University of Chicago Press, 1977).

Lakatos, I. "History of Science and Its Rational Reconstructions," in *Scientific Revolutions*, edited by I. Hacking. (Oxford: Oxford University Press, 1981).

___ . "Falsification and the Methodology of Scientific Research Programmes," in *Criticism and the Growth of Knowledge*, edited by I. Lakatos and A. Musgrave. (London: Cambridge University Press, 1970).

Lakatos, I. and A. Musgrove, editors. *Criticism and the Growth of Knowledge*. (London: Cambridge University Press, 1970).

Lamb, D., editor. *Hegel and Modern Philosophy*. (Beckenham: Croom Helm Limited, 1987).

Lecourt, D. *Marxism and Epistemology: Bachlard, Foucault, Languilheim*. (London: New Left Books, 1975).

Lefevre, S.F. "Science and the Liberal Mind: The Methodological Recommendations of Karl Popper," in *Political Theory*, Volume 2, Number 1 (February 1974).

Leff, Gordon. *The Tyranny of Concepts: A Critique of Marxism.* (London: Merlin Press, 1961).

Lenin, V. *Materialism and Empirio-Criticism.* (Moscow: Progress Publishers, 1970).

Lessnoff, M. *The Structure of Social Science.* (London: Allen and Unwin, 1974).

Lichtheim, G. *Marxism: An Historical and Critical Study.* (London: Routledge and Kegan Paul, 1961).

___ . *From Marx to Hegel.* (London: Orbach and Chambers, 1971).

Little, D. *The Scientific Marx.* (Minneapolis: University of Minnesota Press, 1986).

Lukács, G. *History and Class Consciousness.*Translated by R. Livingstone. (London: Merlin Press, 1971).

___. *The Young Hegel: Studies in the Relations between Dialectics and Economics.* Translated by Rodney Livingstone. (London: Merlin Press, 1975).

Maguire, J. *Marx's Paris Writings.* (Dublin: Gill and Macmillan,1972).

Mandel, E. "Introduction" to Karl Marx *Capital*, volume I. (London: Penguin, 1976).

Mao Tsetung. "On Contradiction," in *Selected Readings from the Works of Mao Tsetung.* (Peking: Foreign Languages Press, 1967).

Marquit, E., P. Moran, and W.H. Truitt. *Dialectical Contradictions: Contemporary Marxist Discussions.* (Minneapolis: Marxist Educational Press, 1982).

Marcuse, Herbert. *Reason and Revolution: Hegel and The Rise of Social Theory.* (London: Routledge and Kegan Paul, second edition 1955).

Masaryk, T.G. *Masaryk on Marx.* Edited and translated by E.V. Kohak. (New Jersey: Associated University Presses, 1972).

McBride, W.L. *The Philosophy of Marx.* (New York: St. Martin's Press Incorporated, 1977).

McCarthy, G.E. *Marx's Critique of Science and Positivism: The Methodological Foundations of Political Economy.* (Dordrecht: Kluwer Academic Publishers, 1988).

McCarthy, T. *The Critical Theory of Jurgen Habermas.* (London: Hutchinson, 1978).

McLellan, D. *The Young Hegelians and Karl Marx.* (London: Macmillan, 1969).

___ . *Marx Before Marxism.* (London and New York: Macmillan, second edition 1980).

___ . *Karl Marx: His Life and Thought.* (London: Macmillan, 1973).

___ . *Introduction to "Marx's Grundrisse".* (London: Macmillan, second edition 1980).

___ ., editor. *Marx: The First Hundred Years.* (London: Frances Pinter Publishers, 1983).

McMurtry, J.M. *The Structure of Marx's World-View.* (Princeton: Princeton University Press, 1978).

Meikle, J. "Dialectical Contradiction and Necessity," in *Issues in Marxist Philosophy*, Volume I, *Dialectics and Method*, edited by J. Mepham and D.-H. Ruben. (Brighton: Harvester, 1979).

___ . *Essentialism in the Thought of Karl Marx*. (London: Duckworth, 1985).

Mepham, J. "From the 'Grundrisse' to 'Capital': the Making of Marx's Method," in *Issues in Marxist Philosophy*, Volume I, *Dialectics and Method*, edited by J. Mepham and D.-H. Ruben. (Brighton: Harvester, 1979).

Mepham, J. and D.-H. Ruben, editors. *Issues in Marxist Philosophy*:

Volume I, *Dialectics and Method*. (Brighton: Harvester Press, 1979).

Volume II, *Materialism*. (Brighton: Harvester Press, 1979).

Volume III, *Epistemology, Science and Ideology*. (Brighton: Harvester Press, 1979).

Volume IV, *Social and Political Philosophy*. (Brighton: Harvester Press, 1979).

Mészáros, I. *Marx's Theory of Alienation*. (London: Merlin Press, 1970).

Meyer, A.G. *Marxism: The Unity of Theory and Practice*. (Cambridge, USA: Harvard University Press, 1954).

Murray, P. *Marx's Theory of Scientific Knowledge*. (New Jersey: Humanities Press International, 1988).

Nagel, E. *The Structure of Science*. (London: Routledge and Kegan Paul, 1961).

Neurath, O., R. Carnap, and C. Morris, editors. *Foundations of the Unity of Science: Toward an International Encyclopedia of Unified Science*:

Volume I. (Chicago and London: The University of Chicago Press, 1938).

Volume II. (Chicago and London: The University of Chicago Press, 1939).

Newton-Smith, W.H. *The Rationality of Science*. (Boston: Routledge and Kegan Paul, 1981).

Nicolaus, M. "Foreword" to Karl Marx *Grundrisse*. (London: Penguin, 1973).

Norman, R. and S. Sayers, *Hegel, Marx and Dialectic: A Debate*. (Brighton: Harvester Press, 1980).

O'Hear, A. *Karl Popper*. (London: Routledge and Kegan Paul, 1980).

Oldroyd, D. *The Archeology of Knowledge: An Introductory Study of the History of the Philosophy and Methodology of Science*. (London: Methuen, 1986).

Ollman, B. *Alienation: Marx's Conception of Man in Capitalist Society*. (Cambridge and New York: Cambridge University Press, second edition 1976).

___ . Dialectical Investigations. (London: Routledge, 1993).

O'Malley, J.J. *Editorial Introduction to Karl Marx "A Critique of Hegel's Philosophy of Right"*. (Cambridge: Cambridge University Press,1970).

O'Malley, J.J., K.W. Algozin, H.P. Kainz and L.C. Rice, editors. *The Legacy of Hegel: Proceedings of the Marquette Hegel Symposium, 1970*. (The Hague: Martinus Nijhoff, 1973).

Parsons, H.L. and J. Somerville, editors. *Dialogues on the Philosophy of Marxism*. (Westport: Greenwood Press, 1974).

Pilling, G. *Marx's "Capital": Philosophy and Political Economy.* (London: Routledge and Kegan Paul, 1980).

Petrovic, Gajo. *Marx in the mid-twentieth Century.* (Garden City, New York: Doubleday, 1967).

Phillips, D.L. *Wittengenstein and Scientific Knowledge: A Sociological Perspective.* (London: Macmillan, 1977).

Plekhanov, G.V. *In Defence of Materialism: The Development of the Monist View of History.* (London: Lawrence and Wishart, 1945).

Poincaré, H. *Science and Hypothesis.* (New York: Dover Publications Incorporated, 1952).

Popper, Karl. *The Poverty of Historicism.* (London: Routledge and Kegan Paul, second edition 1960).

___ . *The Logic of Scientific Discovery.* (London: Hutchinson, 1959).

___ . *The Open Society and its Enemies,* Volume II, *The High Tide of Prophecy: Hegel, Marx, and the Aftermath.* (London: Routledge and Kegan Paul, fifth edition 1962).

___ . *Conjectures and Refutations.* (London: Routledge and Kegan Paul, 1963).

___ . *Objective Knowledge: An Evolutionary Approach.* (Oxford: Clarendon Press, 1972).

___ . *Unended Quest: An Intellectual Biography.* (London: Routledge, 1991).

Poster, M. "Althusser on History without Man." *Political Theory,* Volume 2, Number 4 (November 1974).

Progress Publishers. *Fundamentals of Marxism-Leninism.* (Moscow: Foreign Languages Publishing, 1963).

Quine, W.V.O. "Two Dogmas of Empiricism," in *From a Logical Point of View.* (Cambridge, Massachussetts: Harvard University Press, 1953).

Quinton, A. *The Nature of Things.* (London and Boston: Routledge and Kegan Paul, 1973).

Rattansi, A., editor. *Ideology, Method and Marx.* (London: Routledge, 1949).

Rosdolsky, R. *The Making of Marx's 'Capital'.* Translated by P. Burgess. (London: Pluto, 1977).

Rotenstreich, N. *Basic Problems of Marx's Philosophy.* (Indianapolis: The Bobbs-Merrill Company, 1965).

Le Roy, E. "Science et Philosophie," in *Revue de Metaphysique et de Morale,* Number 8 (1900).

Ruben, D.-H. *Marxism and Materialism: A Study in Marxist Theory of Knowledge.* (Brighton: Harvester, second edition 1979a).

___ . "Marxism and Dialectics," in *Issues in Marxist Philosophy,* Volume I, *Dialectics and Method,* edited by J. Mepham and D.-H. Ruben. (Brighton: Harvester, 1979).

Rubinstein, D. *Marx and Wittgenstein: Social Praxis and Social Explanation.* (London: Routledge and Kegan Paul, 1981).

Russell, B. *History of Western Philosophy.* (London: G. Allen and Unwin, 1946).

Sartre, J.-P. *Critique of Dialectical Reason.* (London: New Left Books, 1976).

Sayer, D. "Science as Critique: Marx vs. Althusser," in *Issues in Marxist Philosophy*, Volume III, *Epistemology, Science and Ideology*, edited by J. Mepham and D.-H. Ruben. (Brighton: Harvester, 1979).

___ . *Marx's Method: Ideology, Science and Critique in "Capital".* (Hassocks: Harvester Press, 1983).

Sayers, S. "Contradiction and Dialectic in the Development of Science." *Science and Society*, Volume 45, Number 4 (Winter 1981-2).

___ . "Marxism and the Dialectical Method." *Radical Philosophy*, 36 (Spring 1984).

___ . *Reality and Reason: Dialectic and the Theory of Knowledge.* (Oxford: Blackwell, 1985).

Schmidt, A. *The Concept of Nature in Marx.* Translated by B. Fowkes. (London: New Left Books, 1971).

Shapere, D. "The Paradigm Concept." *Science*, Volume 172, Number 3984 (May, 1971).

Singer, P. *Hegel.* (Oxford: Oxford University Press, 1983).

Sohn-Rethel, A. *Intellectual and Manual Labour: A Critique of Epistemology.* Translated by M. Sohn-Rethel. (Atlantic Highlands, New Jersey: Humanities Press, 1978).

Solomon, R.C. *In the Spirit of Hegel: A Study of G.W.F. Hegel's Phenomenology of Spirit.* (Oxford: Oxford University Press, 1983).

Stace, W.T. *The Philosophy of Hegel: A Systematic Exposition.* (New York: Dover Publications, 1955).

Stalin, J.V. *Problems of Leninism.* (Moscow: Foreign Languages Publishing House, 1947).

Stepelevich, L.S., editor. *The Young Hegelians: An Anthology.* (Cambridge: Cambridge University Press, 1983).

Stockman, Norman. *Antipositivist Theories of Science: Rationalism, Critical Theory and Scientific Realism.* (Dordrecht: D. Reidel Publishing Company, 1983).

Stove, D.C. *Popper and After: Four Modern Irrationalists.* (Oxford: Pergamon Press, 1982).

Suchting, W.A. "Marx's 'Theses on Feuerbach,'" in *Issues in Marxist Philosophy*, Volume II, *Materialism*, edited by J. Mepham and D.-H. Ruben. (Brighton: Harvester Press, 1979).

. *Marx: An Introduction.* (Brighton: Wheatsheaf Books Limited, 1983).

Suppe, F., editor. *The Structure of Scientific Theories*. (London: University of Illinois Press, 1974).

Swingewood, A. *Marx and Modern Social Theory*. (London: Macmillan,1975).

Thompson, E.P., *The Poverty of Theory*. (London: Merlin Press, 1978).

Timpanaro, S. *On Materialism*. (London: New Left Books, 1976).

Toews, J.E. *Hegelianism: The Path Toward Dialectical Humanism 1805-1841*. (Cambridge: Cambridge University Press, 1980).

Uchida, Hiroshi. *Marx's Grundrisse and Hegel's Logic*. Edited by Terrell Carver. (London: Routledge, 1988).

Vaillancourt, P.M. *When Marxists Do Research*. (New York: Greenwood Press, 1986).

Van Fraasen, B.C. *The Scientific Image*. (Oxford: Clarendon Press, 1980).

Walker, A. *Marx: His Theory and Its Context*. (London: Longman, 1978).

Walton, P. and A. Gamble, *From Alienation to Surplus Value*. (London: Sheed and Ward, 1972).

Wetter, G.A. *Dialectical Materialism: A Historical and Systematic Survey of Philosophy in the Soviet Union*. (London: Routledge and Kegan Paul, 1958).

___ . *Soviet Ideology Today*. Translated by P. Heath. (London: Heinemann, 1966).

Wilde, L. *Marx and Contradiction*. (Aldershot: Avebury, 1989).

___ . "Logic: Dialectic and contradiction," in *The Cambridge Companion to Marx*, edited by T. Carver. (Cambridge: Cambridge University Press, 1991).

Wilden, A. *System and Structure: Essays in Communication and Exchange*. (New York: Tavistock Publications, second edition 1980).

Winch, P. *The Idea of a Social Science and its Relation to Philosophy*. (London: Routledge and Kegan Paul, 1958).

Wilson, H.T. *Marx's Critical/Dialectical Procedure*. (London: Routledge, 1991).

Wisdom, J.O. *Challengeability in Modern Science*. (Aldershot: Gower Publishing, 1987a).

___ . *Philosophy of the Social Sciences, Volume II: Schemata*. (Aldershot: Avebury, 1987b).

Wood, A.W. *Karl Marx*. (London: Routledge Kegan Paul, 1981).

Zelený, J. *The Logic of Marx*. Translated by T. Carver. (Oxford: Basil Blackwell, 1980).

For Product Safety Concerns and Information please contact our EU
representative GPSR@taylorandfrancis.com
Taylor & Francis Verlag GmbH, Kaufingerstraße 24, 80331 München, Germany

www.ingramcontent.com/pod-product-compliance
Lightning Source LLC
Chambersburg PA
CBHW050709280326
41926CB00088B/2903